T0072449

The Journey Home

The Journey Home

Discovering
the Deep Spiritual Wisdom
of the Jewish Tradition

Rabbi Lawrence A. Hoffman

BEACON PRESS
BOSTON

Beacon Press
25 Beacon Street
Boston, Massachusetts 02108-2892
www.beacon.org

Beacon Press books
are published under the auspices of
the Unitarian Universalist Association of Congregations.

Printed in the United States of America

07 06 05 04 03   8 7 6 5 4 3 2 1

This book is printed on acid-free paper that meets the uncoated paper ANSI/NISO
specifications for permanence as revised in 1992.

Text design by George Restrepo

Composition by Wilsted & Taylor Publishing Services

Library of Congress Cataloging-in-Publication Data
Hoffman, Lawrence A.
   The journey home : discovering the deep spiritual wisdom of the
Jewish tradition / Lawrence A. Hoffman.
      p. cm.
   ISBN 0-8070-3620-X (cloth)
   ISBN 0-8070-3621-8 (pbk)
   1. Spiritual life—Judaism.   2. Jewish way of life.   I. Title.
      BM723 .H642   2002
      296.7—dc21   2001008090

Contents

Chapter One

Returning Home:
Spirituality with Jewish Integrity

Return, O Israel, to Adonai, your God.
HOSEA 14:1

Return again, return again, return to the land of your soul.
CURRENT LITURGICAL SONG

My first brush with spirituality came with an unexpected question, back in 1975. Literally and metaphorically, I was far away from home, giving a guest lecture to the theology department of the University of Notre Dame on the rituals of Passover. "What is the spirituality of the *seder?*" a woman wanted to know. "You have talked for a week, covering every conceivable aspect of the Passover experience, but not once have you addressed anything spiritual. Isn't there such a thing as Jewish spirituality?" Unbelievable as it may seem a quarter of a century later, I was at the time completely stumped: I had no idea what to say.

The next day marked my return in more ways than one. I was newly committed to discovering the spiritual foundations of Judaism, and my journey home to Jewish spirituality is still in process.

More than twenty-five years have passed since then, but the curiosity over Jewish spirituality has only grown. Now, not only Catholics at Notre Dame want to know what it is. Everyone is asking the question. And they are mostly getting the wrong answers.

The search for spirituality is endemic to North American society. Its sociological roots lie in the demise of extended families, neighborhoods, and ethnic communities. Demographically, it is an outgrowth of baby boomers reaching middle age; their parents living longer in retirement years; and the generation in their twenties and thirties post-poning marriage and looking for some abiding principles of life as they change careers and try out new identities. It comes from the information explosion that instantly connects us with far-off traditions we once would have considered alien. It arises from the panoply of worldwide religious traditions migrating from countries we never heard of to our own neighborhood and workplace. It is a consequence of feminism, which has successfully critiqued the solo voice of corporate men in church and synagogue seminaries and boardrooms. It is the result of a national distrust of institutional wisdom and a concurrent failure of denominations to speak as compellingly as they once did. Psychologically, it grows from the "me-generation" claim that each of us has a self; that the self is sacrosanct; and that the self needs nurturing within, not just without.

It is especially important to see just how pervasive the spiritual search has become. It is not just a leisure-time project of intellectuals; spirituality has become big business, fueled by rampant marketing in a popular vein. Booksellers stock every conceivable tract on the life of faith. I have yet to encounter *The Underground Guide to the Babylonian Talmud* or *Thomas Aquinas for Fools*, but I know they are coming. They will sit alongside an undifferentiated mélange of offerings on such topics as returning from the dead, health foods from the Bible, channeling, and Rolfing.

Spirituality was mainstreamed in the 1990s. A 1994 *Newsweek* cover trumpeted "The Search for the Sacred: America's Quest for Spiritual Meaning," and two years later, the magazine diagnosed America as "hooked on the paranormal." By 1998, even the *Wall Street Journal* ran a lead story about executives who hunt down spiritual directors to monitor the state of their soul for "internal movements of God"; and as late as July 2001, *Fortune* magazine carried a cover story entitled, "God and Business: The Surprising Quest for Spiritual Renewal in the American Workplace."

This popularized spirituality was a far cry from what anyone could have predicted back at Notre Dame in 1975. My serious questioner at that lecture would have been astounded by the quiet giant of a man I met years later who identified spirituality as the inherent quality of crystals to reverberate sympathetically with the body's hidden reservoir of wholeness; or by another air traveler who thought she was spiritual because she could identify colored auras around the heads of would-be passengers and, from them, determine whether they would arrive safely at their destinations.

Maybe some people do benefit from crystals; maybe the magnetic fields that indeed surround our brains are visible to some. I don't know. I remain open on these things. But I am suspicious of pop interpretations that claim falsely to be scientific and miss the really serious side of the spiritual. Jewish insights that go back two thousand years to the Rabbis and, before that, to the Bible itself may not be scientific; but they are not unscientific either. They avoid the intellectual pabulum that passes for truth these days, offering genuine wisdom instead.

What I find especially troublesome is the way the suspiciously spiritual spirals down into the occult—the realm of Tarot cards, teacup leaves, and the entrails of animals. I am no hardened Philistine, mired so deeply in modernism that I cannot get beyond religion reduced to radical reason. I count myself among the many who suspect they are being had, however, by the more extreme rhetoric of spiritual access to special powers, but who do not on that account want to give up the belief in a kind of spirituality that is very real, consistent with science, supremely important, and (in my case) Jewish to its core. Ever since my Notre Dame lecture, I have been coming home to these authentic roots of Jewish spirituality that had somehow eluded me for so long but that now sustain me. I am discovering that on this, my journey home, I have lots of company.

Jewish spirituality begins with the Bible's claim that there is a region of experience called the Holy. It surfaces in times of awe, or in daring notions of harmony, hope, and goodness—in the prophet Isaiah's vision of the heavens, for instance, and in his older contemporary Micah's demand that we live profoundly here on earth. This biblical spirituality was adopted and then transformed by the Rabbis of late antiquity, who made it part and parcel of the historic quest for meaning that we now call Judaism.

By the nineteenth century, the claim to holiness was being echoed more loudly than ever, but it had been divorced from its spiritual moorings. My own branch of Judaism, the movement we now call Reform, championed the sacred but denounced the mystical. It restricted Judaism to the bounds of modern liberal ethics and the syllogistic sterility of logical rationalism. That was why I was so taken aback by my questioner in the Notre Dame lecture hall. Spirituality? In five years of rabbinic school and four more years of graduate study, no one had ever so much as mentioned the word to me. No wonder I didn't even comprehend the question.

The 1990s spiritual revival is epitomized in Mollie, a Jew by birth and training, who seeks spirituality but not religion, from which she is alienated. She has launched her own private search for a spiritual home. She wants to recapture her Jewish soul, thinks of herself as a Jew, but is investigating other faiths as well to find some generic sense of God, and wisdom enough to unify her world within and the world without. Mollie's spiritual testimony sounds mushy, soft, and soppy, but that is just because she never learned "proper" theological language to describe it. It is the Mollies of the world who become Jewish Buddhists—Jew-Bus (pronounced "Jew-Boos"), as they are known—when they find a ready Buddhist rhetoric for the objects of their inchoate quest; the Mollies, too, who love the idea that Judaism might also somewhere harbor meaningful mystagogy (as Catholics call it)— that is, mysteries to satisfy the soul. Too bad synagogue Sunday schools had all been clones of the no-nonsense schools of rationality described by Charles Dickens in *Hard Times*: all their principals named Mr. Gradgrind; their teachers, Mr. McChoakumchild; all duly appointed "commissioners of fact" (as Dickens puts it), Jewish fact, we should say, "who will force the [Jewish] people to be people of fact, and nothing but fact." From People of the Book to People of the Fact, and for most Jews who grew up the way I did, spirituality failed the "fact test": It was unlike Jewish history, say, or Hebrew grammar. When my wife and I went to enroll my eldest son in a Jewish day school and asked the principal what the school's philosophy was, he replied, "Like the Talmud says, 'When they're young, stuff 'em like oxen.'" Mr. Jewish McChoakumchild: alive and well.

The problem was that my five years of seminary training and four years of doctoral work had been given over entirely to "getting stuffed like an ox" on data—in my case, the history of Jewish prayer and related literature. I could date familiar prayers to their time of origin, trace the history of Jewish prayer books, explain liturgical revision, discuss medieval prayer-book art, and even think through the way prayer worked once upon a time when the absence of cheap paper made a written prayer book inaccessible to all but the elite. But I had never considered Jewish spirituality—the very idea of which sounded strange to me that day at Notre Dame.

It was as if someone had asked me to discuss "national migraines." Now, I know what the words *national* and *migraine* mean separately, but I do not automatically think of combining them. Only after thinking about it for a while does it occur to me that there might be a category of things aptly described by them together: road construction coast to coast, perhaps, or a garbage strike in every city across the nation. Similarly, I recognized both *Jewish* and *spirituality* as perfectly good English words, but it did not occur to me that they went together. The adjective *Jewish* (I thought) described myself and what I and others Jews teach about my tradition; *spirituality* (I imagined) was a particular something-or-other (I wasn't sure exactly what) that Christians talk about. Only relatively recently have we begun to see that spirituality is *not* just Christian. It is not like Christmas carols, the Eucharist, or the Gospel of Luke—things really Christian in their essence. Spirituality is more like ethics and theology, the sort of things you find in many religions but clothed in particularistic religious garb that make them Muslim or Christian rather than, say, Hindu or Native American.

Once upon a time, Jews would have responded equally quizzically to the idea that there could be Jewish ethics and Jewish theology—not because Judaism dismisses morality and belief, but because English is so dominated by two thousand years of Christian thought that Christianity has cornered the linguistic market describing such issues. So, too, the classical Western literature on spirituality is monopolized by Christian authors, but there is no reason to think that spirituality cannot be Jewish. It is just that Jews have not generally thought through what their own kind of spirituality is. No one ever asked. But that day at Notre Dame someone did, and, as a result, I can now see what was not clear to me back then. I know now that *Jewish* and *spirituality* do go together to describe something real.

What the Notre Dame questioner wanted to know (although I am not sure she knew that she wanted to know it) was how learned and spiritual Jews would talk among themselves, if they were to have a readily accessible vocabulary of Jewish spirituality, and how I could describe Jewish spirituality to others in a way that remained true to Jewish experience but understandable to outsiders. She was not the only person who wanted to know that, however; I did, too! There had to be some form of Jewish spirituality, but I needed proper words for it: something other than the Christian lexicon defining Christian experience in the light of Christian theological concepts but tangential to what Jews know as familiar experiential landmarks of their lives.

What most Western thought takes as spiritual rhetoric is largely foreign to traditional Jewish discourse, which, unlike its Christian parallel, did not emerge from the schools of the Roman empire where Greek philosophical thinking was modified for theological debate. The closest Jews come to that Hellenistic ideal is Philo, a first-century Alexandrian philosopher whose topics are marginal to rabbinic Jewish consciousness. By contrast, his Christian counterparts, such as Clement and Origen, were central to early Christian rhetoric. Over the centuries, Christians specialized in talk about the things the philosophers debated: essences, truths, and absolutes. Jews did not. I could not readily answer my questioner at Notre Dame because the language of spirituality (like the language of theology) is a foreign implant for Jews. It is not that Jews have no ideas that correspond to such Christian theological topics as revelation and salvation, but it takes a sort of translation process to arrive at what our parallels are, since we do not normally think in those terms. By now, a hundred years of Jews doing theology has modified the foreign sound of theology; not so—not yet, anyway—spirituality. We have learned to make Jewish sentences about "salvation through works, not just faith," for instance. Parallel sentences about spirituality still sound strange to Jewish ears; they are like tomorrow's spring fashions imported from a Christian designer to be tried on for size. As Jews using Christian terms, we may be like women trying on men's jeans during the period when women wore only dresses and skirts; it was not as if women couldn't wear them, but the jeans weren't exactly contoured for their bodies. It took good designing to reshape jeans as women's wear. So, too, with ideas clothed in words. It is not as if Jews can't use those words, but it takes work to make them fit. With words and ideas, the redesign is best thought of as translation.

Here is the problem: Jewish categories can end up being translated in such a way that they become utterly Christianized, in which case they cease being descriptive of what Jews actually experience. Or Jews can answer questions about Christian categories by simply translating old Hebrew documents into modern English and then pointing to them as if to indicate what the Rabbis would have said if they lived in our time and spoke English. These two pitfalls can be called, respectively, "satisfying the anthropologist" and "going native."

Satisfying the Anthropologist and Going Native

I keep a cartoon on my office door that pictures a family of natives living in a thatched hut in some far-off jungle. They are frantically carrying off their television set, freezer, and stereo system to a hidden alcove. The caption reads, "Quick! Get these out of sight; the anthropologists are coming, the anthropologists are coming."

Inquiring about Jewish spirituality is like being an anthropologist in a strange culture called Judaism in that we want to know what Jews have to say about topics they never actually talk about. Anthropologists who set up camp in a strange village might, for instance, be interested in family relationships, which they have learned in their doctoral studies to call *kinship systems*, a term the natives have never heard. So, the field workers have to ask the natives about other things to get to that information: how do males "get a woman" perhaps, or "why do people call their mother's sister's daughter their sister rather than their cousin?" Imagine, however, some crafty native informants who have gotten hold of an anthropology textbook, figured out what information the anthropologists want, and have decided to save their questioners a lot of trouble by answering right away, "Oh, the kinship system; certainly. We are matrilineal and matrilocal." Unwary anthropologists would record such statements at their own peril, even if they were true. The anthropologists would have translated the culture into proper scientific categories but missed the whole point of what they were there to find: how these people may be similar to others, but still special in their own way. Alternatively, imagine that all the anthropologists get is the usual native interpretations, which they dutifully record but then decide not to translate into scientific categories. They would then publish a book that transcribes in English exactly what they were told by the natives; but, again, they would have missed the point, this time capturing native perceptions but never conceptualizing them in a way that is useful to people other than the natives, who hardly need anthropologists to tell them what they already know.

In the first instance, the natives would have *satisfied the anthropologist*; in the second, the anthropologists would have *gone native*.

Studying Judaism is like visiting a far-off society whose native informants are the Rabbis and whose testimony about what Jews think and do is available in the books the Rabbis wrote. Unlike anthropological field workers who really visit the culture in question, all we can do is visit the books we have inherited, asking questions of their contents the way we would if we were actually to have their rabbinic authors before us. Asking the questions, however, is not as simple as it looks. Everything depends on which language we use to express the questions and (even more important) what we decide counts as good answers.

Questions about Jewish spirituality are difficult because, if we limit ourselves to sentences that describe it in terms of modern spiritual jargon, we may satisfy the spiritual anthropologists among us but not learn anything valuable about the way the Rabbis really thought. If, however, we endlessly reiterate the stock phrases that come naturally to the native lips of the Jewish authors, even though we are replicating authentic medieval or ancient sentences, we are not coming to terms with what those sentences mean for our own lives today.

The Jewish case of *satisfying the anthropologist*, then, consists of imposing on our sources the foreign categories of Western thought. In theology, for instance, it would be inappropriate to limit the Jewish question to "the doctrine of grace." Jews may have one, but even if we knew what it was, we would miss the subtlety of the Jewish way of arriving at theological reality. It would amount to asking Jews to talk like Christians about content taken from Judaism. Even if it is possible to teach Jews to talk that way, the fact is they don't, and we would miss knowing what Jews have to say when they speak their own authentic language of Jewish tradition. Similarly with spirituality: Whatever the categories of Christian spirituality turn out to be, they may not be the ones that best describe the Jewish side of things.

Alternatively, we could *go native*. We might just replicate in English the content of old Jewish books, figuring that if it was good enough for the learned authors, it ought to be good enough for us. We would be collecting everything spiritual that native Jews have had to say over the centuries, but compiling it in a language that we can all understand. Most people who write about spirituality use this strategy; they know there are authentic spiritual masterworks that ought to be consulted, and they figure that the easy way to write a book is to translate from old Hebrew or Aramaic to new English and then to string together a summary of what they have, whether it actually means anything or not. Imagine, by analogy, that someone discovered the work of Lewis Carroll and decided to reprint it with a synopsis. A summary of *Jabberwocky* might include the presumably meaningful explanation: "Jabberwocks and Jubjub birds can be frightened off, but only like frumious bandersnatches, and only by the beamish among us who are not shy to use their vorpal blades"—perfectly grammatical English that sounds positively proverbial in its wisdom, even though most of the words mean nothing at all.

Translations of medieval cabala are often an example of going native. Cabala comes loaded with technical vocabulary. Summing it up by saying "Creation proceeded through stages of *s'firotic* unfolding in which emanations of light smashed the vessels that held them, thereby giving us evil" is not necessarily any more enlightening than the preceding Lewis Carroll summary. Just repeating medieval language in modern English gets us nowhere, unless we can somehow interpret what that language means in terms that modern people can comprehend.

The pop spirituality market is filled with such translations of Jewish spiritual masters, as if simple translations of other people's recorded experience are sufficient to allow us to share that experience. Were that the case, we would all know the wonders of falling in love just by reading romance novels, and we could experience financial success by devouring biographies of millionaires. Alas, the world doesn't work that way. That is the problem of going native. It is not uninteresting to hear the natives talk; it is just unsatisfying.

In the realm of Jewish spirituality, Jewish wisdom called cabala stands out in this regard. The Cabalists were genuine religious pietists who lived largely in Provence, France, and Spain in the twelfth and thirteenth centuries, but then migrated throughout the Mediterranean region in the late fifteenth and sixteenth centuries. They spoke regularly about angels and a creation tale of mythic proportions wherein the cosmos was more or less spoken into existence by a God who is both masculine and feminine. Their account features a primeval burst of divine light that emanated through space and filled up glass-like vessels, which then cracked under the intensity of their contents, leaving those contents to harden like gas that cools into matter. And the Cabalists spoke of absolute evil embodied in a sort of counteruniverse called "the other side." Today's thirst for spirituality has made endless varieties of cabalistic works available, either word-for-word translations of medieval tracts or popular descriptions of the way the medieval authors thought and wrote. If they are done well— that is, if the modern-day populizers remain faithful to an authentic recapitulation of the original texts they are translating—such texts are useful glimpses into a particular Jewish universe of discourse. But translated cabalistic works alone are of limited value in providing modern readers with answers to today's spiritual questions.

To begin with, even the original writers did not intend their remarks to be taken as a snapshot description of the reality they experienced. They knew all along that they were giving only metaphoric descriptions of something that went deeper than literal imagery had the power to capture. Imagine young Einstein ruminating over the ultimate nature of physical reality. He is overwhelmed by the grandeur of it all, the fact that light travels at a steady speed while everything else—even such seeming constants as what we weigh, how tall we are, and how old we claim to be—is merely relative. Then suddenly it hits him: $e = mc^2$. Let us now imagine that centuries later, higher mathematics and physics have altogether vanished from a world that has been practically destroyed by nuclear war. People remember, however, that once upon a time, a realm of experience existed in which mathematical formulas evoked a deep appreciation of the coherence of all reality. One day, someone comes across the remains of an old issue of a scientific journal in which the formula of relativity is used to discuss some further theory regarding the way light bends through the space–time continuum. What good would it be to average readers in the context of that postnuclear wasteland, people with no prior imaginative leap of insight into the nature of time, space, or light itself, merely to repeat literally Einstein's mathematical equation?

Cabalistic description is the mathematics of medieval spirituality, but written out in sentences rather than abstract symbols. Merely replicating in modern English sentences that speak of the angel Metatron or the smashing of the spheres sounds good but goes nowhere for people who have no immediate experience of whatever it was that prompted the original Cabalists to talk that way. Going native works only for natives; not for moderns who cannot go home to the Middle Ages.

We can, of course, memorize the translations of old native talk until we learn to speak the way they did and then form sentences as if we knew what we were saying. That is what pop-cabala tends to be: a dialogue that has ceased being about anything rational and is wrapped in language that makes it sound deep. Using the cabala as a vehicle for spirituality may work for some, but for most, it is far likelier to frustrate, since it is so hard to find real experience these days to which the kabbalistic system can be made to fit.

In any event, the cabala arose only late in the Jewish story. It is not the only way Jews have talked about spirituality. There is another entryway to Jewish spirituality that avoids generic New Age rhetoric and gets us beyond going native as well. It is a deep reading of Jewish texts to elicit the underlying construction of reality that the authors took for granted; and then a consideration of the texts' grid of reality as an alternative to the way we usually think about things. Imagine a world made entirely of colored squares and circles on an invisible background. Raised in such a world, we might be taught to think of the universe as a warlike conflict in which a person must choose to be a circle or a square and then face off for a lifelong fight to the death. Then we discover a literature in which authors talk little about shapes, but instead describe golden sunsets, red-hewed landscapes, and lush green pastures. Awakened to the categories of color, we return to our world to discover that the shapes are indeed colored, with the colors blended almost equally among the various shapes. Exchanging our rhetoric of shape for the language of color, we begin to talk about rainbows, pastels, and harmony. The world hasn't changed, but we have. We see it differently.

Reasonable Spirituality: A Way of Being in the World

When natives satisfy the anthropologist, they frame their authentic spiritual experience in the foreign scientific rhetoric that dominates anthropological literature. Anthropologists writing up this rhetoric lose the sense of the spiritual that it was supposed to describe.

When anthropologists of Judaism go native, they sound spiritual, but check their rational capacity at the door. As long as the sentences make grammatical sense, they will use them, even if it comes out sounding like *Jabberwockian* prose. If we try to explain Jewish spirituality in words taken only from authentic Jewish sources, albeit translated into English, we have spirituality that is not unreasonable, but not reasonable either. It simply would be a grammatically correct treatise in fantasy, an intriguing account of light-filled vessels, smashing glass, sexual energy, and left-handed "otherness" engaged in cosmic conflict with the primeval good—all great stuff for nighttime winter reading, but requiring translation yet again into something else if it is really to make sense. If we do not insist that native speech must mean something in modern experience, we get spiritual talk that corresponds to nothing the average person knows as real.

Finally, we have the fuzzy pop talk about angels, demons, crystals, and auras. This is media fluff, a comic-book reduction of the way the natives used to talk prepared for people who cannot even bother to read the natives. For most people, it is apt to be neither spiritual nor reasonable. There has to be another way.

One of the most surprising aspects of the Jew-Bus is the particular tradition these alienated Jews choose in order to find the spirituality that they miss in their Jewish synagogue experience. It is Buddhism, the one world religion that has least to do with God! It would not be entirely correct to say that all Buddhism is Godless, but theology plays such a minor role in Buddhism that scholars of religion regularly turn to it as a favorite test case of how a religion can be religious even without a Western-style notion of the Divine. Classical Confucian culture is another instance of a religion that no one ever accuses of lacking spirituality, even though God is hardly at the center of Confucian experience. Some twenty years ago, my Notre Dame informant explained to me that spirituality is the way we relate everything we do to God; and, recently, a colleague told the student body at the Hebrew Union College that, to him, spirituality is acting as if God is looking over his shoulder. Are they right? Must God be central to our experience of spirituality? The counter cases of Buddhism and Confucianism suggest that many Muslims, Jews, and Christians may want to talk that way, but a more fruitful beginning is to leave God aside for a moment and start with ourselves, the human situation that we all know quite well.

Religions are ways of conceptualizing the entire universe of existence. Spiritual discourse is thus a particular way to live in the world—one that leads us to appreciate things that we would not be conscious of were we to limit ourselves to the way our secular culture describes reality. What makes religions unique is the way they order the world. There are Jewish ways of doing this, as there are Christian and Muslim and Buddhist ways. This book is about the uniquely Jewish way of mapping reality. Getting in touch with the Jewish map is the beginning of Jewish spirituality.

Spirituality Is Drawing the Big Picture

Finally, we are ready to define reasonable spirituality—at least in a Jewish mold. First, it is worth reviewing what spirituality is not, or, more precisely, what it need not be (even though for some people, it clearly is). There are people, for example, who find spirituality in angels and unseen forces, just as popular culture these days imagines it. The "why" of life is answered by reference to the will of beings beyond our own realm: not God, but angels, poltergeists, and ghosts. To some people, to be spiritual is to be in touch with those unseen but very real wills and forces beyond the material level of experience and the explanatory realm of science.

Prayer, too, can be a means to the extrasensory beyond, putting us in touch with powers beyond the human. In some traditions, prayers may even be directed through, if not to, angelic intermediaries. Not just God, but an entire realm of the godlike is thus pictured as occupying real territory called the heavens, where our prayers as real things get sent, the way telephone conversations get transported through sound waves to real listeners at the other end of the line. If we feel the presence of ethereal forces or at least believe that we have been in touch with them, we say that our prayers were effective.

Others find spirituality in reading spiritual translations of medieval classics—a practice that I describe as "going native." I do not mean to denigrate such people's experiences, just as I would never challenge other claims—for instance, those of people who define the spiritual as doing good, plain and simple. To look for more, they say, is to be on a search for the pot of gold at the end of the rainbow. Mature adults should be content with goodness. That is the only justification of life that we can expect to know, the only experience we can have that will convince us that we matter.

But this book is written for people who want more. Their search is part of a larger phenomenon, the increasing numbers of people who seek a spiritual home. Until the 1960s, North Americans were generally quite secure in the religious traditions in which they had been raised. Typically, for instance, Lutherans, Catholics, and Jews lived in self-imposed religious ghettoes: They identified with the religion of their parents, moved in social circles with others like themselves, married people from those same circles, and then continued to affiliate only with people of the same denomination as their own. Denominations were entire worlds unto themselves, and hermetically sealed, at that; one was born, bred, married, and buried a Lutheran, Catholic, or Jew. Denominations were identity addresses. They were homes.

All of that began to change in the 1960s for a variety of reasons, but most interestingly, perhaps, because of the political polarization of Americans into liberal and conservative camps. Most religious traditions turned sharply to the left on the social issues that the 1960s brought to the fore. But by the 1970s, and especially during the 1980s and beyond, a conservative reaction produced a split between left and right wings in the once-solid denominational bodies. Now, liberal Jews, Protestants, and Catholics had more in common with each other than they did with the more conservative right-wing branches of their own denominations. With growing dialogue across religious lines, switching religions was no longer out of the question. Religious intermarriage became normative; once beyond the pale, families with blended religious traditions became a topic for TV sitcoms. Being born into a particular faith no longer guaranteed an adult comfort level with it. Spiritually speaking, Americans were on the move.

America has always thrived on restlessness. Historians marvel at this society's continual geographical shifts: the movement west in the nineteenth century, for example, or the opening of the Sunbelt a hundred years later. But new physical homes inevitably bring new spiritual ones: nineteenth-century Methodism or Baptism in the population expansion west and south and flirtations with Eastern religions in twentieth-century California. Geographical mobility erodes religious certainty because it breaks down childhood loyalties to family, church, and neighborhood. But geographical change is no longer required to alter the spiritual landscape. The failure of denominations to speak in a single compelling voice to their constituencies is cause enough to send people searching for new spiritual homes without actually physically moving anywhere.

Once the doors of spiritual restlessness have been opened, other forces make the spiritual search compelling: the Internet, for instance, which brings alternative spiritual traditions immediately into view, and the breakdown of extended families, neighborhoods, and ethnic communities—a phenomenon we look at more seriously in chapter 8. The twenty-first century dawned with a spiritual rootlessness that is sending millions deeper within their own religious traditions or farther out to the traditions of others—all in search of a comfortable spiritual home. The soul knows its own landscapes, after all. We have all become spiritual explorers, seeking new vistas wherever we can find them.

For Jews, as we have seen, this spiritual restlessness has meant experimenting with alternative religious traditions, such as Buddhism. But it has also entailed a spiritual foray back into Jewish tradition. And just as Jews are increasingly willing to look anywhere for the deep-down wisdom they seek, so, too, are others. Judaism's age-old spiritual insights therefore attract not just Jews but non-Jews, too, who are in search of a spiritual home.This book is about that home.

If I were back at Notre Dame, replaying the tape of my questioner on spirituality, I would say that spirituality is our way of being in the world, the system of connectedness by which we make sense of our lives, how we overlay our autobiography in the making with a template of time and space and relationship that is vastly greater than we know ourselves individually to be. It is the way we dimly find our way to how we matter, the maps we use for things like history and destiny, the way we take a jumble of sensory data and shape it coherently into a picture, the way discordant noise becomes a symphony of being, the way we know that we belong to the drama of the universe. It is the wonderfully enchanting but equally rational way we go on our way of growing up and growing older in the mysterious business we call life.

Every great religion has its own patented recipe for doing these

great things, drawn from an eternal retelling and rereading of its traditional wisdom. Religious spirituality cannot come through shortcuts.
It is reached only by serious engagement with ancient texts that can
be made to translate into spiritual answers for modern dilemmas. This
book is a map of such authentic Jewish wisdom. It is what I have found
since 1975, in almost three decades of returning home.

Chapter Two

Connecting the Dots:
The Spirituality of Jewish Metaphor

The entire world is a narrow bridge: the main thing is not to fear at all.
NACHMAN OF BRATSLAV

One who regards life as meaningless is not merely unfortunate,
but almost disqualified for life.
ALBERT EINSTEIN

I am a rabbi, and I am intensely proud of that. I also have my Ph.D., something I earned in order to teach rabbinics in seminary; but, for what it is worth, I managed immediately to lose my doctoral diploma, whereas I still display my rabbinic certificate on my study wall.

By and large, I believe that no other professional calling matches the clergy in its potential for satisfaction. All the same, rabbis are expected to be teachers, counselors, pastors, preachers, youth-group leaders, community representatives, managers, and more—which is to say that they are incredibly overworked and overgeneralized. They are also poorly trained at saying "No." And as public personalities who work in a fishbowl, they can expect to be approached professionally even in a restaurant or a movie line. Lacking communities of friends who are not also their congregants, rabbis tend to suffer from a terrible sense of isolation.

It was just such feelings of loneliness that led me, some years back, to facilitate a spirituality retreat for rabbis who feared professional burnout. As preparation for the retreat, I gave the rabbis this challenge. "Think of a metaphor that describes who you are and complete the sentence that reads, 'I am a ——.' Share with us what you are."

Even though casual attire was called for, one participant came late, ominously dressed in a three-piece suit, as if to say, "I am too busy for this nonsense." Adding to that impression was his habit of glancing anxiously at a magnificent gold pocket watch suspended by a chain on his vest. He sat off to the side, said nothing, and seemed inclined to bolt before we got to him. But his turn duly arrived, and I will remember to the day I die what he said. The words fairly burst from his lips: "I am a wine cup—I mean the large one that we reserve for the person who leads services. I have watched twenty-five years of people drink deeply from it. Well, I am that cup, but what no one knows is that I have sprung a hole in the bottom; someday, someone will lift me up and find me empty."

Then and there, I discovered the power of metaphor. What we are depends partly on the words with which we describe ourselves. No account of the insidious forces contributing to rabbinic burnout could tell the tale as stunningly as that rabbi's metaphor of self.

I have since practiced this exercise with others and have never failed to come away with a deeper understanding of the way people establish an image of self-worth in a world that threatens the very possibility that our lives even have meaning. One woman, married to a man who regularly entertained business guests at home, told me, "I am a hat rack; people hang their hats on me and ignore me." Another woman, a mother engaged happily in nurturing six small children (who ran circles around her everyday), said she was a sprinkler system, watering the shoots in her family. "I am a peacemaker," said another mother, "constantly making Solomonic decisions for my two young sons who quarrel all the time." A man, the inveterate reader of anything nonfiction, called himself a learning machine.

The human need to envision our lives metaphorically is suggested by a favorite childhood pastime. Think back: You are ten years old again, and sick in bed. Someone you love visits you, in her hand a precious present wrapped in shiny paper. It is a "jumbo" workbook filled with games to while away the time: paint-by-number pages, a search for hidden shapes concealed in a picture, and even some elementary crossword puzzles. You turn the pages, however, until you get to the childhood staple: "connect the dots." You stop there.

The page is empty, save for a series of apparently random dots marked by numbers and a few odd shapes and lines scattered around the page. You know what to do because you have done this before, maybe a million times. Starting at 1, you move your pencil from dot to dot, until gradually the array of points becomes a picture: a toy boat, say, sailing in a stream. The squiggly lines in the page's margins turn out to be waves; a triangle in the middle is a flag waving from the boat's mast.

You stare with particular satisfaction at the picture you have just made. Had you been well trained in Bible stories, it might have occurred to you that your own delight was anticipated by the depiction of creation in Genesis.

> In the beginning, God created the heaven and the earth,
> the earth being unformed and void, and darkness over the face
> of the deep. Breath from God swept over the water, and God said,
> "Let there be light." So there was light. God saw how good the light
> was, and God separated the light from the darkness. God called
> the light day and the darkness, God called night. So there was
> evening and there was morning: a first day.

Like God, you have just created something out of nothing, a recognizable shape from a jumble of points in an empty expanse of page. Where things were once "unformed and void," there is now a ship plying across the ocean. From chaos, you have constructed a tiny pictorial cosmos. No wonder you are smiling. The divine part of you is celebrating its capacity to emulate our Creator.

Connect the Dots

The day you learned to connect the dots you began practicing for a larger game that has a lot more riding on it: life. Life is very much the process of connecting the disparate dots of daily events that befall us. These dots may be ordinary or monumental; planned or unexpected; joyous or disappointing; elating or tragic. Some religious traditions deny the ultimate reality of these dots that sweep daily across our lives' horizons. In Hinduism and Buddhism, for instance, sensory experiences are just illusions of reality, no more real than a mirage in a desert. Wisdom consists in withdrawing from these apparitions by diverting the mind from them to the truly real and eternal "allness" that underlies the transitory consciousness of life's day-to-day affairs.

By contrast, Judaism accords these ordinary affairs absolute reality. That is what there is. What we do here and now may have lofty, even eternal, dimensions, but what annoys us, haunts us, entertains us, or otherwise keeps us busy hour by hour is precisely the real stuff of life. Bit by bit—like tiny dots, converging in consciousness to become a pattern—the experiences we undergo add up to an image of who we think we are: "victims," say, or "sick"; "power brokers" or "problem solvers." If we like the image we come up with, it becomes what we tell others we "are," even when they are really asking what we "do." It may ultimately be what we ourselves think of ourselves as, like the man on a cruise ship who falls overboard during a storm. The captain shouts through a megaphone, "We are trying to save you, but cannot see you. Tell us your position." The man shouts back, "I am the president of a bank, a big bank!"

Modern life inevitably challenges us to say who we are: a "doctor," "student," or "mother," perhaps. What we really "are" is always more complex than any single-word summary, but when asked to define ourselves, we necessarily come up with simple answers, reflecting the pictures of connectedness that best encapsulate the experiential dots in our memories.

There are two extremes here, and Judaism walks a fine line between them. For the classical religions of India, ordinary experiences are illusory, transitory, utterly misleading; only a fool would look to them for a coherent pattern that captures anything real about ourselves. In Western thought, by contrast, experience is real enough, but analyzable only through the broad psychological, philosophical, or theological categories it epitomizes. These are the Greek essences, updated to preach an inherent difference between nobles and peasants; or, more recently, between men and women, blacks and whites—because in Western thought, people's differentiated experiences are not just what happens to them, but what they truly are. Judaism accepts neither of these alternatives. It holds instead that our experiences are no more and no less than what they seem: the real stuff of life that cannot be denied (as in the East) but that should not be unduly "philosophized over" (as in the West) either. Composing comprehensive pictures out of disparate events is a human proclivity. We all do it. The challenge is to avoid false pictures resulting from a skewed selection. Judaism urges us to include a broader canvas of dots as we determine the shape of our lives. We should neither (as in the East) reduce what we do to being utterly insignificant in determining what and who we are; nor (as in the West) reduce ourselves to being nothing more than the sum total of what we do.

Still, there is no getting around it: As we draw our self-portrait, the unit of measurement is what happens to us, both the surprising and the ordinary. In truth, they are not usually much different. There are exceptions (a plane crash that kills a loved one), but even unexpected bad news is at first fit neatly into the normal mold of who we are. Mounting bad news slowly builds its own portrait—a negative medical test here; a further finding there. Slowly, these negative dots congeal; they form their own cumulative picture of who we are in the form of a series of unwelcome dots to which we are exposed one at a time. In retrospect we see how our lives have been transformed by them.

Jewish texts, therefore, expend inordinate amounts of space not on ultimate concepts and questions, but on the mundane and not-so-mundane single and singular events—the dots of human existence: tales of what happened to this or that butcher, mother, rabbi, or student; vignettes of life, such as the Roman noblewoman who challenged a Rabbi with a question; a rabbi mourning the death of his son; or a seemingly trivial legal issue that nonetheless becomes a precedent. In Jewish literature, the issues of life are not painted globally. Tip O'Neill, once a Democratic congressman from Massachusetts and the most powerful man in the House of Representatives, is reputed to have said, "All politics is local." So, too, Jewish insight argues, all reality is local: What did you and I do yesterday? How will I react to a specific challenge tomorrow? Did I notice the early garden crocuses that herald spring? These are the events without which no life exists at all. They are our dots. Life is what we get when we string them together.

Some dots are relatively ordinary; they matter because they add up to more than what they individually seem to be. More challenging are the dots that arrive unexpectedly with massive consequences: a lump in the breast discovered while showering, or a call from the police that makes our blood run cold even before the voice on the other end of the line gets to the reason for the call. These are the startling dots that resist easy filing away along with the ordinary things that happen to us. Do you calmly file your divorce papers after twenty years of marriage under "Relationships, bad" or "Marriage, old"?

Simply to be human is to have to struggle for meaningful patterns among life's dots, especially the ones we never asked for. And the pattern may be hard to discern. Still, especially with life-altering dots, we seek such patterns, for that childhood engagement with connect the dots instructs us that without pattern, there is no meaning. Meaning is the way one dot fits neatly with another. I say to you, "Seven!" What does that mean? It is just a dot. But if we are playing dice, it means you win or lose. If you thought of the number of days in a week, it is something else again. All of life is made of such simple atomistic answers that take on meaning only because our metaphoric imagination can connect a one-

word or one-line response with dots that came before and with an anticipation of the probable dots that will come later. We humans are quintessentially "meaning-seeking animals." We look for patterns, wondering always what the larger picture entails. Astrology trades (falsely) on
this wild but wonderful insistence that life is more than the random sum
of its parts by connecting us to so-called universal astral phenomena.
Psychotherapy also seeks patterns in the dots of what we do over the long
haul. As creatures seeking meaning, we need, from time to time, to take
stock of all our dots; our very existence depends on finding a pattern in
the disparate events they represent. What have we made of ourselves, we
wonder. Where do we go from here? How did we get this far? And why
not farther?

Significant birthdays are especially given over to this sort of ruminating. Depending on whether we are twenty, forty, or sixty, we are
likely to say, for instance, that we are "on the way up," "at the peak of our
strength," or "over the hill"—metaphors drawn from the prevailing
American view of a lifetime. For Americans, life is a hill: a lengthy as-
cent to strength and power, then a sharp fall-off into what we call the
"declining years" when we go "downhill" toward old age—which is like
a second childhood. That view goes back at least as far as William Shakespeare, who defined "seven ages of man," beginning with the "the infant, mewling and puking in the nurse's arms" and ending with "that
second childishness, mere oblivion, *sans* teeth, *sans* eyes, *sans* taste,
sans everything." The Irish poet Dylan Thomas pictured life in even
more graphic terms: Not only are we on a straight line leading from cra-
dle to grave, he says, but we feel the hot pursuit of time all along the way,
until, at the end, "Death like a running grave tracks us down."

These are images of the shape that life's dots may take. They are
borrowed from culture at large and are taken for granted by most people
who measure their lives by them without ever questioning their validity.
They are not the only images available, however. There are other ways to
describe the contours of our own mortality.

At a spirituality workshop once, I asked people to draw a line corre-

sponding to the shape of their life's course. A heavy line would correspond to their life lived so far, and a dotted one would portray the way
they expected their lives to continue. Most people reproduced the shape
of a hill with a long upward incline, then a summit, and a short downward slope. The older people ended the first part of the exercise around
the crest of the line or slightly on the downhill slope of the other side;
younger people, who saw their lives in the ascendancy, had stopped their
heavy line before reaching the top, but then continued the hill-like pattern in dotted anticipation of what was sure to come. Both ages assumed
the point of life is to rise to the top, after which you can expect only a de-
cline into retirement and old age.

But a few had different pictures. A woman looking forward to being
a grandmother, but living in any case through her children, drew a line
that looked like a double hump on a camel. The first pinnacle had been
raising her children, and the second one, still in dotted form, was to be
her second family. Some people drew spiral shapes that proceeded
across the page without any rise and fall at all. There was a telling shape
that no one drew: a single line going steadily upward, with old age at the
very top—because old age, for Americans, is not an achievement, apparently, but a free fall downhill from life at its best. One man reported that
the exercise threw him into despair. His life had no shape at all, he said.
He could relate the various events that had gone into making him who he
was, but he could think of no way to formulate any coherent picture of
what they implied. He was all dots; no connections.

It is painful to have no image of our life being in order, as if our allotted years are merely shapeless blips in eternity. Some people may remember an old-time radio show that featured Fibber McGee and Molly.
A favored sound effect came when Fibber McGee's closet door was
opened and everything tumbled out in absolute chaos. What we fear
most is that the door of our lives will open and everything will tumble
out in utter disrepair. We cannot even stand it if our desks are in total
disarray. As messy as we may be, there comes a time when we say enough

is enough and put aside some time to make piles out of the junk that has accumulated through the months. It is consoling at least to have things in piles, even piles that correspond to nothing beyond themselves. So, too, we demand that the dots of our lives have some plan, some order, some direction. If not, we are living a horror tale of total unpredictability. With nothing to be seen on the horizon of life beyond random dots that further disconnect us from our past, we suffer the nighttime of our soul. The science-fiction movie *The Blob* appeals to this primal fear with its image of an undifferentiated mass spreading insidiously everywhere. So, too, the old fairy tale of the sorcerer's apprentice frightens us with the image of water coursing everywhere out of our control. Popular medical language adopts the same nightmarish image in the description of cancer, which is a terrible disease, indeed, but made particularly frightening by the idea of metastasis—a slow "oozing" of the cancer from one organ to another, like the uncontainable sci-fi blob. It is the primeval water that God rolled back on day two of creation. It is a return to the state of chaos before God divided light from dark. It is Fibber McGee's cosmic closet opening onto things that crash down and go bump in the night.

This fear of things being out of control may go back to the very foundations of civilization itself. There was a time, perhaps, when our ancestors huddled around a fire to keep away the wilds of nature. Later, they built cities with walled perimeters. Greeks made up stories of the barbarians pressing in on the city-state; and Romans fenced themselves off from conquered peoples, who might mount assaults on what Romans considered the only civilized way of life. Modern countries, too, fear the arrival of *waves* of immigrants the same way we fear floodwaters and cascades of lava from Mount St. Helens. We do not want to be buried alive, overrun by newcomers, drowned in a flood. There is good reason why the story of Creation is followed by the story of Noah. In Creation, God puts everything in order. With Noah, total disorder threatens to wash away Creation's organization. Our worst fear is Noah's: that God might roll back the cosmos until all we have is chaos once again. The earth might again be "unformed and void, with darkness on the face of the waters." "Unformed," "darkness," and "waters" are all allusions to uncontrolled disarray: what we fear most about our own lives as well. The myth of Noah ends with the comforting assurance that God will never bring a flood again.

So, our most important challenge is to find shape in our lives. We are indeed relegated to playing the child's game of connect the dots, except the real-life game is much harder to complete because the dots are endless and they come unnumbered. There is no ready-made shape to the page of life. We have to make it up as we go along. We never even know for sure that the shape we have in our head will continue to work. We just pick up our pencils each day and continue drawing.

In Search of a Biography

The spiritual question here is whether we can posit an underlying self that will prove lasting. The events of life are not themselves the point; they come and they go, sometimes painfully, sometimes not. But either way, they leave us with memories that we seek to integrate into a time line called our biography. Whether that biography has shape and meaning is the spiritual issue to which we are drawn willy-nilly as the years go by. When we are young, with half-drawn images of what we might become, we may feel that our ambitions are what matter. When we are old and must take stock of what we have done, we want to see a distinguishable life that is our own, regardless of how youthful ambitions turned out. And when we stop along life's way, we need to picture where we have come from and where we hope we are going before the day we die.

Think of a photograph album. We take pictures to preserve our memories and arrange them into albums to organize who we are—no one mounts the pictures in an album randomly! What good is an album that doesn't go anywhere?

The dots (and the pictures of them) are real enough. But what about the biographical line connecting them, the implicit story that the photo album tells? Some three hundred years ago, the famous philosophical skeptic David Hume questioned the conviction that our autobiography is obviously true. The things we recall may all have happened, but there is no evidence for a single unified self beyond the events that make it up. The idea that the self is a sort of underlying magnet to which the events of life adhere like iron filings is just an assumption that we find convenient. All we know for sure is that we are "a bundle of perceptions." Hume raised the frightening possibility that the shape of our lives is nothing but some organizing fiction. And to some extent, he was right.

We do create our lives as God created the world. In part, at least, the shape depends on the shaper. Our singular most spiritual act of faith, therefore, is when we determine that we, like God, will connect random dots into a single shape that tells us who we are; that we will stand before the mirror of life sure of our identity and, without stumbling, answer the question, "Who are you?"; and that we, again like God, will do so at the end of each day, looking at what we have created and saying that it is good.

For the Jew, this is where the Torah comes in.

Life Is a Home

Where do we get our images of the shapes of our lives? How did the people at the spirituality seminar decide they should draw life as a hill? How did the rabbi decide he was a leaky wine cup? Clearly, we get images from all around us, borrowing subconsciously from the general environment in which we are raised. In America, Madison Avenue tells us who we are. Television provides imagery that tantalizes; it supplies idealized others that advertisers hope we will adopt as measuring rods to shape ourselves. Artists throughout time have seen the world through the eyes of other artists who preceded them; that is why there are schools of art, why disciples follow their masters, refining their technique rather than starting all over again. Composers, too, do not start de novo; they write "Variations" on a theme of another composer who came before. It is just not true that we are able to see the world raw. The religious personality, therefore, borrows images from religious tradition. For Jews, that religious tradition is called Torah.

I have much to say about Torah in this book. In the narrowest sense, Torah is the first five books of the Bible. More broadly speaking, it is the entire Hebrew Bible, and more broadly still, it is the totality of rabbinic literature—including the book you are reading even now. Jewish metaphors of who we are come from Torah.

I remember lecturing one Shabbat morning at a synagogue, then going for a walk with a woman in her fifties while waiting for the late afternoon hour when a second lecture was scheduled. It was a day in early spring, the air still winter-crisp but noticeably warmed by a sun that had not forgotten how to shine during the February gloom. As we passed by the still-icy surfaces of a stream, our conversation turned to personal matters.

"Tell me about your family," the woman invited. And so I did, and asked her in return, "And you?"

"Ah," she stumbled, "my life has suffered a tragedy." She paused, wondering whether to go on, and then explained. "Several years ago, I had a daughter. She died horribly in the prime of her youth, just barely twenty. Through no fault of her own, she found herself driving by the scene of a drug dealer being pursued by the police. A stray bullet crashed through her windshield, killing her. And even though it has been years since then, I cannot get her death out of my mind."

The woman grew quiet, and then, as if changing the subject, she asked, "What is that concluding service for Yom Kippur all about, you know—I can't remember now what it is called."

"You mean *N'illah*," I reminded her. "It means 'the closing of the gates.' That's why we leave the ark doors open throughout it. People conclude this holiest day of our year by watching the scrolls of Torah within the ark, and then only at the end of the service, do we shut the doors."

"That's right, *N'illah*—so what is that all about?"

Trained in crisis counseling, I quickly turned the tables. "What do *you* think it is about?" I inquired.

My conversation partner apparently had taken the same psychology course I had. "I asked you," she reminded me sharply. "You are the liturgist. You are supposed to know."

When crisis counseling fails, sometimes God does not. There sprung into my head a Hasidic teaching that I had not thought of for years. "The early Hasidic masters taught that life is a series of doors, or gates, that open and close. But God never allows a gate to close without opening another somewhere in its place. When your daughter died, a gate clanged shut behind you. It is as if you are even now looking back through the gate that closed, rattling its iron bars in hope of going back again. But you cannot return. Your life has changed irreversibly. Somewhere there is another gate awaiting you, but you cannot find it as long as you face the wrong way looking wistfully at the past.

"That is what *N'illah* is about: gates closing and other gates opening. You will never forget this tragedy, but you will be able to move on to another place that lies beyond—through the gate you have yet to find. You might think of life as a home that we build through time. We are born into a single room. Our first door opens and we crawl through it, expanding our universe. For the rest of our lives, that is what happens. More doors open, but some doors close. Each new gate opens on some new room that we inhabit for a while and then move on again. At the end of our lives, we look back at all the rooms, some wonderful, some horrible. All we can hope for is that the total home we construct will have integrity. We look back on our lives, as if viewing our home from above, and want to be able to affirm our home as the place we really lived, for better or for worse."

The next day, the woman came back for my final lecture. She had thought of the new metaphor all night and pronounced it comforting. "Maybe I will find my new gate soon," she mused. "Life really is a series of doors, or gates, and rooms—a home."

Here, then, is a Jewish metaphor drawn from the liturgy, but going back, ultimately, to the Rabbis' understanding of life as more than a hill you climb. We are not simply what we manage to accomplish. We are builders of homes in the wilderness of time.

Life Is Torah

In a famous passage from a fifth-century collection of rabbinic musing, we find the Rabbis wondering how God knew in advance what the universe should look like. If, as the Rabbis staunchly maintained, God created the universe out of nothing, there could have been no preexistent model available. How, then, did God, the divine architect, imagine a universe when no such architecture had ever existed before. The Rabbis solve the problem by imagining that God used the Torah as a primal blueprint. It is as if the Torah is eternal, transcending all time, even the moment of the big bang, when time as we know it began.

So, too, the Torah defines the ideal shape of human life. We think of both, for example, as cycles—the life cycle, for humans; and the annual liturgical cycle of scriptural readings that begins with Genesis and ends with Deuteronomy only to start all over with Genesis again every year. This image of life as a cycle is worth pausing on. Cycles assume recurrence; what kind of cycle can life be if we die at the end of it? Where did the idea of life as a cycle come from? Western culture contains two possible answers, one secular and the other religious.

The secular option is reflected in the Shakespearian "seven ages" that we examined earlier. We begin as a child and end as a child, toothless and witless, utterly dependent on others. The religious option, by contrast, emphasizes birth and rebirth. We are born into this world, but then are born again for life after death. Medieval Christian art frequently portrays life as a clock with a birth scene at the seven, a human being at full strength at twelve, the Grim Reaper striking us down at four, and rebirth to everlasting life at six. Though Jewish culture from that era lacks this wealth of pictorial representations, the idea of eternal life is Jewish to its core. Exactly what kind of afterlife we should expect is not certain: Jewish thinkers preferred leaving the details vague, since we can never know for sure what a nonearthly existence looks like, and the important thing, in any event, is to live in a way that makes us worthy of such a life, whatever it turns out to be.

Still, Jewish wisdom on the subject comes closer to classical Christian thought than to Shakespeare's mechanical movement from one childhood to another. (Christianity did grow out of Judaism, after all.) Shakespeare had it right, physically speaking. We do begin and end life with the equivalent of "no teeth, no eyes, no taste." But no *everything*? Hardly. The Torah corrects Shakespeare with a more spiritual view: Life is no ever-dissipating disease that lumbers linear-like along the road toward death. It is a constantly rejuvenating cycle, where everywhere along the way, "teeth and eyes and taste" or not, we play out a sacred journey through time.

Begin with the beginning: Genesis. Genesis is first and foremost about conception, birth, and childhood. The first man and woman come into existence fully formed, but thereafter, children must be birthed, a process so difficult that the Bible knows it as the curse of Eve. For all its wonderment (many women say that having children is their most spiritual experience), conceiving new life, carrying it in embryonic form, and then giving birth to it is fraught with difficulty, uncertainty, and pain, all of which Genesis records in abundant detail. Not a single one of the foremothers conceives easily. But when they do, the scene shifts to the natural rivalries within the nuclear family—surely our own initial experience as children.

You don't have to be in analysis to see how the theme of Genesis is the twisted legacy of human childhood. The very first children born,

Cain and Abel, build such mutual enmity that one actually kills the other. Of Abraham's two children, one born to Sarah and the other to Hagar, pity Hagar's son, Ishmael, expelled from home with his mother because she was Sarah's rival. Or think of Isaac. Sarah waits decades for the miracle that will finally give her the child she wants, and in the very next chapter, her husband Abraham runs off to sacrifice him. Close readers of Genesis discover that Sarah never speaks to Abraham again.

The theme continues. Jacob bears the stigma of his mother Rebecca's favoritism. She schemes to have him receive his brother Esau's blessing at the hands of his father Isaac, who is too blind to know which son is standing before him. When poor Esau arrives late because he was hunting down food for Isaac, he pleads, "Do you have no blessing for me, father?" Isaac does, of course, but it is a poor one; he will be eternally cursed by having to serve his deceitful brother Jacob. And what shall we say of Joseph, again a favored son, cast into a pit by jealous brothers and sold into slavery? His yearning for home haunts him until the day he dies, when he begs to have his bones returned to the land of his youth.

There are family reconciliations here, too; models to yearn for, if we have alienated brothers and sisters. After some fourteen years of absence from each other, Jacob and Esau finally meet again and kiss, before going their separate ways. What reader can forget the Torah's acknowledgment that Jacob, who had feared his brother's ruinous wrath for so long, looks into Esau's face and "sees the face of God"? And the reconciliation of Joseph and his brothers brings tears to the eyes. We cry with Joseph, as he reveals his true identity to these brothers who sought to kill him, but whom he will now sustain in life because, perhaps, that was his destiny intended all along by God.

Tales like these give us the realistic side of parental pathos. Did anyone really believe the old-time television sitcoms like *Father Knows Best* and *Ozzie and Harriet*, where no challenge to growing up went deeper than a single half-hour's worth of parental wisdom? Genesis knows better. We watch our children play out the very roles of these, our forebears. We do what we can, but in the end, honest parents know how little they can influence the course of their children's lives. No wonder Genesis ends on a note of parental anxiety, with father Jacob blessing his children. Those children, like our own, enter their teenage years with hopes of independence and a double-edged heritage from their younger years. They are heirs to their parents' blessings but they also carry the invisible baggage of childhood. The sins of the parents really *are* visited on the children, just as the Bible claims. We are both blessed and cursed by the way our families formed us when we were young.

Genesis, then, is the first stage of life: It is childhood, our struggles with brothers, sisters—yes, and parents, too—capped in the end by the complex fabric of parental blessing, as if our mothers and fathers secretly collude, each in the moonlight while the family sleeps, to weave visions of their children's futures and pack them like garments into our psyches. It is their version of Jacob's verbal blessing with which Genesis ends. "Take it with you," our parents must have mumbled. "It will keep you warm."

And we do. We enter young adulthood wrapped in our parents' invisible visions, newly woven from our homes. We cross some equally indeterminate threshold into adult life, ready, we think, to take our place as individuals in our own right. No longer mere appendages of our elders, we have our own names now; so Exodus, the second book of the Bible, appropriately begins by listing the Israelites who are in Egypt, preparing for their life as responsible adults. It is in young adulthood that we first become conscious of our own individuality. Grown-up mail, like bills and notices, start arriving—addressed to us, not to our parents; we sign our names on a loan, a bank account, a check—and our names matter.

We shouldn't overdo it. Graduating from childhood and adolescence is not exactly leaving bondage. But children are at the mercy of their parents or guardians. They really do not have freedom. And all too many children are actually abused but dare not speak of it. Mastering the challenges of young adulthood is not easy, but at least you are on your own. The tasks involved are precisely what Exodus is all about.

First, there is the need to take responsibility; second, we look to find a partner with whom to settle down in a permanent relationship of love and faithfulness. Jewish tradition ascribes both these experiences to Sinai. When the Israelites leave Egypt, they are, in the Bible's words (Exod. 12:38) "a mixed multitude," a polite way of saying "a motley crew." In life-cycle terms, they are leaving adolescence, some ready for adulthood, and others not. But by Exodus 19, just seven chapters later, they have reached maturity, sending Moses up the mountain to receive the Ten Commandments. They must now be responsible adults. They have laws to keep, ethics to pursue, lives to lead in community.

Further, the Rabbis liken Sinai to marriage, saying that God and Israel are like husband and wife. The prophet Hosea later casts God as angry husband discharging Israel for harlotry with idols, in a failure of faithfulness. But all in all, the marriage lasts, despite its tensions. The model is far from perfect. God has all the power; Israel, none. But the basic idea is sound. "It is not good to be alone in the world," God had said of Adam (Gen. 2:18). Even God needs a partner, it seems. So, too, though many of us live fine fulfilling lives without a spouse or partner, Judaism advocates an ideal of mutual faithfulness between two committed lovers, who choose to chart life's storms together, come what may. Sinai, then, is the onset of adult responsibility: before the law, within community, and (ideally) within the confines of an intimate relationship that proves lasting.

The first thing that people do after marriage is settle down into a home. Single people do that, too. It is the first sign of adult permanence, instead of the vagabond existence of teenagers, living in their parents' homes, moving off each summer to camp, and then as college students, settling impermanently at college, semester by semester. Fittingly, the rest of Exodus is about the way the Israelites, even in the desert, construct a permanent home that they can at least carry with them: the desert tabernacle in which God dwells.

Quite incredibly, the next, and middle, book of Torah is Leviticus. It gets its English name from the fact that it details the priestly, or levitical, role in the social structure of ancient Israel. The Hebrew name is *Vayikra*, meaning, "God called." As we shall see, both are apt. Scholars who emphasize the Bible as a literary masterpiece that was composed by many generations over time say that Leviticus is the latest piece to be added to the Torah, the product of a priestly ruling class that converted Israel into a theocracy, after the waves of return from Babylonian exile from the sixth to the fifth centuries B.C.E.

Nowadays, writers make sure their works begin and end in interesting ways; if they drag a bit in the middle, they can live with that. In antiquity, however, the most important part of a book often came in the middle, as a way of drawing attention to its centrality. It matters, then, that Leviticus is the third of the five books of Torah. The narrative of Israel's travels from Egypt to the land of promise is not at all advanced here. That story goes on hold when Exodus ends and picks up again in Numbers, the fourth of these five books. Leviticus could have come as an afterthought, Book Five (perhaps)—a lengthy footnote to Israel's story. But it doesn't. By locating it in the middle, the Torah's anonymous editors let us know that its concerns are the very essence of life's journey.

The first two Hebrew words in the book are crucial: *vayikra elohim*, "God called." The centerpiece of a spiritual life is the sense that we are not here by accident. We are called. That is to say, every moment of life, from beginning to end, is a chance to rehear God's love-laden call to purpose. A much-cited aphorism assures us that God is found in the details. Watch a single drop of water slide preciously along a pane of glass, making a pattern that the science of chaos reveals as no less gorgeous than the wing of the monarch butterfly. Observe the furrows etched by time in a worker's wrinkled hands; the translucence of a soap bubble rising in the air, alight with rainbow colors until it pops; and the saucer eyes of the child who blew it. This is the stuff of Leviticus: God in the everyday details of life. Leviticus is a call to ordinariness: to menstruation, and food, and sex, and sacrifice, and the petty little ways that we can be good and decent people. It talks of leprosy and sickness; of bodies running down, and bodies getting better, too. It gives us childbirth as well, not its poetry, but the messy business that it really is—and the mystery in the messiness. Whoever said God's signature was neater than our own?

Jewish spirituality draws courage from the levitical metaphor of the everyday. After settling down in our Exodus-built home, we prepare for that everyday existence that American culture describes as draining. Life as a cycle of Torah tells us otherwise. This is what life is all about. The Talmud wonders where the messiah is hiding out in these pre-messianic years. And it answers: "He is binding up the wounds of injured people who crowd together in the city's gates." Even the Messiah is in part a mother, father, or other family caregiver, who spends life, Leviticus-like, with the daily drudgery of runny noses—and then, later, when the kids have grown up, who is still the family worrier, watching for signs of high blood pressure, cancer, and the thousand other ailments that we think happen only to other people but which are equally likely to afflict those we love—as the "other people" turn out to be ourselves.

Leviticus gives way to Numbers, the forty-year tale of desert wandering—called, in the Hebrew, just that: *B'midbar*, "In the wilderness." Throughout their journey, the Israelites complain caustically of God's "wisdom" in bringing them there. In terms of our life cycle, "the wilderness" is our midlife crisis. We spent Genesis and Exodus with yearly, monthly, even weekly and daily markers of our progress: our first tooth, first step, first date, first job, first pay check, first car. When we are young, we map our progress by the birthday candles people light for us—like the pillar of fire by day that the Israelites used to chart their journey. It's easy to find your way by the light of birthday candles, which grow in number from year to year—harder to do so when the pillar of birthday-candle fire diminishes because your birthday cake starts to come with just a single candle year after year, regardless of how old you are. When that happens, you are likely not far away from finding yourself *B'midbar,* wandering in the desert—maybe not for forty years—but perhaps as a forty-year-old or so, wondering just where your life is heading. Maybe you wake up one morning murmuring about a lack of water, nothing to slake your psychic thirst now that old dreams have dried up. You move on, but the surrounding sands look just the same. You seek out oases but find mirages instead—youthful aspirations that shimmer and dissipate into nothingness. The kids have grown up and are out of the house. You won't conquer the world, it seems. You find yourself negotiating with your dreams, scaling down expectations. Thoreau put it well: It is the time in life when we give up our youthful plans to construct a bridge to the moon and settle instead for a woodshed.

But the wilderness does end. Its purposelessness dissipates. We accept the aging process and look at ourselves in the mirror with a newfound admiration for who we are. We return to work with a passion, perhaps, or take up a second career that makes use of all we have learned from raising a family or doing volunteer work for over twenty years. When we do, we move on to the last book of the Torah: Deuteronomy.

America is not kind to Deuteronomy. It is the autumn of our lives, the years when the next generation supplants us in positions of authority and power. In traditional societies, sages were respected for all that they had learned in life. But scientific culture values visions of tomorrow, not lessons from yesterday. Discoveries in physics, like dot.com start-ups, are likely to come from the young who think in shortcuts, not from people who have been around the block and are happy to go back over old terrain. We value thinking differently above thinking deeply.

That same science is a doubled-edged sword, however. Even as it denigrates old age, it makes old age possible. If we are lucky enough to avoid such terrible afflictions as cancer and Lou Gehrig's disease, scientific medicine can keep us around for a very long time. With fine irony, we are preserved in years only to discover that those extra years are held against us by a culture that marginalizes the elderly. No one asks our opinions; we are shunted off to retirement homes to play endless rounds of golf, take up painting, and discuss the grandchildren.

And eventually, we realize that death is really stalking us. Growing old is not for the fainthearted. The people you know and love begin disappearing. You spend more days at funerals than at weddings. You cross out names in your address book. When you get the morning newspaper, you turn first to the obituaries. And you multiply time with doctors, not just your internist, whom you have been seeing for decades, but specialists who go by titles you never heard of before.

The Jewish metaphor of Deuteronomy does not deny the biological side of growing old so much as it complements it by reasserting the normal process of aging as, potentially, a meaningful exercise that is to be welcomed, not feared. The Book of Deuteronomy gets its name from the Greek *deutero*, meaning "second," and *nomos*, meaning "law." By and large, it restates laws mentioned earlier in the Torah, including the Ten Commandments, which appeared first in Exodus and then reappear here (Deut. 5). Scholars read Deuteronomy as a separate document begun about 621 B.C.E. during the reign of King Josiah and then continued by later writers who shared Josiah's political agenda—first and foremost, the centrality of the Jerusalem Temple, a doctrine that helped Josiah obliterate rival cultic centers while enhancing the importance of the one he controlled in Jerusalem. In the narrative biblical book that describes Josiah's reign, the authors of Deuteronomy supplied an explanation of their work that implicitly denies its overt political and economic ends. For them, "The high priest Hilkiah . . . found a scroll of the teaching in the house of the Lord" (Deut. 22:8). Many religious people still accept that interpretation, which allows them to place Deuteronomy in the reign of Josiah while still holding that its contents go back to Sinai, then somehow got lost and then rediscovered.

Spiritually speaking, exactly how Deuteronomy came into being is less important than the fact that the replication of law and the insistence on Jerusalem's centrality are part of the ongoing Torah narrative that only now reaches fruition. Deuteronomy is composed as a recapitulation of Israel's journey, provided by Moses as he grows older. In the end, his own death corresponds to the last lines of the book. Again, the shape of Torah parallels the shape of a human life. The death of Moses is simultaneously the end of the first cycle in Israel's saga, though both are picked up in the next turn of the page. Israel finds new life in the promised land, and Moses is followed by his chosen successor, Joshua.

The main plot from the Torah's beginning to end is Israel's journey to freedom. A subplot, however, is the career of Moses. The message for our own lives is that we, like Moses, necessarily grow old and die, but that we can use our own Deuteronomy to do what he did: review our story.

For life is not the sum total of all the things that happen to us. The dots of life are too many to be recalled in all their everyday detail. Nor do we even want to remember them all equally. We go to psychotherapists, for instance, to learn how to deal with dots that overwhelm us in their negativity. In the picture albums that we use to organize the selective perception of who we are, we weed out painful pictures and keep the pleasant ones. Deuteronomy is the time of life to get in touch with our own personal master narrative, to be able to own up to who we are, warts and all, and to tell our story to the next generation. For Judaism insistently denies the youth culture that expects life-enhancing wisdom only from the young. It contends that we can learn from the stories of our elders.

Jews tell stories. We positively relish memories. When Jesus instructed his disciples, "Do this in memory of me," he spoke as a Jew. Author Isaac Bashevis Singer is reputed to have said, "We Jews have many faults, but amnesia is not among them." The Jewish funeral liturgy is short; the eulogy is what takes all the time. Life is all about getting our story straight and passing it along in all its street-smart wisdom to the next generation. Jewish literature even knows of a specialized genre called "Ethical Wills," in which parents write out what they have learned from life and pass it on posthumously to their heirs. In the Deuteronomy of our lives, we become Moses, reliving our own tales as he did his, giving our own "Ten Commandments" of living all over again, in case the people we care most about didn't get it the first time.

And then, we prepare to die. Moses did so, says the Bible, on a height overlooking the promised land that he knew he would never personally get to. We, too, will never occupy the ultimate dreams of our youth; we will never know the final destiny of humanity or the denouement of the human saga that began when the first animals crawled out of the sea some twenty million years ago. We are not immortal. But Moses was able to live with the knowledge of his own mortality. He had written his tale and bequeathed it to those who followed. Having charged Joshua as his heir to pick up where he had to leave off, he knew his work was not in vain. And so, says rabbinic legend, Moses died gently with a divine kiss on his lips.

Our deepest desires change with the biblical book we are in. By the end of Deuteronomy, we want nothing more than Moses' fate.

Only at the *end*, of course. By providing its own way of looking at things, religion often "corrects" ideas that our culture presents as obvious, natural, and therefore unassailable. Here, then, we see the Jewish view of aging that altogether contradicts the usual American approach to the subject. American wisdom sees the twilight of our years as an unimportant interlude between adult usefulness and the final process of dying. Every other sector of the life cycle blossoms into a fuller period of strength; old age leads only to diminished capacity and then death. Jewish spirituality offers a critique of this perspective by defining old age as Deuteronomy, an entire fifth of the Torah, which is to say, an entire fifth of our lives, and a fifth that offers as much satisfaction as any other period of life. The truth is, every book of Torah, like every life passage, provides both promise and disappointment. The reason we fear the old age of Deuteronomy more than the childhood of Genesis or the youth-fulness of Exodus is that we think Deuteronomy is really the end. But Judaism denies that obvious assumption, too. To begin with, we have our Joshuas to take over for us, a frightening proposal, perhaps, for Americans socialized into believing that rugged individualism is everything, but a comforting idea for the Jewish mind that knows individual human life as only part of a much greater plan of which we can be only dimly aware. And anyway, Judaism promises more: some form of participation in the whole beyond this earthly existence; further life in a "world to come," the joy of a messianic age; an eternal life for the soul; and so forth. These, too, are metaphors. What life after death will be cannot be captured by minds that know only life in the here and now. But whatever it is, the common hill-shaped structure of life that people tend to draw need not be an accurate portrayal; we need not ever be "over the hill." We should look forward to Deuteronomy. It is the chance to get our story straight and to pass it on as our greatest gift to those we love most.

Life As . . .

I have by no means captured every metaphor for life that Jewish wisdom offers. I mean only to demonstrate that the shape of life is not a given; it is what we make of it. And we have no choice but to make *something* of it. The only question is what that something will be. The dominant secular offerings are terrible. They provide no transcendent purpose and promise nothing more than a return to childhood against our will, followed by meaningless suffering and the finality of death. The spirituality of metaphor demands something better than that. Our deepest traumas can be gates clanging shut with other gates opening somewhere ahead of us. The daily grind of ordinary responsibility can be Leviticus, and, therefore, sacred. Old age can be wonderful, not tragic.

To be human is to share the mystery of existence. The spirituality of metaphor embraces that mystery and invites us to conceptualize a shape out of the dots that comprise it. The alternative is living day by day with no sense whatever of what we may mean to eternity. We can manage that in the short run; but the emptiness of such an approach catches up with us eventually, if not at a tragic death of a daughter (my example here), then when we ourselves begin to feel caught in the end game of our own mortality. What is life, then? It is dots, offered to the only species in the universe able to find connections and to say, each day, as God did when God created a cosmos out of chaos: "This is very good."

Chapter Three

Living with Blessings:
The Spirituality of Stewardship

One should eat nothing before saying a blessing, as it is written,
"The earth is the Lord's and the fullness thereof."
PSALMS 24:1

One who makes enjoyable use of this world
without a blessing is guilty of sacrilege.
TOSEFTA, B'RAKHOT, 4:1

When my grandmother wanted to impress me with her one-line formula for success, she would remind me, *Sei a b'rohkhoh*, the Yiddish equivalent of the Hebrew phrase meaning "Be a blessing." Before eating, she would say, *Mach a b'rokhoh*, "Make a blessing," meaning that I should say the standard benediction that precedes meals, praising God for providing food. When she and the other members of her generation died, we captured their lasting worth in a Hebrew expression, *zecher tzaddik liv'rakhah*, "The memory of the righteous is a blessing." Though Judaism bequeathed the idea of blessing to Christianity and Western culture generally, blessings retain a special flavor in Jewish circles, where they provide ready access to the uniqueness of the Jewish way of being in the world.

To arrive at the root idea behind "blessing"—*b'rakhah*, in Hebrew— we need to set aside its popular connotation for a moment. Its original, more technically precise meaning derives from the rabbinic system of prayer.

People tend to think of prayer as a generic activity common to everyone: Muslims, Buddhists, Jews, Christians, and maybe even atheists

("There are no atheists in foxholes," as the old World War I axiom attested). But not all cultures pray the same way. Christian prayer, for example, has historically highlighted the Eucharist, a ritualized act involving the eating of bread and wine, sometimes called "taking communion." Even people who have never been inside a church have some familiarity with the Eucharist, since it is portrayed in literature, movies, and television. It actually emerged out of first-century Jewish meal customs: Its surrounding liturgy began as a form of the Jewish blessings that were recited at mealtimes. But the Eucharist went on to become something distinctively Christian, while blessings remained particularly Jewish, and to this day, what the Eucharist is to Christians, a blessing is to Jews. Reciting blessings is not the only thing Jews do when they pray, but it is the most distinctive thing, the single act of worship that best typifies the prayer life of Jews. Jews take blessings for granted, precisely because they are so ubiquitous in both the synagogue service and private devotion.

Blessings (also called benedictions) are easily recognizable as that particular literary genre in which rabbinic Jewish prayer is most often cast. They are verbal formulas, then, a form of specialized speech that has constituted the ritual trademark of Jewish worship for two thousand years.

Blessings feature the stock phrase "Blessed art Thou . . ." (Or, "Blessed are You . . ." in more modern English, corresponding to *Barukh atah* in Hebrew). This standard opening is followed by a variable set of words that stipulate the aspect of the universe for which God is being declared "blessed"—as, for instance, "Blessed are You . . . who brings forth bread from the earth" (the blessing that introduces meals), or "Blessed are You . . . for creating the produce of trees" (a variation that precedes snacking on an apple or a pear). Public daily liturgy consists most prominently of one blessing after another, while private spirituality calls forth blessings to match specific events that are apt to crop up as we go about our business in the world: seeing an old friend after a sustained absence, for instance, or observing a rainbow.

Blessings exist for the magnificent and the mundane. The blessing over a rainbow, for example, recollects the rainbow God showed Noah as a sign that the earth would never again be destroyed. Even going to the bathroom has a blessing that marvels at the miracle of the many "ducts and tubes" within the human body. There are blessings also for the most improbable occasions, as we see from an episode related by author laureate of the Jewish People, S. Y. Agnon (1888–1970).

Agnon was born in eastern Europe but moved to Israel as a young man of nineteen. In 1966, he was awarded the Nobel Prize for his literary vignettes that captured the traditional ethos of his youth. When he received the prize, the audience that had gathered around closed-circuit television screens outside is said to have been shocked as they watched him initiate conversation with King Gustaf VI. When reporters asked what he had said, Agnon explained that he had indeed been addressing a king: not the king of Sweden, however, but the King of Kings, the Holy Blessed One on high. There is a blessing for beholding an earthly monarch, and Agnon, a traditional Jew who had undoubtedly said most Jewish blessings at least once in his life but who had never encountered an actual king or queen before, was bent on saying it. Standing before the king, he had prayed: "Blessed are You, Eternal our God, Ruler of the universe, who shares majesty with human royalty."

Jewish blessings have abounded for two thousand years. To some extent, they go all the way back to the Bible, where we find biblical men and women referring to God as "blessed." But Judaism today is the product of postbiblical leaders called the Rabbis. The literary blessing that is so central to Jewish prayer is, therefore, a rabbinic innovation of the first or second century that continued until roughly the tenth century, when the practice of framing new blessings largely ceased. Although some Jews still make up new ones today, most limit themselves to the ones that have been handed down by tradition. Either way, blessings express a singular kind of Jewish spirituality.

For every art, people who are artists have a prior notion of what counts as success when they are finished. In music, for example, composers organize notes on a page only if they already know they are putting together a waltz, not a march, and know the difference between one and the other. Artists who paint landscapes determine in advance that a landscape is an appropriate subject and what rules of composition should be used to reproduce two-dimensionally what the eye sees in three dimensions. Japanese convention, for example, arranges objects that are farther away higher on the canvas than objects that are close, whereas traditional Western art prefers the technique of perspective, representing close objects as larger than objects far away. According to art historian E. H. Gombrich, as much as artists paint what they see, they see what they paint. Art forms depend only in part on what our senses perceive. Culture decides how our perceptions should be portrayed and what counts, therefore, as good art.

Literature, too, is an art form, so here as well culture decides what gets written and how. Nobody wrote novels until Miguel de Cervantes published *Don Quixote* in 1605; Russian novels like *War and Peace* or *The Brothers Karamazov* differ noticeably from American epic literature like *Moby-Dick* or *The Grapes of Wrath*. Unlike novels, poetry goes back in history, apparently, as far as literature of any sort extends. Homer wrote his *Iliad* within an oral culture that allowed him to use stock expressions and phrases that oral performers of poetry carried around in their heads. Byzantine synagogue poets juxtaposed biblical words drawn from here and there in Scripture according to complex rules of acrostics and meter, giving us the impression that they were doing with words what Byzantine mosaic artists were doing with bits of glass—creating a montage of sparkling verbal imagery in which each word is an intrinsic mosaic insert in a larger verbal whole. Then there are sonnets, a purely arbitrary decision to write poetry with fourteen lines; Shakespearian sonnets end with a rhymed couplet, but Petrarchan sonnets (named after Italian poet Francesco Petrarca, 1304–1374) don't.

Prayer is its own art form. It, too, depends on rules and genres. Jewish prayer exists in both poetry and prose, and each of these categories has subclassifications that one age or place has favored over another. Jewish liturgy was first collected in prayer-book form in the ninth century. It was added to (almost never subtracted from) over time, so on each and every page, worshipers can find examples of the aesthetics for prayer that various eras found particularly appealing. Some liturgical staples are pure prose, brief theological essays on reality. Others are prose in form, but so lacking in content that reciting them is almost like speaking in tongues. Jewish liturgy, unlike Quakers', for instance, does not favor silence in which the worshiper listens for the inner voice of the spirit to prompt the outpouring of the heart. The central prayer for Jews, called the *Amidah*, is *technically* to be said silently, but, in fact, people read through it individually, all at once, and in a stage whisper or even out loud, creating anything but silence.

Jewish prayer is "liturgical" like Catholic or Lutheran practice in that it mandates specific words of specific prayers at specific times and in specific ways. Jews feel obliged to read every word of every paragraph rather than make up new prayers. Practice was not always so invariable: The Rabbis who began it all in late antiquity were more like jazz musicians who improvised to suit the moment by weaving together memorized biblical citations and novel poetic imagery within the bounds of the rules of their worship art—much like African-American preachers who use no manuscript and so are free to innovate as they go along. That creative spontaneity was largely cut off when the first prayer book was promulgated, however—which is why new blessings ceased to be created by the tenth century. The invention of mass printing did the rest of the job, since worshipers with official prayer books in hand tend toward rote recitation of what they see and are unlikely to abide the free-flowing jazz artistry of prayer leaders who make up new prayers along the way.

Jewish prayer today is therefore highly dependent on an order of service contained in a printed prayer book. The book is outfitted with liturgical services for particular times of day and special days of the year. Worshipers meet to read through the service, albeit with many different kinds of "reading," ranging from *dav'ning* (a sort of speed-reading of the Hebrew, typical of Orthodox congregations) to English responsive reading (more common in Reform). Either way, the raw "stuff" of prayer is literary, and the literary "stuff" varies from page to page. But a unity of style is evident throughout: Every page is dependent on that particular literary form called the blessing. Without the blessing, Jewish liturgy would hardly be recognizable as Jewish. Blessings are the quintessentially Jewish form of prayer.

Kinds of Blessings

Blessings are categorized as short or long. The short blessings are one-liners, such as the blessings said for whole meals or fruit or the blessing Agnon said when he met King Gustav VI. A variation of this simple one-line blessing accompanies the performance of sacred acts that Judaism calls "commandments"—in Hebrew, *mitzvot*, the singular of which (commandment) is *mitzvah*. Judaism presupposes a universe that is sustained by covenants that God makes with human beings. The Jewish covenant occurred at Mount Sinai when the Torah, God's word to the Jewish People, was imparted. Commandments cover all aspects of human existence, everything from ethics (giving to the poor) to ritual (fasting on the Day of Atonement).

Upon engaging in such commanded actions, Jews say a somewhat different formula: "Blessed are You . . . who has sanctified us by your commandments and commanded us to . . ." Like the prior pattern for apples, rainbows, or royalty, the concluding clause varies with the occasion: ". . . to kindle Sabbath lights," for example, or ". . . to eat unleavened bread" (as part of the Passover seder). One-line blessings are used, therefore, not only for human experience (eating food, seeing

rainbows) but also upon performing commandments. Whether blessings of enjoyment or of commandment, the elementary blessing is a
one-line formula combining a fixed introduction that declares God
blessed ("Blessed are You . . .") and a variable conclusion expressing
the occasion that prompts the blessing.

These short blessings are often memorized—as we saw with Agnon
—so that they are at hand when apt experiences arise. They are, in any
event, personal things that individuals say, not corporate acts of prayer
recited together in a group, because even though Judaism is very largely
a religion that appreciates group experience, and even demands it as a
way to actualize our human potential to its fullest, it is also a religion
that appreciates how personal and private true experience of God must
be. We may eat in a group, but we physically swallow food with our own
body; we may look at a rainbow together, but we see it with our own eyes.
Private spirituality, then, produces blessings that are personal, private,
and short enough to be memorized by individuals who want to greet
God's world in all its majesty.

But Jewish prayer is primarily corporate, a set of verbiage that is recited together in a group; and the blessings of the Jewish prayer book, as
opposed to those an individual says for food, rainbows, and the like, are
not one-liners. These are the long blessings, theological essays, more or
less, on such themes as creation or revelation, running in length anywhere from a paragraph to a page or more before ending with tell-tale
blessing formulas that remind us of the one-liners that we examined
previously: "Blessed are You . . . who creates the lights [of the heavens]"
(for a blessing on creation); or "Blessed are You . . . who loves your people, Israel" (for a blessing on revelation). In English, this concluding
formula is generally called a eulogy, though its Hebrew name, *chatimah*,
is more aptly translated as "seal," in the sense of a signet ring that seals
a letter, allowing nothing more to be added to the letter's contents.
Leading up to the eulogy is the body of the blessing, which develops the
theological thought that the eulogy then seals. Sometimes the body includes a petition, in which case the eulogy celebrates God's power to

grant the request: for example, a blessing for healing, which reads, "Heal us, O Eternal One. . . . Blessed are You who heals the sick." Some of these long benedictions also begin with "Blessed are You . . ." and others do not. But in any case, blessings are easily spotted as either simple one-line proclamations or lengthy prose paragraphs with the requisite concluding eulogy, "Blessed are You. . . ."

Blessings have enjoyed such remarkable liturgical success that even biblical citations rarely occur without them. Individual verses are embedded everywhere in the wording of blessings, but so seamlessly, they are hardly noticeable. Sometimes larger biblical quotations, as much as whole paragraphs, are read independently, and then they are recognizable; but even so, blessings generally introduce and conclude them. Sabbath Torah readings, for instance, are sandwiched by blessings that celebrate revelation. Jewish worship includes clusters of psalms, too, called *Hallel*, meaning "psalms of praise," and they also demand introductory blessings such as, "Blessed are You . . . who commands us to read psalms of praise."

Drops of water contain almost invisible single-celled creatures called amoebas that encircle and swallow even smaller forms of life that constitute their prey. The blessing is Judaism's spiritual amoeba. It has incorporated all other worship forms, dominating the Jewish act of prayer. Alternatively, we may conceive of it as a towering liturgical oak tree whose spreading boughs have completely overshadowed the assortment of other liturgical bushes such as psalms, hymns, poems, and meditations.

By the middle of the second century, the blessing's liturgical domination was complete. Rabbi Meir, an influential Rabbi of the time, advised all Jews to say no less than one hundred blessings daily. He used the number "one hundred" generally to mean "a lot," because he knew that reciting all the requisite blessings was tantamount to going through the entire Jewish prayer regimen. So powerful had the blessing become that even the daily recitation of the Ten Commandments was replaced around the same time by a single blessing thanking God for revelation in general.

In the year 200 C.E., the Rabbis codified Jewish practice in a comprehensive law code called the *Mishnah*. They divided their work into six separate "books," each further divided into "tractates" devoted to specific topics. Nowhere in all six books is there a tractate labeled "Prayer." Instead, the rabbinic discussion of worship is incorporated in a tractate entitled "Blessings," since blessings are paradigmatic of Jewish prayer in general.

In sum, building on the Bible—but in their own creative way—the Rabbis fashioned an entirely novel prayer format that was successful enough to become virtually synonymous with Jewish worship in its entirety. When the Rabbis wanted a catchall title for their worship, they found it in this paradigmatic vehicle for spiritual expression: "Blessings." No wonder blessings entail their own unique form of rabbinic spirituality.

Blessing God, Blessing Food, Blessing Us: Who Blesses Whom?

To get at the spirituality of blessing, we need to grasp what the Rabbis thought blessings accomplish—not an easy matter for us who inhabit a culture where the word *bless* has been generalized to apply to all sorts of things. You sneeze, and someone says, "God bless you." "Count your blessings," we advise anyone fortunate enough to enjoy good health, long life, and relative prosperity. "Blessing," we imply, is something that human beings get from God. We even say of people we love, "You have been a blessing to me," meaning, possibly, that our dearest friends and family are heaven-sent.

Classical Christian spirituality seems to say that normal things come "unblessed," but that God, or God's representative, the priest who acts on God's behalf, can raise them to a level of blessedness. In the Catholic Eucharist, for instance, the priest "blesses the host" and then stores it in the area known as the "tabernacle." Ordinary bread won't do. Only bread that has been consecrated through blessing can be used for this sacred act of worship. The old Catholic rite of confession began with the request, "Bless me, Father, for I have sinned." Protestants, too, are likely to introduce meals with a reference to food that is blessed by God. American culture, Christian in its origins, adapts this Christian attitude in a popularized, even kitsch, way, when tourist stores stationed near genuine religious shrines hawk decorative stuffed pillows reading, "Bless this home, O Lord, we pray." By osmosis, Jews, too, are likely to believe that blessing is something we get from God to raise the ordinary to a higher level of sanctity.

Judaism has known that idea. It is thoroughly biblical—early Christianity drew it from there—but it occurs later also. Sixteenth-century Jewish mysticism called cabala taught that the universe had been created with good divine intention, but had fallen short of the ideal along the way. As boiling water shatters a glass into which it is poured, so God's emanating goodness shattered the cosmos at the time of creation. That is why material reality has blemishes and why evil mixes with good in our world. Not that God intended it that way. But the universe is, literally, broken, requiring repair. In this view, the religious act of reciting liturgical blessings accesses divine blessing from on high. Prayer is like spiritual oil that lubricates material reality, repairing the world.

Cabalistic theology was adopted by eighteenth-century Hasidism, which made its arcane ideas popularly available to average spiritual seekers, most of whom therefore identify religion's task as mending the world's fractures. In this view, blessings do indeed confer holiness on the things over which they are said. Jews today enjoy this Hasidic spirituality of blessing, partly because it is akin to the popularized Christian notion that pervades our culture. It "sounds" right when we encounter it.

But as appealing as it is to think of blessing as raising the ordinary to the level of the profound, the Rabbis offered another idea of what a blessing does. Because it is the perspective with which rabbinic Judaism was born and because it permeates the underpinning of classical Jewish liturgy, it is worth recovering as an alternative way of thinking about blessings. It turns out to have dramatic consequences for our time as well.

For the Rabbis, blessing is neither a boon we receive from God nor a higher quality of things that are otherwise profane. A blessing is a form of worship; it is something that we say. By saying it, we accomplish something in the world. We want to know what the Rabbis thought we accomplish.

Occasions for Blessing

The idea that talk alone accomplishes something goes contrary to intuition. We disparage speech as "just talk" and contrast it with action. But talking really is a form of doing. The most obvious examples are those occasions when language creates what are called "social facts." If I say, "I bet you twenty dollars it will rain tomorrow," and you answer, "It's a bet," then we have established something that did not exist before: a wager—with the real consequence that one of us will gain and the other lose. I can smash a bottle over the bow of my new sailboat and say, "I name you the *Prince William*"—and behold, it becomes the *Prince William*. At a wedding, the officiant announces, "I hereby declare you husband and wife," and two separate individuals become a married couple. What makes them so is a statement of speech recognized officially as having legal validity. Because saying really is doing, it is helpful to think of speech as "speech acts."

Different kinds of speech acts function differently and do not always comply with the content of what is said. I answer the telephone "Hello?" and you answer back, "Hi, it's me." In this example, words do not have precise content so much as they set up a connection so that we can say more. Or, "Hi, how are you?" you ask, as we bump into each other accidentally one day. "Fine," I say (even if I am not). "How are you?" In this case, we have used talk ritually, not to learn of each other's welfare, but to demonstrate that we are friends or acquaintances, not strangers.

Worship, too, is a series of speech acts that accomplish different things. Blessings are Judaism's primary religious speech act. They punctuate the moments of every day. More precisely, they fall into four categories. If we look carefully at the four typical occasions evoking blessings, we discover what the Rabbis thought blessings do.

(1) There are blessings said upon *performing commandments.*
We looked at these previously. They accompany such ritually prescribed acts as lighting Sabbath candles, and they elicit the formula, "Blessed are You . . . for sanctifying us with Your com-mandments and commanding us . . . [in this case, to kindle Sabbath lights]."

(2) There are blessings *to punctuate time.* These are the long bless-ings that comprise the fixed liturgy for synagogue and home: They mark the daily schedule of sunrise and sunset and inaugurate spe-cial days such as the Sabbath and holidays.

(3) There are blessings that *accompany certain voluntary acts.* Bless-ings accompany eating, for example, or donning new clothes, or en-tering a cemetery. These are things we generally have to do at some time or other, but they remain elective in that we plan when and, sometimes, even whether to do them.

(4) There are blessings for *certain involuntary occasions.* These blessings accompany such surprise events as seeing a rainbow, hearing good or bad news, and finding ourselves at a place where a miracle occurred. They differ from blessings in the preceding cate-gory because they accompany events that arrive unplanned and sometimes (like hearing bad news) unwelcomed.

We said above that, for the Rabbis, blessings do not bless things in the sense of making them sacred. A closer look at the third type of blessings (those that accompany voluntary acts) shows, in fact, that just the oppo-site is the case, but the texts where this surprising insight is revealed are not easily accessible to modern readers. They are ancient (bad enough), legal (even worse), and cryptic in the extreme (worse still). Before actually looking at the texts, then, we should look briefly at the nature of Jewish texts generally and the Mishnah in particular. The search for spirituality behind Jewish law is something of a spiritual detective story.

Reading Rabbinic Literature: Spirituality behind the Law

The Mishnah is the earliest Jewish law code, but by Western standards it is a strange code indeed because it is so terse. It seems to be a synopsis of the majority opinion on important and even unimportant matters. A minority view may be included as well.

To make matters worse, the laconic statements are not about principle, but about cases. It would be bad enough if the first entry were, "Red lights mean stop; green lights mean go." At least you get a rule that way. But the Mishnah is more likely to say, "Drivers who go through red lights causing damage are guilty and pay a fine. If the light is covered by a tree branch, they are innocent. The majority say the government pays; Justice Judah says no one pays." What good is that for deriving principles?

But Jews have been deriving principles from such legal fragments for centuries. From the fact that drivers may be governed by a system of streetlights, it may be concluded that "under certain conditions, society may restrain individual freedom." Americans battled over this principle for decades. Radical individualism lost and society won. A second principle follows: Since the government may be forced to pay damages if it does not keep the streetlights visible, it follows that "individuals may hold the body politic responsible, as if society were an individual." That is to say, society itself is not above its own laws.

The Mishnah is not usually about real court cases. It is more akin to what great physicists like Albert Einstein called "thought experiments." The Mishnah imagines legal cases and their consequences. It never actually defines the facts of the case, however; instead, it forces the reader to do so. That is where the fun starts.

Our case must be about a driver who went through a red light and damaged someone else's property or person. It cannot be a case of homicide, because monetary damages are involved here, and elsewhere in the Mishnah loss of life is ruled to be beyond financial compensation. Also, the driver is assumed to have known the law and also that the law can legitimately limit individual freedom. But what if the driver claims that the stoplight was covered by a tree branch and could not be seen? The majority view, which is always probative, is that the defendant can countersue the state for not removing the branch, which, we must imagine, is in the public domain. So, the state can limit individualism, but is subject to its own limitations and may be sued for damages just as a private citizen can be. To be sure, my example is a thought experiment: I made it up. But it demonstrates the way the Mishnah speaks, and my unraveling of the principles is what Jewish jurisprudence has been doing for almost two thousand years.

In chapter 4, I explain how the study of these tangled webs of legal precedent is its own form of Jewish spirituality. We can broach this topic now, however, by asking how dry-as-dust legal literature can contain principles of spirituality. The most serious objection I get from people who think "Jewish spirituality" is an oxymoron is the simple act of pointing a finger at the kind of texts Jews have, as if to say, "How can such legal literature yield spirituality?"

Reading the Mishnah for spirituality seems like reading the raw data of the Census Bureau for world history. What could be more dry than population statistics, infant mortality rates, and patterns of disease distribution? But, in fact, census figures are precisely the background data out of which historians spin their narratives of history. So, too, Jewish legal literature reveals a spiritual substructure. If we define spirituality as the deep and abiding attitude we take to the universe in all its manifestations—as I have called it here, the Jewish way of being in the world —it is hard to see how the Rabbis could not have had spiritual intentions.

This survey of the nature of Jewish texts impacts our view of blessings because blessings, too, are described in the very same legal terms as my example about going through a red light. The Mishnah's legislative rhetoric regarding mealtime blessings reveals an early rabbinic notion of spirituality that is both brilliant and bold in its conception.

Blessings over Voluntary Acts: Take Food, for Instance

Most people know that the synagogue is a primary focus for Jewish public prayer. Less well known is the parallel importance of the home as a Jewish locus for the sacred. Holidays are partly celebrated in synagogues, but partly in homes also. On Shabbat, for example (the Sabbath), there are synagogue services, but Shabbat is inaugurated with a festive dinner and concluded with a ritual of "separation" (*havdalah*)—both at home. Passover, too, has synagogue services, but it is best known for its seder, a ritual meal held around the dining-room table. The list goes on and on, but the point is easily made: Jewish spirituality cannot be fully captured by a study of synagogue ritual. That is why comparisons of church and synagogue attendance, which regularly show Jews attending Sabbath services less frequently than Christians, do not tell the whole tale. Jews who, for whatever reason, cannot or do not appear at public worship may nonetheless be aware of the sacred nature of their calendar and may be observing their sacred times at home.

Home meals especially are sacred within Judaism. It is not accidental that holy days are inaugurated just as dinner begins, that the Passover seder is a meal, and that most of the one-line blessings that Jews know by heart revolve around food. This food-centeredness comes from the Greco-Roman milieu in which rabbinic Judaism was born.

The Greco-Roman contribution to Judaism's sacred meals comes from banquets called *symposia*. The most famous description of such a banquet is in a dialogue by Plato (called *Symposium*) in which a group of Socrates' colleagues meet for dinner and philosophic discussion. A symposium banquet, then, was a combination of lavish food and drink, followed by studious, but not too heavy, conversation. Women were probably present, but they go unmentioned in the sources, which treat the dinners as rituals for men alone. The men ate dinner while reclining on couches; then they'd while away the time with somewhat serious talk, modified by the extent of the stupor into which the heavy food and overflowing wine had put them. Christians, too, should recognize the symposium. Jesus' last supper follows the symposium tradition, albeit in not so festive a way as the Platonic example; and Paul recognizes standard mealtime customs when he writes to the Corinthians to scold them for getting drunk instead of properly remembering their Lord.

By then, the symposium had evolved into informal eating associations—loosely knit social networks in which festivals and life-cycle events could be shared over dinner. The Jewish instance—celebrated also by Jesus, as a Jew—was called a *chavurah* (pl. *chavurot*). Its members (in Jesus' case, the disciples) were *chaverim*, a Hebrew word currently used to mean "friends," but used then to denote those gathered around the table. We have evidence of *chavurot* as early as the second century B.C.E., but by the second century C.E., *chavurot* come more finely into focus. By then, the second temple had been destroyed, rabbinic Judaism was well underway, and a host of religious concerns had been added to the Jewish agenda.

Chief among these concerns was the question of what might substitute for the destruction of the Temple in Jerusalem. The Temple was unlike any institution modern Jews have ever experienced. The actual building was monumental in size and mythic in importance. It was said that long before the first Temple was built, Abraham had attempted to sacrifice Isaac there. At its center was a chamber called the Holy of Holies into which only one man, the high priest, entered once annually on the most sacred day of the year, Yom Kippur. Jews as far away as the Tigris-Euphrates Valley contributed donations to the Temple's lavish functioning. Twice daily, sacrifices were offered with all the pomp and circumstance imaginable, while pilgrims from miles around observed the cult, which was believed to effect atonement for sin and, therefore, to guarantee a future for God's People. Once before, a temple like this had been destroyed, but that was in 587 B.C.E., more than six centuries past. Then, during the bitter Roman siege and ensuing occupation, a second temple even more glorious than the first was burned to the ground, leaving only a single retaining wall standing. The theological issue of the day was whether the end of the Second Temple spelled the end of Judaism, or whether Judaism could continue with some other institution taking the Temple's place.

Continuing the actual sacrifices was impossible, since Deuteronomy had limited sacrifice to the Temple alone. So, homes, where religious table groups were meeting anyway, replaced the Temple. The table was compared to an altar. The food served there was tithed just as Temple produce had been; everyone in attendance was likened to a priest, consuming sacred meals in a state of equally sacred purity.

No wonder blessings over food emerged as a form of Jewish piety. Mealtime prayer underscored how sacred the ordinary table had become in the newly evolving Jewish identity of the post-Temple period.

One-third of the entire Mishnah's tractate on blessings deals with food regulations: the blessings over food that are said prior to meals; the Grace after meals; and various debates regarding further ritual requirements for a proper religious meal. Chapter 6 of that tractate begins with the question, "What blessings should be said over produce?" and goes on to discriminate between produce from trees and produce from the earth. The analysis of this passage is critical; though admittedly not easy, it proves exceptionally rewarding.

- What blessing should be said over produce?

- Over produce of the tree, one says, "[Blessed are You . . .] who creates the produce of the tree."
  - Except for wine, over which one says, ". . . who creates the produce of the vine."

- Over produce of the earth, one says, ". . . who creates produce of the soil."
  - Except for bread, over which one says, ". . . who brings forth bread from the earth."

- Over vegetables, one says, ". . . who creates the fruit of the soil."
  - Rabbi Judah says, ". . . who creates kinds of greenery."

Everything depends on categories. A man beats his wife, let us say. In some societies, she is considered his property and he may beat her with impunity. Our own view is that wives are not property but persons. She may file criminal charges against him. In some societies, children are legally born of their mother and inherit through her. In other societies, children are only biologically, not legally, born to their mother; they inherit through their father. Henry VIII, for instance, didn't much care which wife bore him a son, since any son would inherit the monarchy through him, the father.

Categories have subcategories. Under the category of British royalty, for instance, there are kings and queens; then dukes and duchesses. "Royalty" is the "apex category," the very top of the categorization system under which all other kinds of royalty can be subsumed.

What about food? My very question gives it away. Our culture thinks that "food" is the apex category, under which you have produce on one hand, let us say, and edible animals on the other. We further divide produce into fruit and vegetables; then animals into meat, fish, and poultry. The opening question of our Mishnah, then, seems somewhat odd. It ought to have been "What blessings do you say for food?" rather than "What blessings do you say for produce?" That, at least, is how we would have written it, since to modern readers it is obvious that the topic in general must be "Blessings over Food."

But is it? We should not prejudge the case. The spirituality of blessing that we seek depends on our entering the mind-set of the Rabbis whose work we read. If they began with a general statement about blessings over produce, we should assume that "produce" is an apex category. The rest of the chapter discusses special cases of produce, but never chicken, beef, or fish, for example. There are exceptions, but by and large, *it is not what humans make, or the other creatures that humans eat, but what the earth produces* that dominates the author's attention. Moreover, the blessing content invariably emphasizes the food's "delivery system," that is, *how* a food comes to us from its earthly source ("produce of the tree," "produce of the soil," etc.). The rabbinic editor's concern was to provide blessings for the things we get from the earth and to specify in each case the delivery system, that is, how the food in question becomes available to us.

The theology behind this interest in the earth's produce is set forth in two other remarkably straightforward rabbinic texts.

It is written, "The earth is the Lord's and the fullness thereof" (Ps. 24:1), but we read also, "God has given the earth to human beings" (Ps. 115:16). There is no contradiction. The first verse reflects the situation before we say a blessing, and the second verse refers to after the blessing has been said.

In other words, *food blessings release food of the earth from its natural state of belonging to God.* No wonder these blessings expressly state the food's delivery system! The whole point of reciting them is to effect the delivery of food to humans, to go from Psalm 24:1 to Psalm 115:16, as our rabbinic author puts it.

A variant version of the same teaching instructs us, "One should eat nothing before saying a blessing, as it is written, 'The earth is the Lord's and the fullness thereof' (Ps. 24:1). One who makes enjoyable use of this world without a blessing is guilty of sacrilege."

Sacrilege (*m'ilah,* in Hebrew) is a technical term. While the Temple stood, people donated food or property to it, at which time, the donated items became the irreversible possession of God and God's stewards, the priests. It was "sanctified property" (in Hebrew, *hekdesh*), usable only by priests on behalf of God. Laypeople who were at a lower level of sanctity were forbidden to use it. Sacrilege is the sin occasioned by laypeople who use *hekdesh* as if they were priests. In other words, far from *adding* sanctity to what we eat (the commonly held view that we looked at previously), blessings over food *release what we eat from its natural state of sanctity, so that we, who are not God or God's priests, can eat it in the first place.* In rabbinic tradition, we do not "bless our food" so much as we say blessings over it. By acknowledging its ownership by God and the delivery system by which it reaches us, we may have access to it.

Blessings as Transformations

Blessings over food are thus transformative. They are speech acts that transform the sacred bounty of nature (which belongs to God as *hekdesh*) into the ordinary, so that ordinary people can consume it. Similarly, if we go back to the other categories of blessing, we see that they also transform the cosmos, which is absolutely holy and, therefore, God's, not ours. Blessings raise human consciousness of how sacred the universe is so that ordinary human beings may rightly enjoy it.

The food blessings that we looked at are part of the larger category of "blessings that accompany voluntary acts." Other such voluntary acts are entering sacred space (a cemetery) or seeing friends after the passage of time (and acknowledging God who "has given us life, sustained us and brought us to this season"). No less than when we eat God's produce, these acts put us in contact with the sacred, so require blessings. The category of "involuntary acts" is similar. It consists of cosmic events that intrude on us. We see a rainbow or observe a storm. To the rabbinic mind, these natural phenomena are reflections of God's promise or might—as the blessings themselves say. So, we open ourselves to them by removing them from the category of pure holiness, and, like the food we eat, we render them fit for human enjoyment. Similarly, the normal public liturgy of the category we called "punctuating time" can be explained as the intrusion into our lives of the flow of time. It is God who brings on day and night, the blessing says—again, an explicit reference to the delivery system, this time not of food but of cosmic phenomena that are delivered to our senses regularly and must be *de*sanctified if we are to enjoy them. There are also special blessings for the Sabbath and holy days, not in order to sanctify them—for they are already holy—but to enable Israel to partake of them. And finally, there are the "blessings over commandments," which make it possible for ordinary Jews to do God's sacred work in the first place.

Historian of religion Mircea Eliade holds that religion enables human beings to reenact those moments in history when the divine breaks in on us. For the Rabbis, the divine regularly did so: in sacred time, sacred space, representations of sacred events, God's daily work in the heavens, and even ordinary human activities that took on sacred status by virtue of their being divinely commanded. All of these take blessings. First and foremost, blessings are liturgical speech acts that celebrate the reality of the divine, allowing ordinary people who are not divine to live in a universe that is God's.

The Life of Blessing: Radical Awe in the Face of Existence

This is the question: What is the nature of existence, our own and eternity's? The question is existential, not scientific. It is spiritual to its core. Let us assume the validity of whatever science has to say. Let us grant, for example, that at some point—a "singularity," they call it—time itself came into being with a big bang, so that in an instant the universe was born. Let us grant further that purely materialist considerations explain the chance outcome of our being born. Once matter had been founded, we need reference no hidden hand of God to explain our own existence. Let us grant all that and more. How in the world does any of that teach me to live such that on my deathbed I am ready to die?

There are only three possibilities, and it is purely a matter of faith which one we choose. The most malevolent choice is to play the power game on a cosmic scale, casting ourselves as robber barons of the earth. As a group, we can act like a superspecies dropped capriciously on a planet that we dominate ruthlessly just because we can. The litany of possibilities is well known: pollute its atmosphere, poison its waters, denude its forests. Descartes sought truth in the certainty that "I think, therefore I am." Perhaps a truer estimate of what we may know is "I can, therefore I will." Why not?

The spirituality of blessing explains why not. The universe belongs to God, not us. We are its trusted keepers. It is *hekdesh:* sacred. Yet we may indeed use the produce of the earth, as we may enjoy the beauty of a flower, marvel at an electrical storm, or simply greet a new sunrise—because we have blessings. Blessings transform what we need of creation's bounty into gifts for our use. But only what we need, not more —to waste resources is a sin in the rabbinic lexicon—and only with acknowledgment of the One who made it, owns it, but graciously grants it to us.

The second possibility is not purposefully malevolent, but it is equally destructive. That is to imagine that there are no daily miracles. The classic Jewish prayer that acknowledges God speaks of "daily miracles, morning, noon and night." A miracle, by Jewish standards, need not be the overturning of the natural order. On the contrary, a famous Talmudic passage (that we encounter in detail in chapter 4) describes one Rabbi arguing with his peers and demonstrating his case by his ability to move water upstream and invoke voices from heaven. The Rabbis reject his claims. These are inadmissable "miracles" precisely because God has arranged the world to be what it is, and *that* is the real miracle.

Some sins are not malevolent. To walk sightless among miracles in a state of blasé indifference to the miracle of being is itself such a sin. It is wrong in its own right because it squanders the preciousness of being;

and wrong on a second count: It permits robber barons to do what they wish. Abraham Joshua Heschel (1907–1972), theologian and prophetic champion of social justice, spoke of the religious imperative of facing the world with "radical awe." To exist in the world is itself a miracle. That there should be a universe at all and that it should be ordered as it is—these are miracles that demand our attention.

The spirituality of blessing insists on such radical amazement, for it sees the presence of God behind the diverse phenomena of nature, even the daily rise and set of the sun. Further, it makes us active participants with God in this miracle of the universe, for it prescribes blessings over commanded human actions. We may not take the world for granted; and we may not remain passive recipients of miracle, for we must add to the miracle by our own everyday activities, themselves a miraculous gift for which we acknowledge the unknown and unseen force that we name God.

The third option, then, is what Rabbinic Judaism demands: Heschel's radical awe. We know little or nothing about how we came to be or where we will ultimately go, but we are in charge of what we do while we are here. We can revere a universe as the possession of God, not ourselves; we can acknowledge the supreme gift of life and the willingness of God to share the universe with us to sustain us. We can see the reality of God breaking in on our existence with a gorgeous sunrise, a command to act as God does, the flow of the seasons, life itself (as long as we have it), and even death, when it comes and when we are forced to confront it. We can live a life of blessing, stewards of God's sacred bounty.

Chapter Four

Living by Torah: The Spirituality of Discovery

If you have learned much Torah, claim no credit for yourself.
That is the end toward which you were created.
MISHNAH, PIRKEI AVOT 2:9

The public acknowledgment of Jews as "the people of the book" is generally said to go back to Muhammad. Whether the attribution is accurate or not, the centrality of study in Jewish life is undeniable. What is not so commonly comprehended is the almost sacramental nature of that study. As we saw in chapter 2, the gift of Torah is God's supreme act of grace. In Torah, above all, God's will is known. Where board meetings in churches are likely to be framed with opening and closing prayers, the synagogue equivalents are more usually introduced by a few moments of study called a *d'var Torah,* "a word of Torah." No finer compliment exists than to say that someone is a *yode'a sefer,* "a knower of the book." Or sometimes, in traditional circles, just the Yiddish that means "he/she knows." There is no object for the sentence. It is not a case of knowing something in particular, such as the contents of the latest Supreme Court decision or a recent finding in astrophysics. It is the virtue of knowing one's way around the multiplicity of texts that go by the name "Torah."

Study as Spiritual Artistry

As we saw in chapter 2, in its narrowest definition, Torah comprises the five books of Moses with which the Bible begins. Every Sabbath service features a public reading of a successive section of it, known as "the weekly portion" (*parashat hashavu'a*), so that Jews attending synagogue weekly get to hear it read from beginning to end, annually. But Torah can also mean the entire Bible and Jewish wisdom generally. The whole point of Jewish life is the study of Torah, not because that study solves world problems or provides personal guidance (though, in fact, it does both). The Jewish ideal is a life of Torah study for its own sake.

It is difficult to comprehend the extent to which Judaism casts study as a spiritual enterprise because, in the modern world, the act of study has become so thoroughly secularized. *Rabbi*, for instance, means "my teacher," but the Hebrew conjures up far more than the image of a schoolteacher or even a distinguished university professor. In the secular model, knowledge is presumed to grow with time: Teachers use the most up-to-date textbooks and professors are supposed to read, or even write, the latest literature on a subject. In the academic world, only the most current view on any topic counts. Judaism agrees with this way of looking at things when it comes to secular matters such as science or history, but not in the body of religious knowledge that constitutes the spiritual search for truth. There, the Jewish theory of knowledge assumes that the older the authority, the better.

Take the Bible itself, for instance. The Bible is the source of all Jewish knowledge, but the Bible is not read literally. Whose view of the Bible should be accepted then? Secular authorities teaching in departments of religion at any university assume that they know it best; as the latest experts, they know what everyone who came before them knew, but in addition, they have insights from archaeology, textual criticism, and ancient Near Eastern textual parallels that were not available to previous generations. Jews are distinctly schizophrenic on this score. Except for ultra-Orthodox believers, Jews accept the findings of modern biblical criticism without protest. But when they study Torah as a spiritual exercise rather than an academic discipline, none of that modern knowledge is brought to bear. It is compartmentalized as true but irrelevantly so. Even Jewish members of the university Bible departments who teach their modern discipline with passion revert to a premodern mentality when they study the Bible as a Jew—which is to say, when they approach it as a spiritual discipline.

When it comes to mining the Bible for spiritual wisdom, the Jewish way of study assumes that the people closest in time to the Bible—not those most distant from it—knew it best. These are the scholar class known as the Rabbis, who came into existence roughly in the last third of the second century B.C.E. Those who lived before the year 200 C.E. are known as Tannas (Hebrew, *Tanna'im*; singular, *Tanna*), and those who lived after 200 but prior to the codification of the Talmud sometime in the sixth century C.E. are called Amoras (Hebrew, *Amora'im*, singular, *Amora*). Each group composed its own sacred literature. The primary tannaitic contribution is the Mishnah, which, as I have noted, is a terse and very laconic collection of Jewish law. The *Amora'im* composed a much longer set of books called the Talmud, which purports to explain the Mishnah, just as the Mishnah purportedly draws out lessons from the Bible. When learned Jews study, they study the Talmud. Jews who cannot study Talmud because of its difficulty study other books that quote the Talmud.

It is Talmud study, however, that most clearly sets off as unique the Jewish search for spiritual truth. The ideal is a *daf yomi*, "a two-sided page a day," almost an impossibility for all but a few. Nonetheless, all over the world thousands of Jews arise early enough each morning to master their page of intricately reasoned argumentation about arcane subjects that may have no immediate relevance to their lives and only then go to work. The standard published version of the Talmud contains twenty folio volumes, 2,717 double pages in all. But the language is so terse and the logic so tight that the standard English version takes up 16,114 pages in all. The *daf yomi* averages out at 5.93 English pages a day. In 1997, a number of Jews from all over the world rented New York's Madison Square Gardens to celebrate their completion of the entire cycle; and then they began reading page 1 all over again.

There are actually two Talmuds, one that was composed in the Land of Israel about 400 C.E., and another much longer version from Babylonia that was finally edited and sealed sometime in the sixth or seventh century. The Babylonian Talmud (or *Bavli*, in Hebrew) is considered superior. Both Talmuds, but especially the *Bavli*, attracted authoritative literary glosses, first in Babylonian academies from the eighth to the eleventh centuries, and then in North Africa and Europe from about the tenth to the sixteenth centuries. By then several summary codes of Jewish law had been composed, and they too were attracting commentaries. From the sixteenth century to the present day, the commentaries on the Talmud and the codes proliferated, as did commentaries on the commentaries, and even commentaries on the commentaries on the commentaries. So, too, did various other independent works, including responsa to actual questions of practice, so that Jewish study nowadays generally begins with the Talmud as the authoritative Jewish understanding of the Bible, and then works backward through the Mishnah to the Bible itself and forward through the endless strata of literature pitting the opinion of an eighteenth-century Lithuanian master, say, against that of a fourteenth-century Egyptian interpreter, both of whom have read everything in existence up to their time and who stand in different interpretive traditions.

Simultaneously, the Bible itself was attracting its own immediate interpretations. The most ancient ones, beginning in the second century, were like running commentaries on the biblical text, filling in the gaps of knowledge and asking questions that arise from a close reading of the text—such as why Abraham is never found talking to Sarah after his attempt to slaughter Isaac, or why Noah is called a "righteous" man but only "in his generation." These books were called Midrash. Later, especially in post-Crusade Europe, whole sets of new marginal commentaries developed, drawing on Midrash and on Talmud, but filled primarily with novel solutions to old textual conundrums. Today, even those Jews who have not mastered Talmudic study are apt to spend some time with Midrash and with commentaries. Most synagogues have several Torah study classes, and Jewish newspapers carry articles on the weekly Torah reading that summarize some midrashic and Talmudic wisdom on a section of it, and then propose novel ideas that get added to the inexhaustible sum of wisdom known as Torah.

In the last chapter, I described the blessing as Judaism's unique liturgical art form. Now we see that different commentary traditions are also akin to different schools of art. Thinking through the nature of such schools elucidates the way in which Jewish commentary has tended toward a unique artistic feature called *pilpul*.

Cultures invent their own favorite art forms; then, as their favored art grows in complexity, they organize its kinds of artistic output into hierarchies. In Western literature, for example, the classic essay ranks higher than a newspaper editorial, and poetry is considered better than prose. In music, the symphony outranks a simple march or waltz. Art may tend toward complexity (symphonies) or toward brevity of expression (Japanese haiku)—it all depends on cultural whim and is not predictable from the outside. Westerners may marvel at Chinese calligraphy, but without immersing themselves in Chinese cultural categories, they can hardly understand it. The point is, every culture defines its own idealized version of art and then invests its best resources in deepening its capacity to create and to appreciate the art that it values.

What the blessing is to prayer in particular, study of sacred text is to Judaism in general. It is the overall Jewish art par excellence. The commentaries on commentaries on commentaries are akin to the outpouring of British poetry, American jazz, or Italian opera. Jewish study reaches its zenith in legal commentary, which sometimes evolves into a rarified version known as *pilpul*.

Pilpul *and Pure Law*

Despite its faith in the rule of law as the basis for democracy, Western thought harbors a deep suspicion of law as being merely what is necessary to hold society together, not what is desirable in the best of all human scenarios. Modern Western philosophy takes this grudging acceptance of law for granted in that brand of political philosophy known as social contract theory. According to social contract theorists, law comes about only because human beings would tear each other apart without it. Once upon a time, human beings in a presumed state of nature necessarily banded together and ceded their independence to rulers whose job it was to establish and to maintain laws, since life without human law knows only the law of the jungle. As Thomas Hobbes (1588–1679) put it, life in the state of nature is "nasty, mean, brutish and short." Alternatively, in the famous declaration of French romantic Jean-Jacques Rousseau (1712–1778), "Man is born free and everywhere he is in chains." The arch-conservative Hobbes saw the law as necessary; the radically liberal Rousseau saw it as oppressive; neither saw it as inherently desirable. Law was understood only as a positive or negative social contract imposed on individuals.

As different as they were, both Hobbes and Rousseau were drawing their demeaning views of law from a strain of thought in Christianity. Christianity emerged from within Judaism as a denial of the validity of Jewish law. Its imminent messianism assumed that law, which is indeed necessary in an unredeemed world, became redundant when salvation was introduced into human history with the death and resurrection of Christ. The apostle Paul heralded a second covenant for the new Israel. The first, the covenant of Sinai, introduced God's law into the world, but that law was merely preparatory to the second covenant of Christ, a covenant rooted not in law but in love. Contrary to the Rabbis, for whom deliverance arrives because God's law is scrupulously kept, Paul taught that salvation comes about only through faith in Christ.

As Christian thought became synonymous with European culture, law was increasingly seen as necessary but not ultimately desirable. Sociologist Max Weber taught us that one good way to understand people is to examine carefully a culture's ideal man or woman. Christian social life developed the monastic ascetic who shunned the world with all its necessary legal relationships. That, at least, was the ideal. The same Rousseau who bemoaned the necessary shackling of society contrasted so-called Christian authorities in the France of his day with what he held to be true Christians: people who were "wholly spiritual," he said, because they would be occupied "only with the thought of heaven. The Christian's country is no longer of this world."

By contrast, from the rabbinic era on, the Jewish ideal was the scholar studying the Talmud, day and night. Chaim Nachman Bialik (1873–1934), the greatest Hebrew poet of modern times, grew up in a small Polish village where such scholarship abounded. Later, he would remember the study of Talmud in his celebrated poem, "If You Really Want to Know":

If you really want to know the well
from which our martyred forebears drew
their strength of soul . . .

If it is your fondest wish to see the breast
on which was poured a people's tears,
its heart- and soul-felt bitterness
the place where cries broke out and gushed like water . . .

If you really want to know the fortress
where your forebears stored the treasures of their souls—
their scrolls of Torah, holy of holies—
that it might save them . . .

If it is your fondest wish to know the refuge
where the spirit of your people
was preserved in all its purity,
where even at life's contemptible worst,
the beauty of this people's youth never withered . . .

Tormented brothers and sisters,
If you do not know all this,
then . . .

Turn to the synagogue, old and weathered.
To this day, you may see there
in the layers of shadowed darkness,
in some tiny corner, or before a wood-burning stove—
like skinny stocks of wheat, just a specter
of something long since come and gone—
Jews with faces shrunk and wrinkled
Jews weighed down by *golus* exile,
Who nonetheless
Lose their cares
In a tattered page of Talmud
Or the age old conversations of Midrash,
And wipe out worry by reciting psalms.
How desolate a sight this is to strangers
Who will never understand.
But your heart will tell you
That your feet tread the threshold of our House of Life,
Your eyes see the storehouse of our soul.

Bialik refers both to Talmud and Midrash. We have seen already that
Midrash is the art of elaborating on the biblical narrative, filling in the
gaps between the lines with stories, pithy sayings, parables, and any
other manner of teaching suggested by the biblical text. By contrast, Talmud is the study of Jewish law. In the hierarchy of study, Talmud ranks
supreme. Jewish scholars glory precisely in the laws of this world. Like
Rousseau's idealized Christians, they too focus on the Kingdom of
Heaven. But they know that only punctilious study of the law will get
them there. Indeed, according to the third-century Talmudic master

known as Samuel, "The world to come is just like this world in all respects, except that no one will be enslaved." In other words, the law will hold there as well.

But if the Talmud is a law book, it is a very peculiar one. Though it purports to be a commentary on the Mishnah, most of it has nothing whatever to do with the particular laws of the Mishnah on which it comments. In form, it is sheer argumentation, the combined sayings of several centuries organized into two debating sides, as if three hundred years of Rabbis had been summoned together for the occasion. Most striking is that most of the arguments end without a decision being made for one side or the other. It is perfectly normal to think your way through five pages of densely argued material only to find at the end that you still do not know which side is right. Extra-Talmudic writings eventually codify one opinion or the other, but the Talmud remains blissfully unaware that the whole point of law is for it to be practiced. Real people in the real world need to know the complexities of civil rulings, religious edicts, and criminal law, all of which the Talmud discusses with incredible thoroughness. But generally speaking, the Talmud itself is not the place from which you get those rulings. They appear only in the codes, which dispense with the argument and sum up the law for all practical purposes.

But then the codes attract argument for argument's sake, too, not just legal clarifications for novel cases that arise. Though the whole point of law may be to know what to do and what to avoid in the real world that human beings inhabit, the whole point of studying God's law seems to be something else again. Talmud is to law what mathematics is to science and engineering: Mathematics has its practical side. But there is also pure mathematics that mathematicians study for its own sake. Discovering the equation that makes the numbers come out right can be a spiritually satisfying moment. Getting the argument in the Talmud straight is the same sort of thing.

Talmud, then, is in part pure law—but the law of God. To master it in its incredible detail is to open one's eyes to the presence of God in the details. Its highest form of argument is the legal equivalent of the famous scholastic point of theology: How many angels can fit on the head of a pin? The word for such a display of mental acrobatics is *pilpul*. Jewish history for the last two hundred years is, to some extent, a reaction against this pure Talmudic study, which modern Jews thought inhibited Jewish activism and only made persecution of Jews worse. The mentality that prompted it is the *golus* image of Bialik's poem. *Golus* is Yiddish for "exile," in the sense of powerlessness, living outside one's land in refugee-like dependence on rulers who hate you. *Pilpul* came to be seen as a dangerous waste of time, the study of Talmud taken to a fault. But in truth, it is far from that. *Pilpul* is the ultimate in Jewish art. To be engrossed in Talmudic debate with no practical motive whatever is experienced as a sacred venture. Ideally, one studies every day. For many, it is the surest route to God.

A passage of *pilpul* is so intricate that it would be almost impossible to give an example of it in English. Nearly every word would require a footnote explaining the argumentative presuppositions that the author takes for granted. But the study of Talmud can be demonstrated by looking at an easier sample case. The following example is an important question in its own right: the permissibility of birth control in Judaism. In the next section, we see how a relatively small snippet of Talmud generates an entire literature, which to this day is not entirely exhausted.

The Debate on Birth Control

Many forms of birth control were practiced in antiquity. Various forms of pessary were most common: for instance, the precoital insertion of honey into the vagina to impede the flow of semen. The method mentioned in the Talmud is a device called a *mokh*, probably a type of tampon that worked similarly; but alternatively, and less likely, it might have been a postcoital absorbent that is inserted to draw out the semen before the sperm it carries has a chance to cause fertilization. For our purposes, we need not determine precisely what it is, although whether it is a pre- or postcoital device does matter to the argument. Our question is whether, whatever it is, it may be used, and if so, under what circumstances and by whom.

Out of nowhere, as it were, the Talmud gives us the following ruling:

> Rav Bebai recited the following teaching before Rav Nachman:
> Three types of women have intercourse while using a *mokh*: a minor, a woman who is pregnant and a nursing mother. The minor—
> for fear she will become pregnant and die; the pregnant woman—
> for fear that her foetus become flattened; the nursing mother—for
> fear that she wean her child prematurely and the child dies. How
> do we define a minor? A girl from eleven years and a day to twelve
> years and a day. If she is older or younger, she has intercourse as
> usual. So says Rabbi Meir. The sages say that both these and the
> others have intercourse as usual, for God will have mercy on
> them, as it is said (Ps. 116:6), "God protects the simple."

The debate so far is simple enough. Rav Bebai had memorized a tannaitic teaching (a teaching from the pre-200 era) and repeated it before an *amora* (someone living after 200) named Rav Nachman. The teaching isolates three categories of women who use contraception: minors, pregnant women, and nursing mothers. In each case, the purpose of using birth control is to prevent tragedy, although the elliptical saying assumes we know the state of medicine that the teaching takes for granted and the types of tragic consequences, therefore, that are feared. Rabbi Meir represents the liberal position that at least allows (or perhaps even mandates) contraception to ward off potential danger. An anonymous teaching demurs, holding that God will intervene to save those so simpleminded that they have intercourse even when they shouldn't. Taking Rabbi Meir's position as standard, let us see what the Rabbis were afraid of.

First, the minors. Jews were fully acculturated into Roman society, so shared many Roman views on marriage. Girls were typically married off immediately after reaching puberty, which was widely believed to occur around the age of twelve. They might, however, be betrothed much earlier and then have to wait until their first menses to be allowed to complete the marriage rite and engage in sexual intercourse. Our teaching therefore specifies the unusual case of a girl who begins to menstruate in the year preceding her twelfth birthday. Being already betrothed, she might move in with her husband before turning twelve, but even though she was obviously capable of conceiving a child, it was feared that perhaps her doing so at such a young age might prove fatal to her. The clause "If she is older or younger, she has intercourse as usual" should not be taken to imply that girls under the age of eleven were allowed to have intercourse, but, rather, that girls under the age of eleven and over the age of twelve "follow the usual rules of intercourse"—that is, over twelve, they may have it, and under eleven, they may not, as usual.

Pregnant women pose an oddity, since the fear that underlies permitting their use of a *mokh* is what is called "superfetation," that is, becoming pregnant with yet a second fetus while still incubating the first. Roman medicine assumed that women continue to ovulate during pregnancy, so that a second pregnancy on top of the first might create a situation in which the second fetus pushes up against the first, compressing it to the point that it is born flattened. Elsewhere in the Talmud, the Rabbis themselves denied that possibility, but our teaching here seems impervious to the denials. The denials are amoraic; they date from after 200. Our passage, which is tannaitic, predates them and may assume an earlier stage of medical expertise.

Finally, we have nursing mothers. In fact, ovulation ceases for some time after a child is born and may be delayed even further as long as the woman is lactating. The Rabbis clearly noted the interplay between the end of lactation and the likelihood of a new pregnancy, although they may not have known the exact causal pattern. Assuming that a premature weaning was dangerous to a child's health, they sought to maintain lactation as long as necessary and took pains to make sure that the mother's ability to breast-feed was not diminished. Other rabbinic legislation, for instance, prohibited a man from marrying a nursing mother until two years after her child's birth, for fear that she would become pregnant and find her breast milk abated. Sexual intercourse with one's own wife during the nursing period came under discussion as well, with one authority actually advising coitus interruptus during the entire period. His view did not prevail, so pregnancy while nursing was possible. Believing that such a pregnancy damaged the mother's natural nursing capacity, the Rabbis did not ban intercourse throughout the entire period—a law that could not have been sustained, in any event—but did, apparently, permit (or even demand?) the prophylactic use of a *mokh*.

All of this is presupposed by the Talmudic account. And only now does the debate become interesting, because it hinges precisely on whether the Talmud just *permits* or actually *demands* the *mokh* for the three categories of women named. Ordinarily, we might read the passage with only passing interest, since the physiological presumption behind all three fears is, as it turns out, baseless. The case of the minor is irrelevant now on two counts: first, we do not practice child marriage, so it is therefore a moot point for us; and second, even if we were to allow it, it would make no difference whether a girl conceived at age eleven or at age twelve. The second case, the pregnant woman, is based on a fear of superfetation, which we now know to be impossible. Women do not ovulate during pregnancy so cannot conceive during gestation. Finally, there is the case of the nursing mother, for which, it turns out, the Rabbis had their notions of cause and effect all wrong. It is true that continued lactation lessens the probability of ovulation and, therefore, of pregnancy, but it is not true that pregnancy hastens the end of lactation.

We can learn some things from the rabbinic debate thus far even if the facts that underlie it are wrong. We see that they worried (in case 1) about the health of the mother, (in case 3) the health of the child, and (in case 2) the viability of the fetus. And where the life of mother, fetus, or child was in danger, they at least allowed contraception and maybe even demanded it. The problem is that from the Hebrew verb structure employed here we cannot tell whether it means that three classes women *may* use a *mokh* or whether it means they *have to* use one. The reason we care deeply about the Hebrew is not that we care very much about the three classes themselves, all of which are irrelevant to us, as we just saw, but because we can deduce the rule for all other women by applying simple logic. If we are being told that these three classes of women *may* use birth control, then we have to conclude that all other women *may not*. If, however, we are being taught that these women *have to* use birth control, then it follows that other women *do not have to*, but, presumably, if they want to, they may.

Post-Talmudic opinion differed on what the Hebrew means. The most outstanding medieval commentator on the Talmud, known as Rashi (d. 1105) says simply but clearly, "They are allowed to insert a *mokh*," implying that other women are not allowed to do so. Another commentator of note, Rashi's son-in-law, known as Rabbenu Tam, differs in his interpretation. The issue now revolves about what exactly the *mokh* is. Rashi assumes that it is a precoital device that impedes normal conception by preventing the sperm from fertilizing the egg. Indeed, that would be its whole point. But elsewhere in the Talmud, the Rabbis consider intercourse in which sperm is deliberately withheld—onanism, as it is called—and decide it is a breach of the natural order established by God. They therefore ban it. Rashi's translation of "may" is deliberately designed to produce the logical "may not" with regard to women in general so that he can make the logical consequences of the ruling here mesh with the ruling against "incomplete coitus" elsewhere. Rabbenu Tam, however, considers the possibility of a postcoital device that would not run counter to the ban on diverting semen—some kind of douche, perhaps, or, in our time, even the birth control pill. Assuming the availability of a postcoital method, he sees no reason to ban contraception, so he takes the liberal approach of translating the case as "three categories of women *have to* use the *mokh*." It follows, then, that all other women *do not have to;* but they may.

It is this fine art of legal logic that Judaism has fostered for the last three thousand years. It is easy to see why it would do so for such issues as contraception when practical consequences are at stake. It is not as easy to understand why the finest Jewish minds would spend lifetimes working through the logical consequences of problems that seem utterly irrelevant. But they do. Traditionally, Jewish children are introduced to Jewish study when they are three. They begin with something far less complicated than Talmud, of course: Their first year of study is devoted to the Bible. But they do not begin with the stories of Genesis, the natural subject matter for them as we might imagine—something akin to nursery rhymes, Mother Goose, and tales from the Brothers Grimm. Instead, they start with Leviticus, which is packed mostly with priestly regulations that in their entire lifetimes, the children will never need. But that is the point: Sacred study is not necessarily for the sake of anything other than itself. It is called *Torah lishmah,* "Torah for its own sake." It is the highest form of activity Jews know. Intricacies of the sacrificial cult—destroyed now for almost two thousand years—issues of criminal law that Jews will never use, regulations for rituals that only the Bible describes and that may not have been actually practiced even then—all of these may receive the same attention as the real-life issues of marriage, daily prayer, and Sabbath regulations.

The Spirituality of Discovery

The study of Talmud encompasses every conceivable subject because Judaism is a religion of discovery. Nothing is foreign to human intelligence; nothing too dangerous for human investigation. The Rabbis' positive attitude toward human curiosity is evidenced by their ambivalence regarding the story of Adam and Eve's "fall." The truth is, all things considered, the Rabbis have very little to say about it.

Even the biblical account is quite hazy. We know that Adam and Eve ate forbidden fruit of some kind, but we do not know what it was. Genesis 2:17 implies that it was fruit from the Tree of Knowledge, since God says clearly there, "You shall not eat of the tree of knowledge of what is good and evil, for the day you eat from it, you will surely die." Later, however (Gen. 3:3), the forbidden tree is identified only as "the tree that is in the middle of the garden," leading the careful reader back to verse 2:9 which says, "God planted the tree of life in the middle of the garden, and the tree of knowledge of good and evil."

What, then, was the forbidden fruit? The Rabbis could have declared "knowledge" off limits to humankind. Instead, they let their speculation roam freely, identifying the tree in question as anything but the tree of knowledge, or, for that matter, even the tree of life. It was a wheat tree, one rabbi thinks. Another assumes they ate figs; still another thinks they ate grapes. In short, their sin was not so terrible; if anything, it may even have been necessary. The rabbinic discussion concludes with the notion that we will never know what tree it was; its identity is deliberately withheld from us so that we will never hold it in contempt, saying, "This is the tree that introduced death into the world." For the Rabbis, death is inevitably part of being human, as is seeking knowledge. Medieval exegete Abraham Ibn Ezra (1089–1164) goes even further to protect knowledge as a proper human endeavor:

> Know that Adam was already filled with wisdom, since God would
> never issue commands to someone who was without knowledge.
> He lacked only the knowledge of good and evil. Can't you see that
> he gave a name to every animal and bird according to the proper
> genus and species of every single one? Why, he must have been
> a great sage already, or God would not have brought all created
> things to him to see what he would name them! God even showed
> him the tree of knowledge.

For Ibn Ezra, then, Adam was the quintessential scientist, actually led on in his search for knowledge by his creator. If Adam sinned, God was in collusion. Another commentator, Moses ben Nachman, better known as Nachmanides (1194–1270), adds, "Human beings were destined to die from the beginning. The only difference is that now, they would die on account of their sin." A third strand in Judaism's exegetical tradition notes that Adam should have been struck down immediately, since the Bible clearly says, "On the day you eat of it, you shall surely die." But God said, "I could have counted in human days, but I counted in divine days, giving you a thousand of My days for one of yours." What was the "fall" then? As the Rabbis see it, it was not very much at all. Humans by nature seek out wisdom, and God by nature wants them to. They would have died anyway, and their punishment as a result of their eating of the wrong tree is negligible.

The human thirst for knowledge is a constant theme in the history of science as well. Bertold Brecht imagines a monk who is also a physicist saying to Galileo, "God made the physical world, God made the human brain. God will allow physics." Werner Heisenberg also acknowledges the genuine theological foundation on which modern science actually stood. Galileo, Kepler, and Copernicus, he says, really did think they were reading the mind of God: "Galileo argued that nature, God's second book (the first one being the Bible), is written in mathematical letters, and that we have to learn this alphabet if we want to read it." The rabbinic attitude toward nature is identical to Galileo's: It is God's second book, and the Bible, God's first, but as scientists were charged with the second, so they were to be masters of the first.

The Rabbis, then, accepted the spirituality of dual discovery: scientists, in God's second book, the physical universe; and themselves, in God's first book, the Bible. By definition, there could be no conflict between the two books, if they both came from God. Whatever science discovered had to be consonant with Torah, and vice versa. Greco-Roman scientists and Jewish Rabbis were necessarily partners in the quest to discover the secrets of creation.

But scientists of nature or of Torah discover only because God's secrets are discoverable. So, the Rabbis tell the following tale. It is cited as part of what outside observers would consider an arcane legal conversation, namely, whether a certain kind of oven is amenable to ritual impurity. The issue is worth citing if only to demonstrate the kind of argument that the Rabbis thrived on that might appear absurd to anyone unfamiliar with what I call the spirituality of discovery.

Normally, an oven is not suspect of being rendered impure by outside causes because it has no seams in which the impurity can enter. But Talmud raises the issue of a particular oven made of discrete pieces of tile and held together by mortar. The question is whether the mortar that holds the tiles together makes the tiles cohere enough to consider the finished product seamless. If not—if, that is, the oven is more like the stones around a campfire, with holes between the rocks or with sand in the crevices (through which foreign substances can infiltrate)—the oven cannot be treated like a seamless single utensil for cooking, and greater care has to be exercised to make sure it is ritually pure. The actual legal debate is summarized in a line or two, however, as if the debate is cited more as the excuse for the accompanying tale than for its own sake.

> [Regarding the oven,] Rabbi Eliezer said it was ritually pure,
> but the majority said it was impure. . . .
>
> It happened, that day, that Rabbi Eliezer put forward every
> conceivable argument for his position, all of which the other sages
> refused to accept. He said to them, "If the law agrees with me, let
> this carob tree prove my point." Immediately, the carob tree was
> ripped out of the ground and moved one hundred cubits away—
> some even say it moved four hundred cubits.
>
> But the sages objected, "No proof can be forthcoming from a
> carob tree."
>
> So Rabbi Eliezer continued, "If the law is on my side, let
> this stream of water prove it"—at which time the stream of water
> reversed direction and began to flow backwards.

"You can bring no proof from a stream of water," the other Rabbis retorted.

So Rabbi Eliezer pushed on. "If the law agrees with me, let the walls of this academy prove it. Right away, the walls leaned inward, as if they were about to fall.

But Rabbi Joshua rebuked the walls by warning, "When scholars are engaged in a legal dispute, you have no right to interfere." So in deference to Rabbi Joshua, they did not completely cave in, but in deference to Rabbi Eliezer, they did not stand completely upright again either.

Finally, Rabbi Eliezer contended, "If the law is with me, let heaven itself be my witness—and a voice from heaven cried out, "Why do you argue with Rabbi Eliezer? The law always agrees with him."

But Rabbi Joshua stood up with a shout, quoting Deuteronomy 30:12. "'It is not in heaven,'" he said.

What did he mean by this? Rabbi Jeremiah explained, "Once the Torah was given at Sinai, we pay no attention to heavenly voices any more, because God wrote in the Torah itself, "Follow the majority opinion in making your decisions." (Exod. 23:2)

One can imagine the same argument advanced by physicists against medieval authorities who feared where unfettered curiosity would lead. "Why," says the Aristotelian philosopher to Brecht's Galileo, "the truth might lead us anywhere." Galileo's proper response, no doubt, would have been that truth leads us only to God. The Rabbis concurred. They declared prophecy over because prophets claim direct revelation from heavenly voices. They canonized the "true" prophets of Hebrew tradition, thereby excluding any new ones from consideration. Truth, for them, comes from their own allotted sphere: God's first book, the Torah that God had consulted to create the second book, nature.

Einstein is reputed to have objected to the necessary uncertainty of quantum mechanics by saying, "God does not play dice with the universe." That is precisely the Rabbis' claim with Torah: God does not play dice with Torah either. Every word is there for a purpose. Students of Torah, like scientists of nature, discover God. And God, apparently, likes it that way. The story of the oven ends with Rabbi Nathan meeting Elijah the prophet and asking, "What did God do when the sages ruled Eliezer's heavenly voice out of court?" Now in the rabbinic system, Elijah plays the mythic role of knowing all the answers. He sits in heaven, communing with God, awaiting the day when he will be sent to announce the coming of the Messiah. At that time, said the Rabbis, all uncertainty would be cleared away, as Elijah explained all legal deadlocks. But Elijah appears on occasion, making friendly trips to earth to bring important information that the Rabbis would never be privy to otherwise. He must know, therefore, what God thought about a voice from heaven being systematically dismissed. Elijah's answer is telling: "Elijah responded: God chuckled and said, 'My children have defeated me; my children have defeated me.'"

I must confess that as a student of Torah myself, I often feel that Torah, like nature, exists for the purpose of being found out. When I discover a pattern in the Bible, the logic of a Talmudic debate, a reason behind a position held by this Rabbi or that, or a new way to read my texts such that vistas of human and divine reality unfold before me, I am certain that God, as it were, chuckles with satisfaction and says of me and others like me, "My children have defeated me; my children have defeated me."

Living in the Sacred

Making the life of Torah the ideal preoccupation to the point where legal debate need have no practical consequences leads us directly to the central issue dominating Jewish spirituality: living in the sacred. We saw previously, with regard to the spirituality of blessing, that Judaism divides the world into a binary opposition of sacred (*kodesh*) and ordinary, or everyday (*chol*). But things may be less than absolutely sacred; they may be partially, or relatively, so. The Temple courtyard, for instance, was considered holier than the rest of the Land of Israel, which was also seen as holy, although "outside the land" (*chuts la'arets*) was not viewed as holy at all, but ordinary. Then, too, the Rabbis saw human beings as innately holy—"You shall be holy, for I am holy" is, perhaps, the most frequently repeated admonition in the Torah. The holiness code of Leviticus 19 assumes the possibility of human morality because of our inherent holiness. We are, after all, made in God's image.

But we are not fully sacred. Only God is that. The rabbinic cosmos contains angels as well: more sacred than people, less sacred than God. A dominant metaphysical question, then, for the Rabbis—although never discussed expressly in rabbinic literature, which prefers legal debate to philosophical speculation—is how human beings can interact with the sacred. Our discussion of blessings revealed the Rabbis' attempt to avoid mixing together things that are not of the same degree of holiness. Blessings, we saw are the means of transforming things that are more holy than we are into a lesser state of holiness so that we can interact with them. Our prime example was blessings over food, which transform the food of God's earth from belonging purely to God—and therefore partaking of God's higher degree of holiness—to being accessible to us, in our lower level of holiness.

We now encounter another instance of the holy: Torah. The physical universe and Torah are two parallel God-given "books" that God made available to us for our enjoyment. We eat food for our bodies, see flowers that blossom, treat our eyes to rainbows and our ears to good news. For all these things, there are blessings, since, as we saw, to enjoy the universe without saying a blessing over it is tantamount to making unfit use of fully consecrated objects (*hekdesh*), objects that are holier than we are because they belong to the Temple, which is God's realm, not our own. If Torah, too, is a gift from God—the primary instance of God's grace, in fact—we should expect it to demand a blessing as well, and indeed it does. Several such blessings have come down to us, but the primary one is: "Blessed are You, Eternal our God, for sanctifying us by your commandments and commanding us to remain occupied with the study of Torah." Torah, like the world of our five senses, demands a blessing before it can be brought into our lives in a condition appropriate for human use.

The word *use*, however, is too strong here, since technically speaking, study of Torah should be pursued for its own sake (*Torah lishmah*). Not that insights from Torah are not beneficial. Indeed they are. But even if no practical consequence flows from such study, the study is still commendable, even commanded. One rabbinic axiom holds, "The laws concerning the sacrifice of birds" are essential. What could have fewer practical consequences than the details of sacrificing birds, especially in the era after the Temple's destruction, which is when the axiom was coined? But that is the whole point: Torah study exists for its own sake. It is not a means to an end but an end in and of itself. Though it may have practical consequences, these are secondary to the study of God's word, which is primary. The Mishnah is explicit, even hyperbolic, on this point. "Rabbi Zadok taught: Do not make the Torah a crown with which to make yourself important, nor a spade with which to dig. Hillel used to say: one who uses the crown of Torah will die, from which it can be deduced that anyone who benefits from the words of Torah takes his own life." As something that is holy, Torah must be approached through a blessing that releases it for human study; but that study is, ideally, for its own sake. Being holy, Torah cannot deliberately be used.

Here is a working definition of the holy: that which exists beyond the realm of the utilitarian. It applies to other holy things as well. An extension of the rule against benefiting from Torah is the prohibition against getting paid to teach it. To be sure, teachers of Torah earn a living, but technically, they are reimbursed for work that they otherwise would be doing were they not engaged in Torah.

Then, too, there is the Sabbath, a holy point in time. Normally, time exists so that we can do something with it. But not Sabbath time. On the Sabbath, no work is permitted. The English word *work* fails to convey the essence of this prohibition. The Mishnah defines thirty-nine categories of work, a number arrived at by observing that the commandment to avoid Sabbath labor (Exod. 35:2–3) occurs just prior to the instruction to build the desert sanctuary called a tabernacle (Exod. 35:4–19). The Rabbis therefore classify as "work" any act involved in building the sanctuary. In its typically laconic style, the Mishnah simply lists them without explanatory commentary, but I have added numbers dividing them into their Talmudic categories.

> The main categories of labor [that are prohibited on Shabbat]
> are forty less one: (1) sowing, plowing, reaping, binding sheaves,
> threshing, winnowing, sorting, grinding, sifting, kneading, bak-
> ing; (2) shearing wool, washing it, beating it, dyeing it, spinning,
> weaving, making two loops, weaving two threads, separating two
> threads, tying, loosening, sewing two stitches, tearing in order to
> sew two stitches; (3) trapping a deer, slaughtering it, skinning it,
> salting it, curing its hide, scraping the hide, butchering the meat,
> writing two letters, erasing in order to write two letters; (4) build-
> ing, tearing down, putting out a fire, kindling a fire, striking with
> a hammer, carrying from one domain into another.

As the Talmud explains, there really is logic here. The forbidden activities fall into four categories of activity: (1) baking, (2) preparing fabric,
(3) preparing a scroll (for writing), and (4) building construction. Some
of the forbidden acts are obvious; others, like sewing two stitches, become self-evident when the process of building a loom is explained. All,
however, were involved in building the tabernacle.

But there may be more to the list still. Anthropologists draw our attention to the way cultures divide their perception of the world into bi-

nary oppositions. Indeed, we have already seen that Judaism prefers the dichotomy of holy/everyday (*kodesh/chol*). Other societies have other binary systems, as, for instance, the Mbuti of Zaire, a forest-dwelling people that divides everything into "forest" (which is verdant and life-giving) and "not-forest" (which is dry and life-denying). The systems are arbitrary, and they vary a great deal the world over. There is, however, one system that is universal. Whichever dichotomy a culture chooses, it superimposes its chosen set of contrasting elements onto an underlying opposition that it has simply because it is a culture: namely, nature (which is raw, dangerous, and wild) and culture (which is processed, safe, and tame). People the world over fear nature, even as they are in awe of it. Civilization of any sort occurs because we separate out of nature a certain block of land, time, or activity and domesticate it with social rules. We convert the wilderness into cities with walls protective against the wild. We hunt animals and then cook them in socially acceptable ways. We build homes instead of roaming open spaces, develop friends out of potential foes, and band together against the common enemy: the vast and terrifying world beyond the city walls. The anthropologist Claude Lévi-Strauss offers an apt metaphor for the nature/culture dichotomy: He calls it the raw and the cooked.

The four categories of work do indeed share something other than being involved in the tabernacle's construction. They are all instances of transforming nature into culture, making over the raw into the cooked. The rabbinic attention to the desert sanctuary is itself a metaphor for this primal transformative act by which cultures come into being. Adrift in the wilderness, the Israelites' first activity as a people is the construction of the very symbol of their culture: a tabernacle for God. Even God, who brings fire by night and a pillar of clouds by day, who splits the sea and kills Israel's enemies, who brings plagues and controls human destiny—even God is, as it were, domesticated and made over into a friendly deity who can be visited and consulted at will. Cooking, weaving, writing, building: These are the four classes of action that are prohibited on the Sabbath. As Torah is holy study, so the Sabbath is holy time. The Torah may not be used; nor may the Sabbath. *Use* on the Sabbath amounts to any transformative act by which human beings convert the raw into the cooked.

A final and most explicitly telling instance of the holy as nonutilitarian is Hanukkah lights. Hanukkah has become the most popular holiday for American Jews who are caught up in Christmas culture and yearn for a Jewish equivalent in which joy, lights, and gift giving are central. But Hanukkah was much more humble in its origins. It is said to have originated as a festival to recall the miraculous deliverance from the hands of the Greeks in a war that was fought by a priestly party known as the Hasmoneans, in 167 B.C.E. It quickly attracted the symbolism of light, to the extent that the first-century historian Josephus tells us that it was quite common to have torchlight parades (though, he confesses, he does not know why). The Rabbis adopt the holiday, but emphasize God's role in bringing victory rather than the military exploits of the Hasmoneans, who had established an independent Jewish commonwealth but who were not always friendly to the rabbinic class.

By the second century, torchlight parades had given way to the use of a candelabra that was lit for the entire eight-day festival. The Talmud connects the candelabra with a miracle performed by God in the Temple, which had been restored to use. As background for the tale, it is necessary to know that every night, the priests kindled some oil that burned throughout the night, parallel to the light that God had commanded for the desert tabernacle (Exod. 27:20; Lev. 24:2).

What is Hanukkah? Our Rabbis taught: Commencing on the 25th
of the Hebrew month of Kislev, there are eight days of Hanukkah,
during which it is forbidden to eulogize the dead or to fast. That is
because when the Greeks entered the Temple, they rendered all
the Temple oil ritually impure. When the Hasmonean dynasty
became strong enough to beat them in battle, they made a search

and found only a single cruse of oil marked with the seal of the
High Priest. It contained only enough for a single day, but a miracle happened: it burned for eight days [by which time, new oil had
been procured]. The next year, they fixed those days as holidays
for praise and acknowledgment of God.

Liturgy gradually developed for kindling the lights, and by the
eighth century, the following prayer occurs:

We kindle these lights for the victory and the miracles and the
wonders that You brought about for our forebears at the hands of
your holy priests. Throughout the eight days of Hanukkah, these
lights are holy: we may make no use of them except just to look at
them to acknowledge You for your wonders, miracles and victory.

Again, we see that the essence of the holy is its being unavailable to
us for personal use. The Talmud had declared the Hanukkah lights holy,
their sole purpose being "to proclaim the miracle." Jewish law prohibited reading by them, warming one's self by them, or even using their
light to find something in the dark. Like Torah and the Sabbath, Hanukkah lights are holy and may not be used.

The spirituality of discovery, then, leads us to the anomalous notion
that we study Torah to discover what God has hidden away, knowing all
the while that the purpose of the study is not necessarily to find anything. To be sure, one always finds something, and what one finds may
end up being useful; but the ultimate usefulness is secondary. Jewish
spirituality advises living with the sacred—the Torah, the Sabbath, Hanukkah candles—knowing that the usual attitude of using what we encounter does not hold here, for the sacred may not be willingly used.

Here is an attitude that flies in the face of all that Western culture
holds dear. We are taught that everything we do should yield something.
There is nothing worse than a thing being "useless." Useless things get

thrown out. We say the same of people. We dismiss "useless" people with disdain. We ask of people and of things, "What do they do?" as if the measure of each is the use to which we put them. Judaism has no argument with utility, but limits it to the experiential realm of the everyday. The holy is a higher realm of existence. The ultimate purpose of living by Torah is not to pass a course, get a grade, become a rabbi, or learn how to do anything. The life of Torah exists for its own sake.

Perhaps the most revered rabbi of all time was Moses Maimonides (1135–1204). Born in Spain, he migrated to Egypt, where he ran a family business, learned medicine, emerged as leader of the Egyptian Jewish community, and wrote (among other things) a fourteen-volume code of Jewish law and a philosophical treatise called *Guide to the Perplexed*. Maimonides describes the stages through which someone matures into a Torah scholar. He pictures himself attracting a little boy to Torah study by promising candy as a reward. When the child becomes a young man, the teacher offers a new suit of clothing instead. Eventually, the man becomes wealthy enough to buy whatever he wants, so the teacher changes the promise yet again. "Study Torah," he says, "and you will be honored by all who know you." But one day, it dawns on the student that neither wealth nor honor is the point. The only reward for study of Torah is the study of Torah itself.

Chapter Five

Having a Home:
The Spirituality of Landedness

The air in the Land of Israel brings wisdom.
BABYLONIAN TALMUD, B.B.148B

You shall not wrong a stranger or oppress him
for you were strangers in the land of Egypt.
EXODUS 22:20

It was early autumn, the sun streaming through maple leaves that had just decided to change color. I was a young and struggling scholar, a father of three, and proud owner, more or less, of a heavily mortgaged home outside New York City. My wife and I were sitting at the kitchen table in a rare moment of household silence, when one of us—I forget which one—spoke up. "You know, we are both over thirty, and neither of us has yet been to Israel."

Eight months later, all five of us were on our way to live for a summer in the land that has held the Jewish heart captive for nearly four thousand years, the land we call home, the Land of Israel. Echoing in my ears was a litany of praise for the land that I had internalized from Jewish study and from personal reports of people who had preceded me there.

Israel is the center of the earth, the Rabbis had taught, and Jerusalem is the center of Israel. "The air in the Land of Israel brings wisdom," they promised.

"Just wait until you get there," a student who had just spent a year in Israel explained. "You'll see: Jerusalem really is just a little closer to heaven."

Sacred Land or Sacred State?

When the modern Jewish state was created, it took as its name *M'di-nat Yisra'el*, "the State of Israel." Since both land and state go by the same name, it is important here to differentiate one from the other. Most Jews today feel positive and passionately about both. It is possible, however, to separate them, at least in theory. When the state was first proposed as the goal of the modern Jewish nationalist movement known as Zionism, many Jews rejected the Zionist idea of a state, but remained loyal to the age-old Jewish allegiance to Israel, the Land. That was in the nineteenth and early twentieth centuries, when it seemed self-evident that the world's Jews would soon be welcomed unequivocally as citizens of all the modern states in which they lived. It was before Hitler, and before the discovery that the classless society being built in Russia would oppress Jews just as surely as its czarist predecessor had. Today, it is rare to find Jews who do not somehow support the Jewish state, which welcomed Jewish refugees the rest of the world refused; the state, moreover, that has revived Hebrew as a living language and that exports Jewish scholarship and culture throughout the world. From our home in southern Ontario, for instance, my parents watched the Holocaust unfold and dedicated their lives to donating their spare quarters, nickels, and dimes to Israel's establishment. The money went into a blue box, which was regularly emptied and given to someone who went door to door on Israel's behalf. So, even as a child, I was a Zionist. I still am.

But even Zionists differentiate Israel the country from Israel the Land. The country is necessarily politicized, for good and for evil. Its policies frustrate us, madden us, surprise us, and sometimes (at least) delight us. But no matter what we think of any given Israeli government, there is something about Israel the Land that transcends the state. My Jewish heart and soul were in love with the Land long before the state was ever imagined. There was, for instance, no necessity that the state would even be built where it is today. At one time, the British government offered the land of what is now Kenya and Uganda as a Jewish state. Theodor Herzl, the founder of the Zionist movement, was going to take it. With Jews dying daily in czarist Russia, it seemed absurd to wait until the Ottoman Turks, who controlled the Land of Israel, agreed to part with some of it. But Herzl was an assimilated Jewish reporter from Vienna and had had little or no Jewish education. He became a Zionist in response to the anti-Semitism he encountered in France while covering the Dreyfus affair, an episode in which a Jewish captain was framed for treason and imprisoned on Devil's Island. Herzl watched anti-Semitic riots break out on the same streets that had once echoed to cries of "Liberty, Equality, Fraternity." One night, he went to a concert to hear the stirring nationalist music of Wagner—and then went home to begin his diary with its daring dream of founding a Jewish state for the Jewish People. No wonder he accepted Uganda. Under colonialist conditions at the time, it was "available"; and it would save Jewish lives. But he failed to grasp the Jewish People's love of Israel the Land. When he announced to the delegates of a world Zionist convention that he intended to establish a Jewish state in Africa, it was none other than the suffering delegates from Russia who shouted him down. They would rather die than relocate to a Jewish state that was not at the same time the Jewish Land for which Jews had prayed, mused, sung, and dreamed of for thousands of years.

Love of the Land, then, is related to, but separate from, love of the state. And it is love of the Land that lies at the root of this unique brand of Jewish spirituality. I mean *landedness:* sensing that not all patches of the earth's surface are identical; feeling that somehow you have an attachment to a certain latitude and longitude where, indeed, somehow your Jewish center is located; knowing what it is to have a perpetual home; and knowing also the infinite pain of homelessness.

Many Christians have trouble understanding the spirituality of Land. Christianity, after all, has prided itself on being a world religion. It sends missionaries around the globe converting the world's peoples to its doctrine. Yes, Catholics have an eternal city called Rome that they may visit with special joy, as Lutherans may visit Germany, or Canadian Anglicans, England. But these cannot compare to the way Jews visit Jerusalem. Christianity is a religion of the universal; anyone can join and be equally Christian without giving a thought to the place where Jesus lived or the rock on which Peter erected the Catholic Church of Rome. Anyone can join Judaism, too, but not without adopting the Jew's special connection to the Land that the Bible says God gave to Abraham. Judaism is a religion of the specific: universal in its ethics and its welcome, but particularistic in its sacred geography.

Native American culture shares some of this landedness; so, too, does Latino culture of the American Southwest. For Native American tribes, a particular forest or mountain is uniquely holy. It is where the ancestors live, where the tribe itself was born. Similarly, Latino Americans in New Mexico know that the land on which they walk is not just a chance habitat but a genuine home in ways that New York City, Seattle, and Houston are not. Jews everywhere feel that way about the Land of Israel.

Being "in Israel the Land" is juxtaposed in Jewish literature with being "outside the Land." These are not just chance dwelling places. These are metaphysical constructs. "My heart is in the east, and I am in the utmost west," wrote the medieval poet and philosopher Judah Halevi. One need not move to Israel, most Jews would say, but if you are outside the Land, you must remain connected, as if with an existential umbilical cord, to the Land, without which Jewish life shrivels. I draw my sacred sustenance here in New York by my connection to Israel.

The *state* of Israel, by contrast, is not sacred. It is a political invention of modern times, necessary for many reasons, but completely secular. Orthodox parties want it to be the theocracy of which the Bible dreamed, but they will fail, as they should. State is not land. Most modern peoples have states; only some have lands. And even those who have lands may not be consciously landed, the way Jews know Israel to be their land. What an anomaly. To know we have a land but (as Jews in the Diaspora) not to live there; to know that the Land of Israel is sacred, but to know also that the government that runs it is secular and sometimes even profane. My sacred sense of being a Jew derives in part from my certainty that I am related to a sacred center somewhere else: a center that is charged with my family's history, calling me also to whatever historical role I may have in God's plan for all time.

The Land of Israel in the Bible

The Jew's love affair with the Land of Israel is as old as Judaism itself. The Bible virtually begins with God's promise to Abraham (Gen. 12:1), "Go forth from your native land and from your father's house to the land that I will show you." And the Torah virtually ends with the prescription of a harvest ritual for farmers to recollect the centrality of the Land (Deut. 26:5–9). Annually, the farmer would remember that Jewish history began with a "wandering Aramean" (Abraham) and reached its culmination when "God brought us to this place and gave us this land, a land flowing with milk and honey." Homelessness to landedness: There you have it—the Bible's sense of Jewish history in a nutshell.

When the biblical editor began his narrative with the story of creation, his intention may not have been to describe how all things began, but to create a preamble to his narrative that demonstrated the pain of being expelled from home. Adam and Eve foreshadowed the Babylonian expulsion of 587 B.C.E., an event that remained etched in Jewish consciousness ever after. The first five books of the Bible—the Torah—were all about landedness: how God brought Abraham there to start with, how, because of a famine, Jacob abandoned it for Egypt only to find that outside the land "a new Pharaoh arose" who persecuted the Israelites. But God brought Israel back. Deuteronomy ends with Moses atop a summit staring out at the ultimate destination of God's people, the Land that Joshua would enter after Moses died. The Torah was edited by people returning to the Land when the exile ended. Eden is Israel; Adam and Eve, the paradigmatic exiles. Then the mythic images shift: Egypt is exile; Moses, the new Abraham, bringing the people home.

In biblical theology, Adam and Eve had to leave Eden because they sinned; so, too, the Israelites were taken captive because of their sin. But the theme of return to the Land is sounded immediately by the prophets. An unknown visionary whose words are appended anonymously to the book of Isaiah, and who we call "Second Isaiah," therefore announces to the exiles in Babylonia (Isa. 40:1, 2; 44: 24, 26):

> Comfort, oh comfort my People,
> Says your God.
> Speak tenderly to Jerusalem
> And declare to her
> That her term of service is over,
> That her iniquity is expiated. . . .
> It is I, the Lord who made everything,
> . . . who say of Jerusalem, "It shall be inhabited,
> And of the towns of Judah, "They shall be rebuilt."

References to *Erets Yisra'el*, "the Land of Israel," or even just to *Ha'arets*, "the Land," are ubiquitous in the Bible, so much so that we take them for granted. The sacred dimension of the Land even grows with time. The anonymous author of Psalm 137 reflects on exile in Babylon:

> By the rivers of Babylon, there we sat
> Sat and wept, when we thought of Zion. . . .
> For our captors asked us there for songs,
> Our tormentors for amusement:
> "Sing us one of the songs of Zion."
> How can we sing a song of the Lord on alien soil?
> If I forget you, O Jerusalem, let my right hand wither.

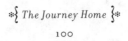

Let my tongue stick to my palate, if I cease to think of you,

If I do not keep Jerusalem in memory

Even at my happiest hour.

Second Isaiah's "comfort" consisted in the promise that "the Lord shall comfort Zion . . . make her wilderness like Eden, and her desert like the garden of the Lord; joy and gladness shall abide there, thanksgiving, and the sound of music" (Isa. 51:3). Another exile, the prophet Ezekiel, conceptualized it as "the most glorious of all lands (Ezek. 20:6) and even the geographic center of the universe (Ezek. 5:5), a claim that the Rabbis would later take literally, describing the Temple in Jerusalem as the axis around which the world spins. Ezekiel gives us the image of a "holy mountain" (Ezek. 20:40), and his prophetic successor, Zechariah, coins the phrase "holy land," by which Israel has been known ever since (Zech. 2:16). The Hellenistic world developed the notions of "homeland," "fatherland," and "motherland," all epithets that have been applied to Israel ever since the Apocryphal book of 2 Maccabees was composed sometime around the first century.

Being a Jew without regard to the land that God granted Israel is inconceivable to the Bible and the Rabbis who canonized Jewish scripture and then built on it. The Jewish tale is a story of a covenant between God and a particular people. Other peoples have their own covenants, the Rabbis taught. Even the universalistic covenant, the one God made with Noah, was a covenant of "land"—the whole earth, rescued from the flood. God tells Noah (Gen. 9:9–11), "I hereby establish my covenant with you and with your offspring yet to come. . . . Never again will there be a flood to destroy the earth." So, too, Israel's covenant was about land, this time a particular plot given to Abraham (Gen. 12:7), as God promises him, "I will assign this land to your heirs."

I do not mean to imply that all Jews today know by heart or are even able to recognize all these citations from the Bible. They may know some of them, but how many they can cite or whether they can cite any at all is not my point here. I am not describing Jewish theology, but Jewish spirituality; and even though spirituality and theology are related, they are not identical. Spirituality is the way we relate to the world. Jews relate by assuming a special plot of land called Israel. Two thousand years of studying Torah have left an indelible mark on Jewish culture that now incorporates love of the Land even by people who cannot quote a single biblical verse on which that love is predicated. Some Jews, who study the Bible, find this landedness writ large on almost every page and discover the historical reason for their passion. Others do not. Some do not feel that passion at all, but are still Jews. My argument is not about what people *have to do* to be good Jews. But Jews who investigate their heritage find a challenge to take biblical landedness seriously—not an easy task in an age in which land and state are often confused and sovereign states have all too often meant nationalism, jingoism, conquest, empire, and war.

Before moving on to the consequences of taking landedness seriously, we should survey postbiblical thought to see what happens to the idea of the Promised Land. What makes the survey especially interesting is the fact that the writers often lived outside the Land and never intended returning to it. They faced a basic conflict: While living outside the Land, they yet maintained the theory that only within the Land could life as a Jew be fully realized.

Landedness after the Bible

In part, the spirituality of landedness came about because Jews who lived outside the Land had to think consciously about what their relationship to the Land might be. If Israel had not been exiled, the entire Bible might have been put together differently. The creation narrative and its emphasis on exile might have been omitted. Warnings of imminent exile by such prophets as Jeremiah and Isaiah would be lacking. We would never even have heard of Second Isaiah, who would have had no return from exile to write about. Precisely the lack of land made Jews think through land's meaning. But once Jews had reestablished themselves within the Land's perimeter, the Rabbis who canonized the land-centered biblical narrative turned to a consideration of how and why the Land of Israel loomed so large to them. And once again, it was not just Jews living in the Land of Israel who faced those questions. From the first century of the current era onward, substantial Jewish communities existed outside the Land, especially in Babylonia, where the concept of landedness loomed large.

Still, the Palestinian Jewish community remained uniquely in touch with the sacred soil they called their Land. As farmers, they followed what they could of the biblical legislation regarding the land that they still tilled. In principle, the Land had been God's gift to all the people, not just to the gentlemen farmers who happened to own deeds to it. The concept of landedness thus took on ethical consequences. When the owners gathered their crops, they left the corners of the field unharvested for the poor to glean; they were also prohibited from picking up grain that fell to the ground after being plucked—it, too, was left for the homeless to collect.

Not all the biblical laws could be followed. In words that Americans might know from the inscription on the Liberty Bell, for instance, Leviticus 25:10 announces that every fiftieth year "You shall proclaim liberty throughout the land to all the inhabitants thereof." At issue biblically, however, is land, not people. In the Jubilee, or fiftieth year, all ownership of land becomes null and void and the land returns to all the people. When that proved economically unfeasible, the law was dropped; but it remained on the books as an ethical ideal and a reminder that the people were the land's true owners.

In other ways, too, daily life in Palestine put the people in touch with their Land in ways that were impossible outside of it. One way the Palestinian Talmud differs from the Babylonian is that it is filled with land rules: what property people tithe, how orchards must be pruned, and what special rules apply to produce grown in the Land of Israel since the Land is sacred, hence its produce cannot be treated lightly.

Babylonian Jews were not unaware of all this legislation, much of which had been set down in a previous book, the Mishnah, which had been promulgated before the Babylonian community was firmly established. The Mishnah formed the core of rabbinic discussion both in Palestine and in Babylonia. But the Babylonians largely ignored the lengthy agricultural sections on which the Palestinians waxed most eloquently. The Babylonian Jews too were mostly farmers, but they farmed ordinary soil outside the Land, so they remained unconcerned about the complex agricultural laws that applied to the Land of Israel alone. Their silence regarding the Land of Israel and its produce tells us much, however. Both Palestinians and Babylonians were tacitly in agreement regarding the metaphysical superiority of the Land of Israel. Being in the Land was equivalent to being on sacred soil. You were closer to the earth's center, closer to the presence of God. Not that God was limited to appearing there. It was said that divine compassion was so strong that the presence of God, called the *Sh'khinah*, accompanied the Jews who went into exile. In time, the *Sh'khinah* became a more or less feminine manifestation of God, a divine Mother who cries for her children in exile and awaits their ultimate return to rebuild the Land and welcome the Messiah who will inaugurate the end of history.

The basic rabbinic dichotomy of Jewish life had been established. For the Bible, it had been the contrast between "holy" (*kodesh*) and "ordinary" (*chol*). Now those categories were applied to real estate. You were either "in the Land" (*ba'arets*) or you were "outside the Land" (*chuts la'arets*). "In the Land" was sacred; "outside the land" was ordinary. One might remain outside it for any number of reasons, but ideally, one would try to move there. In theory, Jewish law actually permitted a man who wanted to move to the Land but whose wife refused to go with him to sue for divorce. In theory, also, even the Babylonian Talmud held that "whoever dwells outside the Land is as one who has no God."

To be sure, reason prevailed, as later commentators diffused the stark reality of both precepts. The latter was said to apply only to antiquity when special divine providence was available to Palestinian Jews, not to medieval conditions when access to God was available worldwide; the former was honored in the breach; when husbands sued for divorce on the grounds that their wives would not follow them to Palestine, medieval Jewish courts generally denied the husband's request because (as one ruling put it) "From now on, everyone who dislikes his wife and wants to divorce her without paying the necessary divorce settlement will fabricate this claim." Writing from his home in Egypt, Maimonides added, "It is a light matter for most men to cause grief to their wives, and we must guard against such a sin."

In principle, however, the dichotomy between "the holy land" (*erets hakodesh*) and living outside it remained. It was given lip service in daily prayers that petitioned God to rebuild Jerusalem and return the exiles from the four corners of the earth. Synagogue worship the world over was conducted facing Jerusalem. At weddings, a glass was smashed underfoot to symbolize mourning for the Temple. Myths arose explaining that when the Land was finally redeemed, the dead would roll underground from cemeteries everywhere until, finally on holy soil once again, they would be resurrected. And, particularly after the Crusades had forged roadways through Europe to Palestine, many Jews did indeed try to return "home" instead of remaining "in exile." The land of Zion became widely known as the Mother; Israel's scattered communities, the children. Judah Halevi (1075–1141)—like Maimonides, a widely read philosopher but also a poet and romantic, was certain that prophecy had ceased because Jews outside the Land had incomplete access to God's word. In what can only be considered a form of mystical geography, another philosopher, known as Gersonides (1288–1344), held that God had chosen the Land of Israel because of its climate, which bears "exceptional readiness to receive divine emanation." A mystical work of the seventeenth century summed up the medieval Jew's exceptional longing for the Land by saying that every section of the earth's surface is given to a particular nation, with which it is inextricably connected, so that there is a three-way tie that binds the people, its land, and a guardian angel responsible for that people's powers of soul and cognition. Israel is thus tied to the Land of Israel. It has no guardian angel, however; instead, it is bound directly to God, who oversees Israel's destiny without any mediation.

Spirituality of the Land and Modern Zionism

I have already described the hold that modern Zionism had on Jews during the first half of the twentieth century. Theodor Herzl was both dreamer and activist. He did more than write a novel describing an idealized Jewish state; he literally worked himself to death visiting prime ministers and potentates the world over in hope of attracting them to the idea of returning the Jews to their homeland. When he died in 1904, he had yet to attract a single world power to his cause. But he had built a movement and a political infrastructure from which success would later come.

Neither Herzl nor most of the leaders who succeeded him, however, had any notion of the spirituality underlying the Jewish vision of living on the Land. As secularized products of nineteenth-century nationalism, they saw the return geopolitically, not religiously. The anti-Semitism they faced was all consuming, far worse than the animosity medieval Jews had known. In many ways, it was a new phenomenon altogether. To begin with, modern nation-states possessed the technological capacity to execute masses of Jews on a scale unimaginable centuries earlier. Even more important was the nature of the hatred itself. Medieval animus was religiously based. Jews could always convert to escape being killed. In addition, the Church's attitude toward Jews was ambivalent. On the one hand, it preached an anti-Jewish doctrine, charging Jews with denying their savior and then conspiring to crucify him. On the other hand, however, Church authorities frequently worked to save Jews from the masses and even held that a Jewish presence among Christians should be retained, if only as a sign of Jewish guilt in killing Christ. In the nineteenth century, however, hatred toward Jews became the tool of ardent nationalist leaders who co-opted the Church's message and replaced its religious content with racism. Jews could hardly convert from race to race. They were doomed from birth, waiting targets for anti-Semitic demagogues whose careers depended on fastening all of society's woes on convenient Jewish scapegoats.

As the rhetoric of religion became the rhetoric of politics, traditional religious promises were recast in terms of national interest, colonial expansion, and defensive alliances. For nineteenth-century Jews, old ideas such as exile and landedness were not just metaphysical constructs; they were realities affecting flesh-and-blood people every single day. Massive government-sponsored pogroms in Russia in 1881 moved one Jewish observer, Leo Pinsker (1821–1891), to describe his people as "a nation long since dead" in desperate need of "a single refuge—politically assured," ideally in Israel, but (as Herzl later agreed) if need be, anywhere at all where Jewish bodies could be safe and sound.

As the Zionist dream played itself out, then, ideas about the spirituality of landedness were largely lost in the storm of political realism. The Jewish leaders to whom European powers felt most comfortable talking were those who spoke the language of the times: such men as Chaim Weizman in England and David ben Gurion from Poland. Weizman was a successful industrialist who had abandoned Judaism as a religion altogether. Ben Gurion, destined to become Israel's first prime minister, was similarly secularized through and through, but typified the ideological bent of eastern European Jews by adopting socialism as his messianic dream. In Israel's early years, it was May Day, not Rosh Hashanah and Yom Kippur, that attracted the masses. Some early settlers still kept the Passover seder, but transformed it into a celebration of the work of their hands in draining swamps and building settlements.

Gone was any mention of God. Since the early Middle Ages, the Passover *Haggadah* had ended with a plaintive cry, "Next year in Jerusalem!"—a hope for the end of history, but an appeal to Jerusalem as a metaphysical concept as much as an actual city. Israeli Jews said, "Next year in Jerusalem rebuilt," subtly transforming the hope for an end to history to their own personal project, the restoration of a real city for real Israelis.

But even in the midst of secular politics, the spirituality of the Land was never totally absent. Even Jews who disavowed God and abandoned religious practice could not entirely forget the age-old attraction of the Land. A. D. Gordon (1856–1922) and Abraham Isaac Kook (1865–1935) illustrate two diverse kinds of spirituality that remain to this day among Jews who move to Israel to experience the reality of a Jewish People at home on Jewish soil.

Gordon is remembered as one of the founders of the Kibbutz movement, collective settlements that returned to the land to till the soil and share the harvest equally. But Gordon was passionate about the redemptive power of the work itself. In exile Jews could own no land; they were often relegated to becoming intermediaries between the aristocracy and the peasants, playing a role that they and their detractors alike thought of as economic parasitism. Spiritually, they had become orphans cut off from their motherland and from the sacred work of caring for it. Utterly dependent on foreign cultures, they had learned to grovel and plead for scraps from the foreigners' tables, forgetting how to work for themselves. A return from exile meant the opportunity to return to the literal landedness of Judaism's sacred center, where they could buy land, till it, and harvest it, recognizing that their honest backbreaking labor was the very essence of redemption. It wasn't even necessary for all Jews to return. Even if just some did, their labor would teach Jews outside of Israel the value of independence. The entire Jewish People would emerge as a new creation, self-consciously pursuing a proud destiny among the nations. A. D. Gordon thus preached spirituality without God, but not without Jewish values. He was an atheist, a socialist, and a spiritual Jew all at the same time.

Kook took a radically different approach, marrying traditional religion to Zionism. He synthesized the traditional love of the Land with the secular Zionists who were redeeming it. Even the atheists among them were instruments of God, cleansing Judaism from the superstitions that had attached themselves to the Jewish core during the long Middle Ages. Return to the Land was tantamount to that religious return to God called *t'shuvah*, "repentance." The magnet drawing Jews back home was the mystical center of Jewish life, the Land whose holiness was utterly unique and beyond reason, but whose hold on Jewish consciousness was the invaluable beginning of Jewish renewal. As Kook saw history, Jews had gone into exile armed with a finite store of spiritual sustenance that they had forged during their long years on the Land. But that store was now depleted, so that exilic Judaism was becoming fossilized. The only hope for a Jewish renaissance was a return to the Land by enough Jews to recover the genius for creativity that Jews had known, as long as they remained in physical touch with their Land. Moreover, the spirit of Israel remained pure, whereas the spiritual energy outside the Land had long ago become sullied by sin and violence. The whole world required redemption, which could come from Jews who would radiate their own redemptive power to others, thereby becoming God's agents at world salvation, not just Jewish deliverance. The stakes were still metaphysical for Kook, who believed that human redemption worldwide depended on a Jewish return to its Land.

All of this is the ideological and religious backdrop for the founding of the State of Israel in 1948. Both the secular spirituality of Gordon and the religious spirituality of Kook suffused the thinking of the early pioneers. The Jewish Commonwealth founded by King David had ended with the Babylonian exile. A second commonwealth begun by émigrés from Babylonian captivity had ceased with war against Rome in 70 C.E. Almost nineteen hundred years later, and against all odds, a third Jewish commonwealth was born. Though officially secular, the state nonetheless preached the Land of Israel's sacred centrality for all Jews. Ben Gurion maintained that no Jew could ever be complete without returning home to the Land. And to this day, the Hebrew term for settling in Israel is *aliyah*, "going up"; leaving Israel is *y'ridah*, "descent." Immigrants usually arrive for extrinsic reasons, usually to escape persecution. But many Jews, even today, certainly do feel incomplete living in "exile," as they still think of it. They will indeed tell you that Israel is just a little closer to heaven.

Their spirituality is a deeply rooted experience of living on the Land. No longer farmers, they nonetheless walk the streets where Isaiah trod, eat the harvest that Deuteronomy describes, and feel the desert sun the way Abraham and Sarah did. For them, every alleyway and riverbed echoes the Jewish People's story. Here is where the twelve tribes settled, where David fought the Philistines, where Solomon built the Temple, where Elijah ascended to heaven. Modern Israel, however, is often secular to the point of being profane. Its politics can be noisy, nasty, and negative. The Kibbutz socialist experiment has failed, and farmers hire Arab labor rather than work the land themselves. Religious warfare between right-wing zealots and everybody else is rampant. This is no idyllic social order. But Jerusalem flourishes in the middle of a desert, with flowers everywhere because someone gets up early each morning to water them by hand. Israelis are still proud of the acres and acres of farmland planted on land where they rolled back the swamps and desert dunes. More than a handful of Israelis will tell you that they relive the Bible daily; that a sunset bleeding into the Mediterranean or the lush oases in the desert are the age-old hand of God operating today with the same natural precision as the psalmist experienced when he wrote "How glorious is your name in all the earth" (Ps. 8:2, 10).

Spirituality of the Land for Jews Who Live Outside It

Having a land to call home is equally important to Jews who do not live there and never will. To begin with, Jews visit Israel not just as tourists but as pilgrims coming home to find the wellspring of their souls.

The attitudes that make us tourists or pilgrims are poles apart. Tourists are prototypically despicable the world over; no one wants to look like a tourist, after all. Tourists ravage the landscape, buying their way, as loudly as possible, wherever they can go. Natives put up with them, but do not respect them. They go to whatever is the "hot spot" of the year, the untapped places that the *New York Times* Travel Section discovers, and return to boast that they got there first before the masses found it. They are the ultimate consumers, driving up prices to whatever the market will bear, and driving the natives to market even their own sacred land-scape as honky-tonk glitz decorated with kitsch art.

There is plenty of this in Israel, too. At the Western Wall, for many the most sacred place in Israel, strobe lights illuminate the evening prayer service so that tourists can film the worship of pious Jews gath-ered on Tisha B'av, the day that recalls the destruction of the Temple. In the cemetery in Safed, tourists can descend a series of steps to visit the grave of Isaac Luria, the most famous Cabalist of all time—but not, alas, without first being propositioned by a Yeshivah student "to buy a Coca-Cola in honor of the saintly Rabbi Isaac." Tourism and banal indecency go hand in hand; they feed each other in Israel as they do everywhere else.

And yet, less readily observable are the thousands of Jews who travel to Israel because their Jewish souls draw them there. The synagogue offers them a prayer before they leave. They pack tour guides but also Bi-bles and prayer books that they haven't looked at in years. Unlike tour-ists, when they get to Israel, they speak their own language out of neces-sity, not pride—they secretly say, or even openly admit, that Hebrew is the sacred language of Jews, and they wish they spoke it like the natives. They can't get enough of it, in fact: They stare in awe at *Coca-Cola* written in Hebrew letters.

They mumble silent prayers at the Wall, filling its cracks with the written petitions of others from home who asked them to follow the time-honored practice of inserting one's most private musings into the stones where God, presumably, hangs out to read them. They visit graves of every patriarch, matriarch, rabbi, and seer they can find, more or less aware that maybe the famous departed aren't really buried there—but they may be, and, in a way, it doesn't matter. The people who tend the graves as a matter of religious conscience are convinced that this place is authentic; and if you ask, or even if you don't, they may offer a blessing to your children.

These visitors take rolls of pictures, sensing somehow that they are a modern version of relics. Once upon a time, pilgrims brought back pieces of the landscape as tangible reminders of the sacred center they had visited. Now they put you in prison for doing that. So Jews take photos instead, arranging the best ones in albums and proudly displaying them the way they would their wedding pictures. They don't do that for trips to the Greek Isles, the Spanish Riviera, or Club Med.

Then, too, the presence of Israel drums home the lesson of belonging to a worldwide family called the Jewish People. All cultures have their fatal flaws, and the less–than-spiritual side of peoplehood has included times when Jews took jingoistic stands against the world as if to say that just being born a Jew is better. Even as alienated a Jew as Sigmund Freud believed that deeply. He wrote to his Jewish colleague Karl Abraham that C. G. Jung could not be expected to understand psychoanalysis as well as Abraham did; Jung was not Jewish. Freud was the product of racist European culture, and even as he feared and despised the Nazi version of it, he adopted his own subtle Jewish variety, but hid it as best he could lest it damage his standing in the academic community.

Other Jews less famous than Freud concurred; a response, in part, to inhabiting a world that treated Jews with contempt. Jewish immigrants from eastern Europe at the turn of the twentieth century were often outright racist in their pride of Jewish character. It was commonplace to believe that Jews were innately smart, that Jewish marriages lasted longer, and that Jews could not be alcoholics. Of course, none of this turns out to be the case. Being chosen, as the Bible puts it, does not mean being especially genetically endowed. Jews today have rightly denounced that kind of pseudoscientific understanding of what is a theological category not a biological one.

So, peoplehood has to mean something other than ethnic or racial pride. And Jews today are discovering that it does. Despite the deep divide that separates some Jews from others (the religiously Orthodox from the religiously Reform, say), Jews never splintered into warring factions the way Protestants and Catholics did at the time of the Reformation. Such Talmudic one-liners as "All Israel is responsible for each other" turn out to be more than simplistic truisms. Even as Jews practice universalist ethics, there is a sense in which Jews feel a deep sense of kinship with other Jews, even Jews half way around the world who differ in native language, favorite foods, ritual practice, and even race—as in 1991 when Jews raised millions to transport the oppressed Jewish community of Ethiopia to Israel. The first Jewish law passed by the state made every Jew in the world a potential citizen, so that never again would oppressed Jews have nowhere to go and no one to take them in. Israel acts as a visible symbol of worldwide Jewish peoplehood. In this single tiny country, the gathering place of the exiles, as tradition would have it, you see Jews who are nothing like you, but who, you feel, are your family, bound in common destiny for better or for worse just because they, like you, affirm the history that runs from Sinai to Israeli statehood and beyond.

Finally, there is the matter of symbolic geography. All geographic systems tell us as much about the geographers as they do about the earth they map. Most Americans, for instance, have grown up using atlases containing a map of the world known as the Mercator projection—a name derived from the map's originator, Gerardus Mercator of Belgium (1512–1594). The map usually stretches across a double page, with Europe and most of Asia on the right-hand page and the rest of Asia and the Americas on the left. The map is designed so that if you glance casually at it, your gaze rests naturally on Europe. It was revised for the colonial politics of England, where, not coincidentally, the zero-degree line of longitude runs. To fit the information on a double page, the map converts the earth's global surface into a quadrangle, distorting the corners to highlight the British empire and the world centrality of the United Kingdom.

Maps, then, do not describe the world so much as they help us think differently about it. Hikers and bicyclists use maps measuring elevations and declines. Highway maps distinguish expressways from old county roads. Political maps provide national boundaries and starred capital cities. Maps in a war room reveal movements of troops. Maps are just lines on a page connecting arbitrary dots to each other, and which dots we connect are the inventiveness of the geographer. Whether the map is true or false depends on the goal for which the map was designed and how well it facilitates the design. A hikers' map is useless for political purposes, but excellent for walkers who want to avoid steep elevations; we measure its utility by how accurately it gauges the hills and valleys.

Most people, therefore, carry in their heads a variety of personal maps that they have memorized through experience and on which they can draw for practical purposes. For instance, parents usually have a "children's activity map" in their heads. They can drive the usual routes to retrieve their children without even thinking about where to turn. They can instruct the baby-sitter on where to go by leaving a hand-drawn account of the relevant roads and landmarks, such as the fire station, where you bear left, and the candy store next to a friend's house. Here is a highly idiosyncratic map that is utterly useless except for driving the kids around.

Religions, too, have their own maps of the world. When possible, they may even design actual spaces with their map in mind, as in Salt Lake City, Utah, where Mormons plotted their entire city with the temple precinct in the center and all roads extending out from it in a perfect grid, numbered according to how far away from the temple they are. In

Jerusalem, you can buy Jewish, Christian, and Muslim maps, all of which are different portrayals of the same city. The Christian map highlights the Via Dolarosa, where Jesus carried the cross to Calvary. The Muslim map provides detail of the Temple Mount, where the El Aksa Mosque and the Dome of the Rock are found. Neither map includes much information about the part of Jerusalem that Israelis have constructed around the historic old city of the Bible. The Jewish map, however, includes it all, juxtaposing landmarks of modern Jewish history alongside sites from antiquity. Same city: different maps for different religious ends.

There is, then, a Jewish map of the world, no more arbitrary than the revised Mercator projection, which portrays how British politicians pictured reality. The Jewish map is my spiritual map of the world. It is how I, as a Jew, think about space.

To begin with, my Jewish line of zero-degrees longitude, so to speak, runs through the city of Jerusalem. We saw before that for the Rabbis, "in the Land" was holy; "outside the Land" was not. But their view was more nuanced than that. They believed that concentric circles of holiness radiate out from Jerusalem's center. Most holy was the central room of the Temple, the Holy of Holies. Less holy is the rest of the Temple precinct; less holy still is the rest of Jerusalem; and least holy of all is the rest of the Land of Israel. The boundaries of the Land mark the all-important changeover from holy to ordinary.

Problems arise when we juxtapose the political map onto the religious one, since the borders of the State of Israel and of the Land of Israel are not the same. Hebron, for instance, where the matriarchs and patriarchs are buried, is considered by many to be a holy Jewish site second only to the Western Wall. But it is in the area now known as the West Bank, where Palestinian Arabs want to establish a state. Muslims have the reverse problem regarding the Temple Mount, which is in Israel now, but where their sacred places are. Zealots on both sides want to match politics to religion by altering political realities. But the problem need not be seen as political. Cooler heads will see it as a spiritual challenge: regardless of who owns the real estate, the issue is how to show due regard for other peoples' religious maps. Pilgrims need not own a place to go there. State and Land need not be identical. Sovereign nations can carve out the spiritual oases of other peoples' religions as potential places of pilgrimage.

It would be difficult for Jews to have no state at all in the sacred Land of Jewish dreams. That is because history is not reversible. The Jewish story is inconceivable without the Jewish Land. In addition, like Muslims in Mecca and Catholics in Vatican City, we decorate our sacred sites with religious artifacts the way we decorate our homes with personal memorabilia. The places we hold sacred are homes for us, places, as they say, where they have to let you in, where you know you will be met by family, where no one will laugh at the way you pray. There must be, then, some correspondence between Land and State, as the Zionists who rejected Uganda knew full well. But complete equivalence is impossible and not even desirable. Wealthy Americans may own summer homes in France. They do not need to own France the way French citizens do. All they ask is that France allows them to decorate their homes the way they want and to be able to come and go at will and in safety.

Having a Home

I do not know the extent to which other religions think of their sacred sites as homes. I do know that Judaism insists on this point. And I know that other schemes are possible. Sacred sites could be pictured instead as awesome places that we enter only at great risk, for instance. That is a common image of the sacred that even the Bible explores on occasion. When David rescues the ark of the covenant from the Philistines and transports it to Jerusalem in a wagon, Uzza, one of the men transporting it, reaches out to steady it and is killed (2 Sam. 6:6). The Rabbis, too, flirt with the idea of the sacred as dangerous when they imagine the high priest remaining only briefly in the central Holy of Holies, lest the Jews waiting outside suspect that God has struck him dead. It is all too human to fasten religious attention on awe—the "fear of God," as the Bible puts it.

In modern times, theologian Rudolf Otto characterizes the holy in that way. Otto's book, *The Idea of the Holy*, is still basic college reading material. Thousands of undergraduates every year learn that the holy must be awe inspiring, if not downright frightening—like Moses at the burning bush. But theology is one thing; spirituality is another. *Spirituality* is our direct experience of God's reality; *theology* is the intellectual scheme we manufacture to explain it. And direct experience of the sacred may be far from what theologians tell us. Psychologist C. G. Jung (1875–1961) got it right when he described "belief and disbelief in God" as "mere surrogates" of the real thing. The question is not belief in God so much as the willingness to say that we have experienced God's reality. Jung described the inhabitants of what he called "primitive" cultures, where people do not just "believe"; they "know." That is because they "still have no theology" and are not yet "fooled by boobytrap concepts." They live in a single integrated and coherent world, whereas "we live only in one half and merely believe in the other or not at all. . . . We live by self-fabricated electric light and—to heighten the comedy—believe or don't believe in the sun."

Biblical *theology*, then, does include images of the sacred that are awesome. But it also recalls God as a shepherd and loving parent, and that is the part of the Bible that Jews carried with them as a practical matter of knowing God's reality. What was indelibly encoded in Jewish memory was the compassionate *Sh'khinah*, mothering Israel in exile and then patiently accompanying her home. Home is not frightening; it is just the opposite: safety, nurturing, love, and promise.

Modern Jews differ on the meaning of *exile*. Some Jews, mostly Orthodox, hold that exile is, literally, living outside the Land, even of one's own free will. These Jews correct the situation by making *aliyah*—"ascending" to Israel. Other Jews limit *exile* to enforced exclusion from the Land. That was a basic tenet of Reform Judaism, the movement that emerged in nineteenth-century Germany and was brought here by German immigrants. In the Babylonian exile, for instance, Jews were forcefully removed from their land—hardly the same as choosing freely to live in New York City rather than Jerusalem. Most Jews agree with this perspective. They may visit Israel, but are not likely to move there. Israel is their spiritual home, even if they do not believe that life outside it is necessarily life in exile.

The immediate knowledge of a Land that is home coupled with memories of medieval exile and enforced Jewish homelessness through the centuries allows Jews nowadays to draw a world map where the contrast between "at home" and "not at home" is everywhere. Police maps record incidents of homicide and grand larceny. Corporate maps chart headquarters and branch offices. Jewish maps feature a network of homes.

Home, then, is the core geographical unit for Jewish maps. Because Jewish spirituality knows the Land of Israel as our paradigmatic sacred space, Jews have systematically built other sacred spaces that we call home as well. Jewish communities are homes where people care for each other and where strangers find a welcome. Three institutions, especially, constitute the centers of this communal home. Each is even called a home—in Hebrew, *bayit*, or (when used with other Hebrew words, the shortened form) *bet*.

First, there is our actual home, the house and household where we literally dwell, called our *bayit*. The English phrase, being "at home," conjures up comfort and safety. But being "at home" is a spiritual, not just a physical, matter. That is why Jewish worship is not simply synagogue-centered. As we saw, every Jewish holy day has its home component too, not just Sabbath meals and the Passover Seder, but others as well: The festival of Sukkot (booths) is a sort of Jewish Thanksgiving that falls during the Autumn harvest. Jews keep it by building a *Sukkah*, a booth in the back yard, from which they hang produce as visible tokens of gratitude for what the earth yields. On Rosh Hashanah, the Jewish new year, Jews symbolize their hopes for a sweet year by serving apples dipped in honey. On Yom Kippur, we seek forgiveness for wrongdoing. Pious Jews begin the process around the dinner table, where family members apologize to each other for words spoken, deeds done, and harm committed, intentionally or inadvertently. Private homes are oases of the sacred, set apart by love and prayer from the symbolic world of "exile" that is the street, the subway, the office, and the shopping mall.

Then there are the communal homes we call synagogues. The word "synagogue" comes from the Greek *synagoge*, meaning "assembly." The parallel Hebrew term also, *bet hak'nesset*, means "home of assembly." Like a home, the synagogue was originally just a place for people to gather. In time, the synagogue became also *bet hamidrash* and *bet hat'fil-lah*, "home of study" and "home of prayer." In Judaism, neither study nor prayer is a private matter. They are communal pursuits of responsibility by a covenanted people.

As a visible reminder of the synagogue as such a sacred "home," the arks of synagogue sanctuaries are outfitted to look like the primal home in Jerusalem, the ancient Temple. Medieval Jews read the biblical description of the desert tabernacle. Assuming that the ancient Temple must have looked like that, they made their synagogues into little "local temples." As the Temple had boasted the Holy of Holies, where God's presence was said to dwell, so synagogues contained arks to hold scrolls of Torah, the source of God's presence in our time. The Bible calls for various tabernacle appurtenances—an eternal light, for instance, a valence, and a curtain—all of which are now standard fare in synagogue arks as well. The synagogue thereby came to mirror the home we once called the Temple: a sacred space for sacred community.

And last, there is the grave. A cemetery, too, is called *bayit*, in this case, *bet olamim*, meaning literally "the eternal home" to which we go when earthly life is done. Death is not something to be feared. We were made from the earth and our bodily remains return there, a final home of homes from which no more exile is ever possible.

The Ethics of Home

Knowing the difference between home and exile carries moral consequences. To begin with, there is the obvious obligation of seeing to it that other human beings have homes. Homelessness is a particular horror for Jewish spirituality. In the Middle Ages, when Jewish mystics adopted the belief in the transmigration of souls, the dismay of homelessness was actually transferred to the fear that some souls on their way from one body to another would end up in eternal wandering. All the more so does Jewish ethics care about actual human beings who lack homes of their own. Here is where Jewish spirituality departs decisively from the pop spirituality of angels and crystals described in chapter 1. Spiritual commitment to the primary metaphor of "home" requires a particular sensitivity to homelessness.

Being without a home is so devastating an experience to the biblical author that he has Moses name his son Gershom, meaning "stranger there." And in case the reader misses the allusion, the author explains (Exod. 2:22), "He named him Gershom, for he said, 'I have been a stranger in a strange land.'" The same information is given yet a second time, in precisely the same words to Jethro, Gershom's maternal grandfather (Exod. 18:3). He, too, is to know what crushing significance Moses' stay in Egypt had been. And the Torah never forgets the moral attached to that experience. Immediately after the Ten Commandments are received, Moses settles down to explain "the rules" that come with the covenant. Prominent among them is, "You shall not wrong or oppress a stranger for you were strangers in the land of Egypt" (Exod. 22:20). Just one chapter later (Exod. 23: 9), this all-important law is reiterated, "Do not oppress a stranger, for you know the feelings of the stranger, having yourselves been strangers in the land of Egypt." Leviticus 19:34 builds further on this central moral tenet, which flows from the spirituality of landedness. "The stranger who resides with you shall be as one of your citizens; you shall love him as yourself, for you were strangers in the land of Egypt." Four more times we get it—in Deuteronomy 5:15, 10:19, 15:15, and 24:22! No other law is stated even remotely as often as this one is. Care for strangers is built into the very fabric of the Torah's account of moving from slavery to freedom, from exile to landedness and home.

There are political consequences, to be sure. Stateless peoples deserve a state, as Israel claimed its own. Continual wars between Israel and its Palestinian neighbors have made it hard, in practice, for Jews to support a state for Palestinian Arabs. But originally, the mandate was to have made room for an Arab state as well as for a Jewish one; eventually a Palestinian state, too, will come into effect.

Last, there is an ethical claim made in Hasidic literature that should not go unheeded. Though some Hasidic masters made *aliyah* to fulfill the commandment of living in the Land, most did not. With brazen boldness, they likened the actual Land to their own centers in eastern Europe, thereby building on the metaphor of synagogue and home as "Land," but ignoring the plain and obvious meaning of the Bible and Talmud. The most striking such claim is by Menachem of Chernobyl, who held that what puts people in the Land is the purity of their prayer and intentions. If they occupy themselves with vain thoughts, even if they live in Jerusalem, they are not considered in the Land. Landed people are those who pray and study with full intentions of carrying out their consequences. Staying in the Land then becomes a generalized ethical impulse that worshipers or students of Torah anywhere in the world retain even as they go about the ritual acts of Jewish life.

It is often thought that spirituality and the real worldly concern of social justice are incompatible, or at least unrelated: Spiritual seekers may be moral beacons as well, but they just as easily may not be; and the other way around—ethical activists are considered less likely to be spiritual. Again, it is the popular view of spirituality as private and self-serving that brings about this misunderstanding. Polls reveal that one-third of Americans identify as spiritual a whole host of things, including "a calmness in life," "believing in myself to make the right decision," "living a life that I feel is pleasing," and "living positively," without any reference to God, a higher power, or a higher morality. Sociologist Robert Wuthnow sees this privatization of spirituality as the domestication of God, who now conveniently serves us, not the other way around. That is distinctly not the Jewish view of covenant. Our relationship to God surely ought to move us internally, but if it does not move us also to a better code of behavior, something is distinctly missing.

In 1998, the president of the national synagogue body of the North American Reform Movement stepped down after almost forty years of service. When two prominent rabbis emerged as final candidates, one known for social justice and the other for work in Jewish prayer, a Jewish newspaper ran a story stating that the Reform Movement was choosing between ethics and spirituality. Nothing could have been further from the truth. No matter which candidate they chose, the electors would be opting for both: They exist together. "

Chapter Six

Spiritual Thinking:
The Spirituality of Translation

What is French for London? Maybe "Paris."
EUGENE IONESCO

The spirituality hype in the media is apt to make a lot of people feel guilty because they don't seem to be as religious as everyone else. That is because, despite our constitutional right to believe anything we like religiously, in practice, we are pressured to believe the right thing—or at least not to disbelieve what Americans take to be religious verities. We may have the sense that we are being admonished by the White Queen in Lewis Carroll's *Through the Looking Glass*. A clergyman in the Church of England himself, Carroll has the Queen tell Alice, "Why, sometimes I've believed as many as six impossible things before breakfast."

In 1989, the Gallup Poll constructed an index of religious belief, a cumulative measure of the extent to which people hold such "basic" Christian views as faith in a personal God and belief in life after death. Out of a total possible score of 100, meaning that you professed every single one of the beliefs mentioned, the average American response was 67, second only to the Republic of Ireland (whose average score was 73). By contrast, West Germany scored only 37, the Netherlands and Great Britain, 36, France, 32, and Denmark, 21. A whopping 97 percent of Americans said one year earlier that they *never* doubt the existence of God. And as the year 2000 dawned, American faith in faith scarcely dimmed: 96 percent of all Americans told George Gallup that they be-lieve in some kind of God; 75 percent say they pray daily; 90 percent believe in heaven; and 77 percent think their chances of going there are good.

When a serial killer, captured in the 1960s, told police he had no religion, columnists and preachers alike drew the inference that everyone devoid of basic religious belief would be likely to engage in monstrous behavior. Atheism, in other words, is held to be not only stupid but morally dangerous as well.

The Eisenhower years are responsible for that belief. Communism, after all, was proudly atheistic. At war with Marx's heirs, we seized on the godlessness of the Communist system as the root of all evil. By contrast, suburban American religion—though not always deep and engaging—thrived. Eisenhower brought Billy Graham to the White House as his guest. We added "under God" to our pledge of allegiance.

Are People Really That Religious?

But Americans might well ponder the degree of religious certainty that polls seem to reveal. Can it really be true that for the past twenty years or so 97 percent of our neighbors have *never* doubted the existence of God? Or are such respondents just supplying pollsters with answers they think are supposed to be right? Polls tell us that from 1944 to 1999 the percentage of people who affirmed a belief in "God or a universal spirit" vacillated between 94 percent and 99 percent, with a high of 99 percent in 1952, the year Dwight D. Eisenhower took office. Maybe so. But polls can be deceptive, as the following instance shows.

In 1986, 93 percent of all Americans said that they were either "very satisfied" or "mostly satisfied" with their family life, an increase in two percentage points since 1980. But that very same year, one-half of all marriages ended in divorce, and the divorce rate had actually risen since 1981. Why do 50 percent of marriages fail if 93 percent of the people in them are either "very" or "mostly satisfied" with their family life?

Now it may be that Americans are telling the truth when it comes to religious matters, at least since 1980. We are (as we shall see in chapter 8) in the middle of only the third religious awakening in American history. In 1960, John F. Kennedy, the first Catholic president, had to guarantee American voters that his personal religious views would not influence public policy; whereas by 1980 Ronald Reagan assured voters that he was a creationist because they confidently expected that as president he *would* run the country with his deepest Protestant convictions guiding his acts of state. The extent of the religious swing is evident in other ways as well, some of them small, but telling: In January 1996, on a trip to Phoenix from Denver, an airline offered me *Christian Parenting Today* magazine along with the usual choices of *Time* and *Newsweek*.

Still, the contrast between people who report high family satisfaction and the rise in divorce rates suggests that we ought not to take at face value what polls report. If "generic" religious belief is something people think they ought to have, and if expressing religious doubt is tantamount to being a bad American, the polls that document religious certainty might be leading us astray. Take the issue of attending weekly worship.

For over fifty years, the Gallup organization has been tracking religious attitudes and behavior. A lot has changed in that period of time. When Gallup began keeping records, there were no microwave ovens or computers. We have seen the hippy sixties come and go, flower children metamorphose into stockbrokers, and Vietnam vets return from the first war that America clearly lost and then tried to forget. Science has landed men on the moon and mapped the human genome. And yet, through all of this, the Gallup poll finds that American churchgoing patterns have remained the same. Week in and week out, roughly 42 percent of Americans say they attend church services every Sunday morning.

But do they? In 1994, a team of sociologists decided that instead of asking people what they do, they would watch them do it. They hired observers to stand at church doors and count the people entering. It turns out that 42 percent of all Americans *say* they go to pray every week, but only 21 percent really do. People tend to say what they think researchers want to hear or, more likely (but amounting to the same thing), what they themselves want to think that they do. So, too, they may answer questions about religious belief in terms of what they think they would like to think, not what they really do believe.

It is probable, then, that internal pressure to think of ourselves as virtuous citizens, not amoral atheists, prevents us from owning up to the extent to which we really are baffled by the complex issues that pollsters blithely put to us. It takes courage to admit that sometimes we are not sure if God exists.

We have no models of healthy uncertainty. Public personalities practice speaking like parents for whom everything is clear. They may be mediocre senators, governors, and presidents, their closets stocked with skeletons, but they sound like theological geniuses. No one ever says, "Well, I do believe in God, but I wonder why a good God allows bad things to happen to good people" or "I shudder at the thought of an aborted fetus, but especially in cases of rape, I can see arguments on both sides of the abortion issue." Oh, no. Waffling politicians are dead politicians, so we have no cultural model for doubt; no examples of people we admire who are anything but absolutely sure about answers to moral questions that the wisest minds in human history have debated for thousands of years. If God is good, why do children get sick and die? America's religious climate is not conducive to questions like this, which are not discussed so much as they are dismissed by firebrand moralizers who castigate doubters as irreligious radicals and un-American agents of moral decay.

American religion is amazing in its easygoing conviction that faith is obvious. By contrast, think of Martin Luther who was wracked by questions of what God wanted from him; or of Blaise Pascal, the seventeenth-century philosopher who acknowledged God's reality only as a wager—knowing that proof would never be forthcoming, he would bet on

God's existence, because he had less to lose thereby. The nineteenth-century existentialist Søren Kierkegaard rightly called it a leap of faith. Today's polls, by contrast, treat religious belief as so patently evident that anyone who expresses intellectual doubt should be suspected, not respected, for the insistence that the only God worth believing in is a God who challenges our minds as much as our hearts.

Are the 96 percent of Americans who say they believe in God really as religious as they seem? Maybe; but maybe not. Lots of people do not write off as utter nonsense scientific challenges to religious cosmology or geological evidence that the earth is older than the Bible says it is. They know, too, that people suffer pain they do not deserve and that the same public personalities who claim to know what virtue is don't always act virtuously. They must therefore know that the world is not as simple as simpleminded people like to imagine. Questioning so-called verities is not irreligious; it is profound and it is what Jewish wisdom values as the ideal.

The columnist and social critic of the 1920s and 1930s H. L. Mencken once said that for every complex problem, there is an answer that is simple, obvious—and wrong. Brilliant, if acerbic, Mencken was a card-carrying professional atheist who got only part of the truth straight. He should have added that for every complex problem there is also a complex answer that may be right. Really spiritual questions are complex. And they invite properly complex answers, not parroted pieties that leave a lot to be desired by anyone whose mind is really functioning.

Thinking about spirituality is like thinking about anything else. Conclusions come at the end of the process, not at the beginning. But even though we think all the time, we don't spend much time thinking about thinking. Before launching the exercise in thinking through some basic spiritual truths, then, I need to say something more about what it is to think.

Thinking about Thinking

Thinking comes naturally to human beings. We all do it, but do we all do it the same way? Nineteenth- and early twentieth-century anthropologists who were discovering so-called primitive cultures believed that we do not.

French theorist Lucien Lévy-Bruhl (1857–1939), for instance, wrote a book in 1922 called *Primitive Thought* and another in 1910 entitled *Mental Functions in Inferior Societies*. He attributed to "primitives" an inability to distance themselves from their world, so that they suffered from a false sense of "mystical participation" with their surroundings. Unable to understand the scientific notion of cause and effect, they attributed even such obvious phenomena as birth and death to mystical forces that attack or otherwise infect human beings. By the end of his life, Lévy-Bruhl had largely rethought his simplistic dichotomy between primitives and moderns, but it remained fashionable nonetheless.

Others cast doubts not on primitives in general, but on specific peoples or groups of people. This often meant injecting racist or gender-biased presumptions into the conversation. At its extreme, we find the Nazis, who were quite convinced that only bona fide Aryans could think clearly. But Nazi doctrine goes back to earlier racist theory. Its chief proponent, Count J. A. de Gobineau (1816–1882), wrote, "This is what the whole course of history teaches us. Every race has its own mode of thinking . . . which it cannot engraft upon any other except by amalgamation of blood, and then only in a modified degree." Gobineau's studies became very popular and were refined by many, including such unlikely candidates as a self-hating Jew named Otto Weininger, who called his own contribution to the evolving pseudoscience of racial and genetic difference *Sex and Character*. Weininger believed that clarity of thought was the sole possession of men—and only white men, at that. T. S. Eliot and Ezra Pound, inheritors of Victorian beliefs that painted women as more emotional and men as more logical in their respective genetic endowments, were among the intellectuals who would have agreed. Alan Jay Lerner captured the accusation against women's rationality brilliantly in his lyrics for *My Fair Lady*, when he has Professor Higgins accuse women of constantly straightening their hair, never their thinking apparatus (act 2, scene 4).

These early evolutionary schemes that attributed fully rational thought only to modern European men attracted critics as well as supporters. In the 1920s, the Polish anthropologist Bronislaw Malinowski studied a Melanesian people in the Pacific called the Trobriand Islanders. He conceded that magic did inform the way they lived. But it was ludicrous to conclude that they thought differently from scientific Europeans. Regardless of what "superstitious" ritual they resorted to in order to insure pregnancy, for instance, they certainly knew where babies come from. Rather than imagining that they had no concept of science, we ought to say that they had their own body of incomplete science on which to depend. They did not think differently; they were just uninformed about much that was taken for granted in the West.

There are certainly differences in the ways that cultures assemble their thoughts, but these differences do not derive from any innate discrepancy in the way their collective gray cells function. From the most "primitive" cave dweller to the most "advanced" co-op owner, we all think the same, and we do it equally logically.

The difference lies in the implicit models of the universe that cultures provide their followers. College courses used to feature the most famous examples: anthropological studies that sought to demonstrate the psychological conditioning of cultural responses. Some cultures were Apollonian: They stressed a detached, passive, and coldly logical approach to life. Others were Dionysian: They favored an aggressive, actively engaged, and emotional citizenry. Most people now would agree that "patterns of culture" (as they were called) went too far, but clearly, there are significant differences in the way that members of one culture and members of another choose to conceptualize their world. If thinking is an art, we can say that all cultures paint pictures, and they do so equally well, but using different colors and having different models of what a successful picture looks like.

One way to think of theology is as a set of ideas with which religious people color their world. Inuit find snow; Christians find the word that became flesh; Jews find blessings. What matters is partly what the world gives us and partly what our culture teaches us to find.

Jews through time, therefore, have been taught to think in a particular conceptual framework. We paint the world in cultural colors that read "God," "Torah," and "a People called Israel." Time comes prepackaged as Shabbat and holidays; space is segmented into places called home. These are the categories of Jewish spirituality that occupied our attention in earlier chapters. Not all Jews through time have believed the same thing about these ideas. But you cannot be a Jew without drawing on them somehow. Jewish spirituality uses Jewish ideas, Jewish rhetoric, Jewish concepts, Jewish words, and Jewish analogies. That is what makes it Jewish.

But modern Jewish spirituality need not accept exactly what bygone Jews have done with these things. As I have said already, regarding the Jewish penchant for blessing and for study, it helps to use the metaphor of art.

The thinking process is the brushwork, which does not change. All cultures use brushes to paint their canvases, although they may use different kinds of brushes or expand their elementary brush repertoire by the creative addition of other brushlike elements in their environment or even (from time to time) by technological improvement—computerized brushwork, for instance, which increases the speed at which colors are applied. In the world of thought, too, computers have increased our thinking speed, but have not allowed us to think better or more clearly than Aristotle and Plato did some twenty-four hundred years ago. All religions think with the same thinking mechanism; they are all answerable to the natural limits of the evolving human brain; they all use metaphors of one sort or another; they all process thought in the same ways.

But, however they are the same in terms of how they function, cultures do differ from one another. They are like different traditions in art, which may share the common characteristic of having to apply color to canvas, but have different models in mind as they do their brushwork. An art tradition runs like a vertical line through time, piercing different horizontal axes that represent the eras in which they have existed. Each intersection of the vertical and the horizontal lines gives us a stage in the unfolding story of how the art tradition evolved. As the line of Western art moves upward from point zero on the chart, we can watch it progress through classical Greek experiments with the human figure to the Renaissance discoveries of human musculature to cubism and Picasso's geometric abstractions of his human subjects. Similarly, we can look at the culture we call Judaism and watch it develop from biblical concepts to classical rabbinic texts and then medieval or modern variations on the same themes—themes like holiness, Torah, and a sacred Land. The reason authors can write a book on the history of Western architecture or Buddhist thought or Christian theology—or Jewish spirituality—is that each of these topics is just that: a historical description of different stages in the evolution of a single subject.

Many people mistakenly believe that in order to think spiritually they have to swallow uncritically the literal truths they find in traditional writings. The writings, however, are like diary entries at earlier intersections of the vertical and horizontal lines, where their religious tradition has met other historical eras. Reading old diary entries and knowing they are part of our own evolving life story as members of a single tradition is not equivalent to thinking the same thoughts all over again and feeling the same way about what we wrote when we were younger. Spirituality is the conviction that the old diary entries continue to engage us; they define our way of seeing the world; by rereading our traditional affirmations of faith, we rethink the world using the themes that our religion has bequeathed us. But using the colors and models that past generations gave us is not the same as settling for a photocopy of the same pictures that they drew.

Take the question of God. Believing that spirituality implies a belief in God, pollsters ask, "Do you believe in God?" But serious Jews do not just parrot back affirmative answers. Knowing the shades of meaning that Judaism has presented in its understanding of God, they may want to qualify the question: does it assume a God who literally answers prayer, for instance; or a God who rewards virtue and punishes vice; or a God who inhabits the heavens and spoke to Moses on Mount Sinai; or a God who created the universe out of nothing. What kind of God does the questioner mean? These are all pictures of God now hanging on some wall or other in the museum of Jewish spiritual thought. We need not accept them all; indeed, we cannot, since some are inconsistent with others.

The easy and automatic answer to the question "Do you believe in God?" is always "Yes." That is what 96 percent of all Americans told the Gallup pollsters. The more honest answer, however, would have been, "Yes (to some things); no (to others); maybe (to most)." The right answer ought always to start with, "It depends what you mean by that. Let's talk about it."

Some Age-Old Jewish Certainties

Jewish culture encourages this kind of measured response to all questions of belief, including the existence of God. Jews tend somewhat maddeningly, therefore, to refuse to give absolute affirmations to things that everyone else seems to know for sure. The same polls that measure the overall rate of American belief thus regularly report a falloff when it comes to Jewish respondents. There are so few Jews in national samples that we are always warned by researchers to be wary of making too much of the Jewish findings. But nonetheless, it cannot be an accident that Jews always score lower on matters of faith than Catholics and Protestants. For example, 83 percent of Protestants and 81 percent of Catholics say they are "sometimes very conscious of God's presence"; 61 percent of Jews agree. Eighty-six percent of Protestants and 84 percent of Catholics say they believe that "God performs miracles even today"; only 46 percent of Jews say so. Don't Jews believe in anything?

Of course we do. Our low scores on matters of faith are partly the result of the fact that Jews tend to live in cities, and Christian city dwellers also score lower on such things. Jews are highly educated, too—99 percent of them have attended college, for instance—and college-educated people generally doubt the veracity of simple one-liners. But even if you compare only college-educated urban residents, you find that Jews score lower than Christians. So, more is at stake than education and urbanity.

Partly, Jews are "handicapped" by the fact that their religious tradition never trained them in statements of belief. Christianity was erected on a foundation of Greco-Roman philosophy, where right belief mattered more than anything else. Early Christians excommunicated heretics because they believed differently; a whole field called Christology developed to determine what the true Church believed about the Trinity. Protestants broke away from Catholics over matters of faith and then fractured into separate churches over similar matters, most of which Jews fail to understand altogether because Judaism never played the Western game of theology. When Jewish sects broke away from the mother religion, usually they did so on the basis of what they thought God wanted them to do, not what they were supposed to believe. It came more naturally for Jews to question certainties, therefore; there were fewer truths they had to accept. Even if Jews didn't accept any truths, as long as they acted like Jews in matters of conduct, they were apt to find broad leeway within which they were permitted to exercise their doubts.

Judaism did pass down a set of truths to which Jews were supposed to give assent, but Jewish literature never developed them into a creed the way Christianity did. There was never a centralized rabbinic authority that could pass one, for one thing; and for another, even the greatest minds who tried to decide what lay at the center of Jewish faith usually found some other great mind who thought differently.

But part of the Jewish way of conduct is the commitment to daily prayer, and part of that daily prayer is a set of prayers that come close to being a creed. Jews do not have to accept it all—they may even doubt a good deal of it, even as they pray it—but it comprises the best index of Jewish wisdom over the course of Judaism's three-thousand-year-old history, and if we look at it, we learn a good deal about Judaism as a faith and even more about serious religious spirituality for minds that have not forgotten the fine art of honest inquiry.

The prayers in question constitute that section of the service known as the *Sh'ma* and its Blessings. The *Sh'ma* is known to most Jews as a liturgical "one-liner" from Deuteronomy 6:4. Translations of the Hebrew vary, but the essence of the line is an affirmation of monotheism: "Hear O Israel, the Eternal is our God; the Eternal alone." In fact, the *Sh'ma* extends beyond that one line. In its entirety, it encompasses several more verses from Deuteronomy 6, and then two other biblical snippets. Moreover, the entire collection of biblical citations is bracketed by blessings.

These blessings are said both morning and night, but with different wording. The following quotations give a good indication of their contents.

(1) *Blessing of Creation:* Blessed are You, Eternal our God, ruler
of the universe who forms light and creates darkness, who makes
peace and creates all things. In mercy You give light to the earth
and to those who dwell on it; in your goodness, You renew the work
of creation every day, constantly. How great are your works, O Eternal One. In wisdom You have made them all. The earth is full of
your creations. . . . Blessed are You . . . creator of the lights.

(2) *Blessing of Revelation:* You have loved the house of Israel your
People with everlasting love; You have taught us Torah and precepts, laws and judgments. Therefore, Eternal our God, when we lie
down and when we rise up we will speak of your laws and rejoice in
the words of your Torah and in your precepts evermore. Indeed,

they are our life and the length of our days. We will meditate on them day and night. May You never take away your love from us. Blessed are You . . . who love your People, Israel.

(3) *Blessing of Redemption:* You were the help of our forebears in days gone by, and have been a shield and savior to their children after them in every generation. . . . You are the first and the last and besides You, there is no ruler who redeems and saves. From Egypt You redeemed us, Eternal our God, and from the house of bondage You delivered us. . . . Blessed are You . . . who redeemed Israel.

As my italicized titles indicate, it has been commonplace at least since the nineteenth century—and perhaps earlier as well—to describe these three blessings as essays on the threefold Jewish theme of creation, revelation, and redemption. God is a creator of the cosmos, the revealer of truth, and a God of history who saved the Hebrew slaves in Egypt and will similarly redeem the world entire at the end of time. Among other things, the three blessings give us a time scheme from beginning (creation) to midway in history (revelation at Mount Sinai) to the end of time (redemption). But we have considerably more than that. These three ideas are a photograph in time of the way Jews thought when the vertical line of Jewish tradition met the horizontal line of the late Roman Empire. Spiritual thinking is the way we wrestle with old ideas in a new way.

Let us look at each of the ideas in order, to see how the Jewish line of tradition has carried them forward to our time. The Rabbis bequeathed to Jews ever after these three unique claims regarding the spiritual essence of God and God's world; what have Jews done with them up to our own day?

Creation

Jews have taken it as axiomatic that God created the universe. This belief has generally been expressed by the phrase "creation out of nothing." According to Jewish lore, God first created Torah and consulted it like a blueprint to find a model for the universe. This is another way of saying that the cosmos appears to be logically ordered and systematically arranged.

But even as Jews have insisted on the divine origin of the world, they have not demanded that the creation account in Genesis be taken literally. The Rabbis insisted that the stories in the Torah do not follow the laws of chronology; as they put it, "There is no 'earlier' or 'later' in Torah." So, how long the creation process took, exactly how it occurred, and similar questions were considered unanswerable from the biblical pages alone. They were reserved for the rarefied discussions of philosophers and mystics. In the second century c.e., for instance, "Creation Doctrine," known as *Ma'aseh B'reshit*, comprised a distinct field of academic expertise for a very few mystical adepts intent on facing issues of ultimacy—akin, perhaps, to the unbounded awe a scientist feels today when the Hubble Space Telescope beams back information about the billions of light-years during which the universe has been in existence; or the grandeur that brought the psalmist to marvel, "You have stamped your glory in the heavens. . . . How majestic is your presence in all the earth!"

The Rabbis of two thousand years past struggled, as we do, to comprehend the process that even today takes our breath away: not just how a creative order came into being, but the awesome fact that it did at all—that there is something rather than nothing.

As they struggled with the ultimate nature of reality, Jews freely admitted scientific findings into their calculus of creation. Moses Maimonides, for instance, whom I have already cited, lived when Aristotelian doctrine dominated people's thoughts. But Aristotle had taught that the universe was made out of matter which itself was eternal, so that creation consisted only of applying distinctive form to primeval shapelessness. Here was a theory that ran counter to the age-old rabbinic notion of "creation out of nothing." Maimonides, therefore, might have championed the rabbinic doctrine insisting that God and God alone was eternal. But interestingly enough, he flirted with the possibility that raw matter might indeed be as infinite as its Maker.

But God would, in any event, still be the world's Creator, in a deeper nontemporal sense. Creation is an infinitely ongoing thing, in the sense that everything other than God is dependent on something else for its continued existence. The universe would then be composed of a chain of dependent entities—except for God, who, by definition, would be the sole entity on which all else depends, but which itself depends on nothing such that if all created matter were to die, only God would still remain; but if God were to disappear, everything else would vanish.

Maimonides' speculations demonstrate the extent to which Jewish spiritual thought is far from a simple literal repetition of what inherited Jewish texts say. Jewish tradition demands continual interpretation as it grows through time and comes into contact with new eras of thought. To be a Jew, then, is not necessarily to accept the literal doctrine of biblical creation. It is, however, to take seriously the claim that there is one God who is somehow intimately involved with the universe the way a creator is involved with something that is created.

The Jewish view of creation fits harmoniously with the state of scientific knowledge in every age. Scientific theory changes. The Jewish interest in creation as a manifestation of the divine touches not on scientific truth or falsehood, but on the values implicit in the universal order, no matter what science has to say. The universe is valuable because however it came into being, it is in some way indissolubly linked to God. Its order is assumed somehow to be a manifestation of the divine blueprint we loosely call Torah. The rules by which it operates cannot be random, and human life, as part of a larger cosmos, must be tied to a greater scheme of things that escapes the eye of any part of the cosmos itself, including the humans within it. One way to think of the Jewish affirmation that God created the world is to say that the world is not without inherent order and that we humans, who ferret out what we can of that order, are as much a part of what we study as we are the curious seekers after the very order that we ourselves help to constitute.

Revelation

Our second blessing asserts the Jew's faith in revelation. Revelation, however, is best considered from the perspective of what I call an *idea complex.*

Ideas are like diamonds: They have several facets, not all of which sparkle at the same time. Imagine a diamond on the end of a string, twirling very slowly in the sunshine. Our eye catches the reflection of the sun off of only one facet at a time, so that depending on which side we face, the diamond lights up brilliantly in a different way. So, too, with great ideas. The limitations of our minds may necessitate our thinking clearly about different facets of ideas one at a time, but the idea itself is a complex of related notions grafted on to one another like different sides of a conceptual diamond. The French Revolution, for instance, was fought for "Liberty, equality, fraternity." But these are not so much three diverse ideas as they are three sides of a single complex notion. Accept any one of them, and the others follow as well. So, too, the Jewish idea of revelation is just one way of describing a set of associated beliefs. Judaism takes for granted an idea complex of "Exodus, freedom from bondage, chosen peoplehood, revelation at Sinai, and being at home in the sacred soil of a Land called Israel." Revelation is just one of the facets of this larger idea complex.

Broadly understood, revelation is the process by which God and God's will are known to human beings. The Bible assumes that God addresses people to inform them of their duty and to clarify the nature of reality. People need only remain open to the word of God as it breaks in on human consciousnesses from time to time—in a burning bush, perhaps; atop a mountain, maybe; or in this or that miracle that flashes unannounced on the scene of history.

But the Bible is not the work of just one author, or even of a single generation. So, this simple and straightforward view of revelation has to be modified to fit the specific circumstances of the part of the Bible we are considering. Sometimes God speaks through prophets, for instance, as in the eighth to the sixth centuries B.C.E. when people like Amos, Jeremiah, Hosea, and Isaiah claimed to be special recipients of God's messages. Before that, monarchs like David and Solomon relied on court prophets who saw it as their task to correct the kings whenever they went astray. In other parts of the Bible, no prophets exist at all: God converses instead with ordinary people—Cain, for example, after he kills his brother Abel. So, even in the Bible, the ways that God communicates with people vary, as does the nature of the divine message and even the time, place, and vehicle in which the message is carried. What does not change is the firm belief that the message is there to be known and that life is meaningless without our finding the message.

Prophets present a peculiar problem to society, however, in that it is hard to decide whether to trust their words. They may be lying, suffering delusions, or misinterpreting. Even when prophecy was at its height and there were certain accepted behavioral symptoms by which true prophets might be recognized, prophets were still apt to be opposed by the powers that be, whose politics they decried, or by other would-be prophets, who claimed to have equally decisive albeit contradictory messages from God. Thus, a new stage in the history of revelation was reached when one specific revelatory message, the Torah, was canonized as the central word of God, given at one unique and historic event: Sinai. In the fifth century B.C.E., the age of Ezra and the return from Babylonian exile, a single Torah came into existence as the accepted record of God's will, and from then on, Judaism has been a religion of the book, not of random prophecy. All religious debate was henceforth theoretically able to be settled by reference to the one book that Jews call Torah.

But who would be the determiners of the Torah's true interpretation? No book is without ambiguity, especially one with such diverse material, compiled over the course of ages so long ago. Jewish society was a theocracy then; its leaders were priests, like the famous Ezra himself. Unsurprisingly, the Torah that Ezra and his fellow priests compiled vests the final interpretation of its contents in other priests. For many years, it was the priests who established God's revelatory messages for Israel. Judaism had moved from a system of direct revelation to revelation through Torah, and from prophets to priests.

But again, it was the Rabbis who left the most lasting stamp on the Jewish doctrine of revelation. They canonized the remaining books of the Bible and did away with direct revelation through prophets. Their very act of biblical canonization ended the possibility that someone might write, or even uncover, yet another source for direct apprehension of God's will. It was this issue of revelation that divided Jews from the early Christians because, for Christianity, God had not ended direct prophet-like discovery of the divine will. For Christians, that knowledge was now vested in Jesus, its content recorded in a new set of holy books called the New, as opposed to the Old, Testament. As proof of his divinity and prophet-like status, Jesus regularly performs miracles on the sick and the multitudes that gather to hear him.

We saw earlier that for the Rabbis, even patent miracles were declared out of bounds in the determination of God's will. They did not doubt that God could and did perform miracles, but they refused to classify the miraculous as evidence of revelation. Even the voice from heaven was not enough to establish the truth of a rabbinic debate. Now Rabbis—not priests, prophets, or miracle workers—held the key to revelation. Technically speaking, they remained convinced that their interpretations were already implicitly contained in the words of the written text they were interpreting. More precisely, they held that when Moses received the written Torah on Mount Sinai, he also received an oral commentary that revealed the written document's true meaning. The Rabbis saw their task as determining the content of that oral amplification, which—they believed—had been handed down from Moses to Joshua, and then to successive generations, including their own. Revelation was now not only a book, but also a commentary endlessly spun out in the process of rabbinic study and argumentation.

Most Jews today accept the idea of ongoing revelation beyond the written Torah, but they have modified even further the rabbinic doctrine of an oral Torah, too. They find it difficult to believe that every single statement of Jewish wisdom actually derives from a single revelatory moment on Mount Sinai. Ongoing revelation is, rather, an indefinable process by which God's will is made manifest anew in every age. Implicit is the notion that truth itself is not permanent, unchanging, and immutable, but is instead part of the very process of change and development that scientists assume with regard to evolution in general.

This, then, is the general outline of the history behind the revelation part of the idea complex. But the fullness of the doctrine can be understood only when we pay attention to the way the blessing on revelation emphasizes the related concept of God's love. The blessing is bracketed by opening and closing statements telling us that God loves us: "You have loved the house of Israel your people with everlasting love; You have taught us Torah and precepts, laws and judgments. . . . May You never take away your love from us. Blessed are You . . . who love your People, Israel."

The idea complex of which revelation is a part displays a world in which God's love is paramount. The gift of Torah and the manifestation of divine love are interdependent ideas. To allude to one notion is simultaneously to imply the other. Why this emphasis on love?

Idea complexes take their shape against the backdrop of real life. They hardly ever are arrived at in the luxury of an historical vacuum. This one emerged when the vertical line of Jewish tradition met the horizontal line of first- and second-century religion in the late Roman Empire, the very time when Christianity was taking shape and when other religions less well known to us were equal candidates for people's allegiance. The common factor that influenced them all is a worldview called Gnosticism.

The word *gnostic* comes from the Greek *gnosis*, meaning "knowledge," not in the sense of ordinary knowledge of mathematics or current events, say, but knowledge of ultimate things. An "agnostic" is someone who has no certain knowledge of ultimacy. The classic statement on Gnosticism is from the second-century Church father Irenaeus of Lyons, who composed argumentative tracts polemicizing against what he considered heresies in Christianity. At one point he refers to "the so-called Gnostics" as a brand of such wrongheaded Christian belief. Based on Irenaeus, it became common for nineteenth- and early twentieth-century scholars to imagine a single wayward church called Gnosticism.

But Gnosticism really was no single church at all. It is a way of thinking that permeated even Irenaeus's own doctrines. He fulminated against a particular version of Gnostic speculation perhaps, but his own brand of Christianity was Gnostic through and through, as was Judaism. Among other things, Gnosticism was the general belief that the cosmos was divided into two warring realms, light and darkness. Christianity shows Gnostic influence when the Gospel of John calls Jesus "the true light . . . which shines in the darkness but is not overcome by darkness" (John 1:9, 5). Judaism's Gnostic basis remains evident to this day in a Saturday-night ritual that distinguishes the departing Sabbath from the workweek just beginning and also dividing "light from darkness."

Gnosticism provided an entire spectrum of opinion, with some thinkers going further in their dualism than others. Some took the final step of imagining that two diverse realms of experience, light and darkness, required two gods as well. How could a good God of light also create the evil kingdom of darkness? Judaism's strong monotheism prevented the Rabbis from taking this logical leap from one God to two, but did not on that account deny the inherent opposition between the two realms of light and darkness.

If we return to the Creation blessing, we can see how it was influenced by Gnosticism. It ends specifically with praise of God for creating light. "Blessed are You . . . creator of the lights." On the other hand, wanting to deny the possibility that some other deity created the dark side of the universe, the blessing holds at the very outset "Blessed are

You, Eternal our God, ruler of the universe who forms light *and creates darkness*, who makes peace *and creates all things*."

There is more: The introductory line of the blessing is built on a citation from Isaiah 45:6–7, in which God announces, "I am the Lord and there is none else. I form light and create darkness; I make peace and create evil" (Isa. 45:6–7). Isaiah was a prophet who lived before the Babylonian exile, warning the corrupt Judean monarchy of the consequences of its morally bankrupt policies. Isaiah 45, however, is not really written by Isaiah, but by the later anonymous author we met in chapter 5, who is known as Second Isaiah. An unknown biblical editor appended a message to the prophecy of the real Isaiah, as if they were both by the same man.

From the content of his writings, we surmise that our anonymous Second Isaiah was a Judean captive living in Babylonia many decades after Isaiah had died. Babylonia had invaded Judea in 587 B.C.E. and transported the intellectual and political elite back into the heartland of the Babylonian empire so as to prevent them from exercising leadership within the captive Judean state. Only fifty years after the Judean war, Persia overran Babylonia, allowing those Judeans who wished to return home. Most did not, however, and among those who remained was Second Isaiah.

The religion of the Persian empire was Zoroastrianism, a relatively new faith promulgated by a sixth-century visionary who preached a doctrine of absolute dualism. Here was early Gnosticism in extreme form: the good god of light at war with the evil god of darkness; the entire cosmos locked in mortal combat between good and evil. Second Isaiah was responding to Zoroastrian claims that a good God who provides light cannot possibly be the same deity who manufactures darkness. Not so, says God to Second Isaiah; rather, "I am the Lord and there is none else. I form light and create darkness; I make peace and create evil."

Six or seven centuries later, the Rabbis faced the same cultural struggle. Could a single God provide light and darkness, people wondered. The rabbinic blessing on creation retains monotheism at all costs. God has made light, but the same God made darkness, too. Nonetheless, the blessing avoids saying explicitly that God actually brings *evil* into the universe, because when it borrows the Isaiah verse, it changes the word *evil* to *all things*: "Blessed are You, Eternal our God, Ruler of the universe who forms light and creates darkness, who makes peace and creates *all things.*"

A second Gnostic tendency was to identify the realm of light and good with love, and the realm of dark and evil with law. Some groups chastised Judaism as the religion of the devil, in that the Torah seemed to be so legalistic. Reflecting this view in his own way, Paul preached a Christianity that annulled Jewish law on the grounds that it had been superseded by a new dispensation offering unbounded love instead. Similarly, the Gospel of John, written during the stormy years of the second century when rabbinic Judaism and early Christianity were at odds with one another, holds, "The law was given through Moses, but grace [that is, love] has come through Jesus Christ" (John 1:17). So, the Rabbis wrote into their second blessing, the one on revelation, a further polemic, this one directed against their detractors who contrasted law and love as if the two were irreconcilable opposites. As they saw it, the same God who gave law also gave love: Love and law were two sides of the same coin.

The "grace" to which John refers is the gift of Jesus into the world. As he puts it elsewhere, "God so loved the world He gave his only begotten son." Christians take this gift to be a freely offered gift from God, in no way deserved by human beings, but a sign instead of God's limitless love. It is this love that Christians call "grace." Jews tend not to use the English word *grace* because of its overwhelmingly Christian connotations; but the idea itself is by no means foreign to Judaism. The Rabbis too have a concept of grace, meaning divine love freely given even to the undeserving, but their example is God's gift of Torah. They therefore bracketed the blessing of revelation with lines affirming God's love through the gift of Torah.

My point so far is that each of the first two blessings, creation and revelation, is not only about an idea in the abstract, but an idea as determined by a specific historical milieu. The beginning of spiritual thinking is the contextualization of the ideas in our texts against the backdrop of the times in which they emerged, a step that becomes clearer still when we look at the third blessing connected to the *Sh'ma*, the one we call redemption.

Redemption

We like to believe that events are connected to each other like links in a chain of time. History is the discipline of finding out what holds the chain together. Perhaps events are linked economically, as, for instance, when we argue that the American Revolution was caused by the antagonism of the American colonists, who saw the mother country systematically loot its raw materials and carry them back to Europe to support British manufacturing; or that the Civil War occurred because the agrarian cotton economy of the South made slave labor economically beneficial, but the urban economy of the North did not. Alternatively, we might opt for great- (or poor-) leader theories, attributing the Civil War to Lincoln, and blaming King George III for American secession. There are political explanations, and psychological ones—was George III crazy perhaps? Some historians posit principle, plain and simple, as the dominating factor of history—the North fought slavery because it was wrong.

We cannot be certain why things happen as they do. History is less the marshaling of new facts than it is the organization of old ones into different narratives that support new explanations. World War II turns out to be the result of Hitler's megalomania, or Germany's resentment following its crushing defeat in World War I, or the German psychological conditioning that allowed the masses blindly to follow charismatic leadership; or the economic threat of Communism in the depression era; or deeply rooted anti-Semitism and paranoia; or all or none of the above. We do not know. History is as much an art as a science. It is the fashioning of convincing stories. The individual facts may be certain enough: Hitler did invade Poland, burn down synagogues, meet with his advisors on specific dates, and issue orders with specific wording. But the glue that organizes individual events into narrative form is supplied by the historian, who, in another time and culture not our own, might attribute the whole series of events to divine intervention, the activity of demons, or any number of alternative explanatory systems that we would simply laugh out of court.

However uncertain we may be about any particular historical explanation, we remain convinced that some true cause exists. What we cannot abide is the possibility that events occur inexplicably. History is the frantic denial of randomness. Individual episodes follow, somehow, from what precedes them. History, we say, is a chain of happenings linked together by time. The present is assumed to follow logically from the past.

Can we also explain the present by the future? Granted that events have a cause, but do they also have an end or purpose that determines them as well? The study of history's ultimate destiny is called *teleology*—from the Greek, *telos*, meaning "goal." Once upon a time, most Western minds spoke as convincingly of teleology as we now do of causality—they sometimes combined the two, thinking that the cause of an event is identical with what has to happen for the future to work out the way it is meant to be.

Religions once preached both teleology and causality. Causal explanations, however, tended to be moralistic. Both Jews and Christians, for instance—each for different reasons—thought the Temple was destroyed because Jews had sinned. That kind of simpleminded logic is less likely to be convincing today: Can we really imagine (to cite a more recent tragedy) that six million Jews died in gas chambers or at the hands of death squads because they had sinned by not keeping God's commandments? Some Orthodox Jews said so at the time, but most people found the idea repugnant. Modern religions have therefore tended to leave causality to the secular science of history.

As science has so strikingly dismantled the old moralistic explanation of history, however, religionists have held all the more tenaciously to teleology, about which science, by definition, has nothing to say, since the probability of a final messianic era or the second coming of Christ can by definition have no proof. Nonetheless, religions must face up to the fact that a scientific study of what has happened so far in human history is not necessarily supportive of the existence of a grand scheme that leads to an ultimate end of days. The sum total of all that has occurred so far does not immediately seem to be directed toward any particular aim at all. Human history often seems repetitive. Rather than heading toward a glorious or cataclysmic end, it is at least equally likely that there is no end at all, just a sorry reiteration of what has already happened in one way or another: wars, famines, economic cycles, and so forth.

Alternatively, history may be completely determined from the very beginning. The universe may resemble a giant machine that was wound up at the beginning of time and now plays itself out in fully predictable ways. If those predictions elude us, it is because we are incapable of knowing all the causal factors. But once again, the only pattern here is the repetitive playing out of the laws of physics and chemistry. We are born by chemical processes, and we die when those same processes determine that we should; other human beings take our places, and they too die, having their places taken by other generations still. We may evolve more powerful brains and use them to create more and more advanced technology, but war, disease, and death will never disappear. There is, therefore, no progress, no plan, no hope beyond this life, which is all we have.

In these scenarios, human hope is discouraged. There is nothing an individual can do to move history closer to its ultimate end, either because there is no such end toward which history moves, or because we are just cogs in a machine, utterly unimportant to the grand scheme of things. Human consciousness is a cosmic joke, a huge bit of irony that makes us think we make a difference, even if we do not.

Religious thought struggles with these issues of purpose and pattern. All the talk about God and salvation, reward and punishment, karma or nirvana is really about the way things fit together in time and space and the place we humans occupy in the chain of history or the purpose toward which that history is heading. Spiritual thinking takes these basic questions about the universe seriously, positing meaningful patterns in the face of randomness or pure blind fate. The most important question is whether humans really matter in the long run, and if so, how?

Judaism says that we do matter because, as much as the course of human history is governed by historical cause and effect, it is also directed toward a teleological end, which Judaism calls the messianic age or the world to come. The process by which that better era comes into being is called redemption.

As with creation and revelation, however, redemption is no simple unidimensional idea. For most of Jewish history, Jews have held that God, who set history going to start with, will end it as well, whenever the right time arrives. Humans were given some role, in that good deeds were believed to hasten the end, but it was generally thought that only God could decide when the end should arrive and that it was fruitless for human beings to try to force God's hand. In the nineteenth century, however, when faith in the overall pattern of human history engendered hope in what became known as progress, Jews began referring more and more to redemption as something God and human beings would together accomplish over the course of centuries. So, as with the other two concepts that make up the Jewish creed called the *Sh'ma* and its Blessings, the particulars of the belief in teleology have varied, even though the belief itself has not faltered. Jews continue to believe somehow that history has shape, life has meaning, and humans should have hope.

Here, too, it was the uniqueness of the late Roman era that determined the content of our blessing. If the Gnostic environment explains the rabbinic fascination with the creation of light, in particular, and a revelation marked especially by love, it was a parallel philosophy of the same time period that determined the shape of the third idea, redemption. In this case, the dominant influence was Epicureanism.

Epicurus (341–270 B.C.E.) was a philosopher of ancient Greece who taught a brand of sophisticated hedonism. The end in life, he said, is simply to maximize pleasure and minimize pain. Wisdom enables us to take a long-range view by which we avoid paltry pleasures at the expense of enormous pain later; but the pleasure/pain calculus leaves no room for the commanding voice of the gods. So, even though Epicurus believed that the traditional Greek pantheon might actually exist, he was certain of the gods' indifference to human affairs.

If the events of the world are not controlled by the gods, he thought they must be fully scientific, brought about by mechanical interaction of the parts of the physical universe. In this regard, he drew on the opinions of two philosophical predecessors, Democritus and Leucippus, who were two thousand years ahead of their time in that they had already arrived at the idea of the universe being made of tiny particles called atoms.

Our information comes from later Greek treatises reporting on the early masters:

> Leucippus of Elea or Miletus (450–370? B.C.E.) . . . posited innu-
> merable elements in perpetual motion—namely, the atoms—and
> held that the number of their shapes was infinite. . . . As the
> atoms move, they collide and become entangled in such a way
> as to cling in close contact to one another. . . . The reason he
> [Democritus (460–370 B.C.E.)] gives for atoms to stay bound
> together temporarily is that some of them are angular, some
> hooked, some concave, some convex. So they cling to one another
> until such time as some stronger necessity comes from the sur-
> rounding and shakes them apart.

Epicurus thus held that "the whole of being consists of bodies and space. . . . [There are atoms] out of which composite bodies arise and into which they are dissolved. These vary indefinitely in their shapes, and are in continual motion through all eternity." It followed that the universe is without moral pattern and human beings have no purpose in life beyond seeking out whatever pleasure life has to offer. As Epicurus put it:

> Death is nothing to us, for the body, when it is resolved into its ele-
> ments, has no feeling, and that which has no feeling is nothing to
> us. There is no absolute justice, but only agreements made for re-
> ciprocal relationship in this or that locality, now and again, from
> time to time. Justice is just something found expedient for mutual
> relationship. . . . No pleasure is in itself evil.

Though Epicurus preceded the Rabbis by centuries, Epicureanism was a popular ethical alternative to the Rabbis' own views throughout the period when rabbinic Judaism took shape. There is reason to believe that the Rabbis were attracted to the physics of the Epicurean system; they had no problem at all with the idea of a universe made of atoms hurtling through space and combining into material objects. That part was science, and, as we have already seen, Judaism has no quarrel with scientific thought. But the Epicurean ethics were another matter. They flew in the face of the morality that the Rabbis preached in their teleology, which promised that, at the end of days, "all Israelites have a portion in the world to come." They expressly excluded an Epicurean. The Hebrew for *Epicurean*, borrowed directly from the Greek, is *apikoros*, and to this day, *apikoros* is the Yiddish epithet for freethinking atheists who characterized eastern European socialist circles roughly a century ago. But originally, an *apikoros* was an Epicurean: someone who denied the possibility of divine providence extending to the end of time.

The final blessing of redemption is a response to the Epicureans who thought history had no purpose. Jewish prayer insisted instead that God cares about human destiny; so history must have an end toward which the Jewish People contribute. God had entered history once to save Israel—in Egypt. What had happened in Egypt would happen again, but on a cosmic scale sufficient to end the evil Roman regime as quickly as—and even more surely than—it had the paradigmatic Egyptian tyranny.

Translation Thinking: From Literal to Contextual to Spiritual

Most people who regularly attend synagogue services pray their way through the liturgy with hardly any idea at all that it has a structure. They are amazed to discover that the first line of the *Sh'ma*, which they may even know by heart, is part of a larger liturgical unit with blessings that express classical Jewish thinking about the nature of God. They react with pleasant surprise to hear that Judaism has something more to say about God than the truism (nowadays) that God is "one." They may be told, in that regard, that Judaism is built on the threefold scheme of creation, revelation, and redemption. And so (as we have seen) it is.

But that explanation does not go deeply enough. The Rabbis invented the blessings in question, but they did not label them "creation, revelation, and redemption"; modern critics added those titles. The threefold theological scheme that they summarize is the invention of the nineteenth century. Not that Judaism altogether lacked these ideas before that. The philosophers and mystics of the Middle Ages certainly had a lot to say about creation, revelation, and redemption. But they were already far removed from the world of Gnosticism, Epicureanism, and late antiquity. They had necessarily read their own conceptual framework into rabbinic texts so that the texts they read came out speaking to them in terms that were useful to their time. They were doing what we all must do when faced with echoes of voices that preceded us by centuries: translate their words into our own vocabulary of concepts.

Spiritual thinking follows from the recognition that conversation on ideas operates on different levels of translation. We begin with the *literal* level: memorizing the actual sentences that people made long ago and learning how to make meaningful sentences ourselves using their words. Seeing that they spoke of God as *yotser* and knowing the word *yotser* means "Creator," we say to ourselves, "The Rabbis believed in a God who created the universe."

The next step, however, is unveiling the context in which ancient sentences were made. Such *contextual* thinking is what this chapter has been about so far. We have looked at the Rabbis' blessings surrounding the *Sh'ma* and put them into historical context, saying, for instance, that to the Rabbis, God as creator meant God who created everything, in-cluding the darkness—in opposition to the good Gnostic deity, who cre-ated only light.

But now we see that one more step is necessary. We have to translate ancient words beyond their original context into our own. We are not Gnostics, after all. As interesting as the historical backdrop may be, prayers against Gnostics are irrelevant now. Why should we continue saying prayers that arose as polemical statements against rival religions that do not even exist anymore? The answer ought to be that those same statements have meaning that transcends the historical circumstances that produced them. Contextual thinking takes us from the literal to the historical; we need one final step to take us from the historical to the spiritual.

The challenge of translation is usually put: "How can we render some old passage exactly as the original writer did?" But in truth, we ought to ask the very reverse: "How would that original writer have put it, if that writer had been one of us?"

An unsophisticated witness for this process of translation is the late Whitey Ford, who became famous as a New York Yankee pitcher, but who also is reputed to have commented, "I don't know why they keep talking about God as King. I've never even seen a king. I think they ought to refer to God nowadays as the Chairman of the Board." A more sophisticated approach that says something similar to Whitey's statement is to consider translation as a problem of identifying functionally equivalent parts of diverse systems. The equivalent of a chicken's wing is not a human wing but an arm. *Chairman of the board* is to Whitey Ford's universe what *King of Kings* was to the universe of the Roman Empire. Using what I call "translational algebra," we should write the equation this way:

CHAIRMAN OF THE BOARD : AMERICA :: KING : ROMAN EMPIRE

Now the Hebrew for *king* is the word *melekh*. So, most literal translations just insert *king* whenever they come across *melekh* and consider the matter closed. *Melekh* does, after all, mean "king" in the context of the Hebrew universe in which the classical rabbinic texts about God as *melekh* were originally composed. But the equation "*melekh* = king" does not go far enough. It is like insisting on talking about human wings, as if "chicken wing = human wing," when the proper equation should be:

WING : CHICKEN :: ARM : HUMAN

In order to convey what writers about chickens would say if they wanted to write about humans, we would have to translate *wing* as *arm*. Similarly, were the Rabbis alive today, what would they say about God? What, functionally speaking, plays the same role in our universe of discourse that *king* did in theirs? I don't think *chairman of the board* captures it: It has negative connotations of being driven by corporate profits, not universal virtue. But the question remains: What, for us, is the same idea that *melekh* was for ancient writers?

The philosopher, linguist, and mathematician Douglas Hofstadter frames the problem well when he asks, "What is the French for London?" A *literal* translation would be the French word *Londres*, which is what French speakers say when they refer to the city that holds Big Ben,

Westminster Cathedral, and Buckingham Palace. But if you think in terms of a higher order of translation, says Hofstadter, you get a different answer entirely. The French playwright Eugene Ionesco got it right when he said, "The French for London is Paris." What he means is

LONDON : ENGLAND AND ENGLISH SPEAKERS ::
PARIS : FRANCE AND FRENCH SPEAKERS

Therefore:

LONDON = PARIS

Here is a more complex example that Hofstadter supplies. How would we best translate into French (for instance) the book title *All the President's Men*, an account of the downfall of President Richard Nixon. Going word for word, he substitutes French for English and gets *Tous les hommes du président*, which is acceptable as far as it goes. But it does not go far enough; it lacks the necessary allusion that the original English had to the nursery rhyme Humpty-Dumpty. The authors of *All the President's Men* meant to imply that, like Humpty-Dumpty, Richard Nixon fell out of power and "All the president's horses and all the president's men couldn't put Nixon together again."

Hofstadter does not have an answer for his own question, but he does show us what real translation must do: It cannot just supply a word-for-word equivalence of what some ancient author of a prayer once had to say. The best translation of someone else's sentence must do in our language and context what the old sentence did for people who heard and used it when it was written. What would those writers have said if they had existed in our context instead of their own?

Now we can move on to genuine spiritual thinking for our time. *Literal* thinking limits us to imagining what it might mean to have a king whose name is God; or how a being called God could have created the world. These are not unimportant questions—they are precisely what theologians look at—but they are not necessarily spiritual. *Contextual* thinking explains what our ancestors meant when *they* thought of God as a king or a creator. It puts us into their universe as an enlightened visitor so that we can read their prayers with some appreciation for why they opted for words or statements that might never occur to us. If literal translation evokes theological discussion, contextual translation spawns history. Both are primarily cognitive enterprises, intellectually interesting but not necessarily spiritual.

Spiritual thinking is intellectually sophisticated, too, but instead of explaining ancient thought in terms of ancient culture, it transports ancient thinkers into modern times, demanding that we, the translators, confront ultimate issues in the language of our day. It occurs when we translate old ideas into whatever the functionally equivalent new ones are; when we ask what the old authors would have said if they were our neighbors instead of our ancestors.

From Projection to Introjection: Pattern, Purpose, and Hope

The Rabbis conceived of the universe as a set of concentric circles with the earth in the center, around which the vastness of star-studded galaxies swirled. God was in heaven far, far away, at the other end of space, where angels, cherubim, and other assorted heavenly hosts abounded. The great questions that haunt human beings were therefore couched in projective imagery: of a God "out there," prophetic messages from afar, apparitions of angels, voices in space, and physical signs from heaven like a pillar of cloud by day and fire by night.

We think differently today. Instead of projecting our thinking beyond ourselves onto the canvas of space, we prefer metaphors of introjection that evoke imagery of some interior space we imagine as existing inside ourselves. People who scoff at the existence of heavenly hosts "out there" may accept the Freudian notion of an id, an ego, and a super-ego inside our psyche. For similar reasons, we speak easily of a "the voice of conscience," but not "the voice of God." We advise each other to "get in touch with our deepest selves" and look "inside ourselves" to find out who we are, rather than "outside ourselves" for signs of our "real" identity. We are contemptful of people who "put on a show," pretending on the outside to be other than what they are "really" on the inside. We think inwardly nowadays, not outwardly.

How, then, can we recast the concerns of Judaism's liturgical creed so that the three blessings that surround the *Sh'ma* discuss the same ultimate issues they always have, but in imagery consonant with inside, not outside, thinking? Spiritual thinking demands our translation of old projective metaphor into new introjective concepts that may look different on the surface, but are actually the same thing, in modern conceptual dress.

The doctrine of creation is actually an affirmation that the universe has shape, pattern, or order; that it is not a total accident lacking all design or logic. That was why Maimonides could translate creation in time into a case of logical dependence. In both cases, the universe is revealed as something defined by a plan larger than itself. Both are projective schemes, however, attributing order to the world because of some external orderer, either a God who creates at a given point in time, the way humans do, or a philosophical first cause that works its magic on the universe by a series of interrelated logical processes of cause and effect.

But what if we ask what that same idea of creation looks like when it is set free from its projective metaphors? We are left with the question of whether the universe is internally ordered or merely random. Philosophically inclined mathematicians have asked this question when they wonder aloud if it is just an accident that geometry works on physical space or whether the universe is actually designed mathematically. In either event, the math works—cause for spiritual excitement in itself. Einstein had to wait years to confirm his mathematical insight into the theory of relativity. He had predicted that during an eclipse of the sun, the sun's rays would bend around Mercury. When an eclipse actually occurred, and astronomers proved him correct, he is reputed to have replied, "The excitement came when the mathematics worked out; the sighting of phenomena that agreed with the math is anticlimactic."

Einstein therefore laid claim to being spiritual in the modern sense of being in awe of the universe's intricate set of necessary patterns. When quantum theorists expressed doubt about the necessity of things, he answered with his famous line that we already looked at, "God does not play dice with the universe." He knew that discussions about the universal pattern were in essence the same as discussions of the way God had one day put the universe together. The only difference was whether we prefer the traditional religious rhetoric of projective metaphor or not.

The charge today that the universe has no pattern or plan is equivalent to the ancient heresy that denied divine creation. We cannot abide the awful possibility that the universe is senseless. The claim that God created it is inseparable from the assurance that we can count on its order. In translational algebra:

CREATION : RABBINIC THINKING :: PATTERNED UNIVERSE : MODERN THOUGHT

The Rabbis assure us that the universe comes patterned.

If creation assures us of the universe's orderliness, revelation assures us of the existence of purpose. We all have a subjective sense of doing things on purpose. We differentiate things done spontaneously from those done with purposeful forethought, giving precedence to the latter in our scheme of things. If someone plans on obtaining a good end but fails along the way, we say that at least the motive was honorable. And at the other end, we recognize degrees of evildoing by the extent to which purpose was involved. Killing someone, say, is differently labeled according to the extent that the killer purposed the deed before doing it. If it was done by chance, we declare it an accident or charge the guilty party with manslaughter; if the killing was an act of rage, motivated by purpose but not thought out in advance, it is considered second-degree murder. Worst of all, a killing planned coldly in advance is first-degree murder, for which the full measure of the law is brought to bear.

Purpose presupposes pattern, without which all planning would be fruitless. Having determined in blessing 1 (creation, renamed for us "pattern") that the universe works according to predictable laws, we declare in 2 (revelation, renamed now "purpose") that those laws allow human beings to plan their future and even to contribute to the overall purpose of the divine plan of which they are part. Here, then, is where ethics enters the equation. Pattern alone is neutral: It may be complex or simple, pleasing or ugly, gaudy or plain, but it is neither good nor evil. Purpose, however, is tied to an ultimate end that we evaluate in advance as desirable. Just as the universe turns out to be mathematical in its essence, so, too, Jews say, it is amenable to purposeful planning that is morally responsible, not ethically repugnant. Torah, as that which God revealed, provides the highest kind of purpose we can imagine. To say God loves us or that God chooses Israel is tantamount to acknowledging the existence of purpose in the very fact that Jews have stuck it out through all these years of human history. Jews believe that something incomparably precious would be lost to the world if the Jewish People were to disappear. We think we are part of history, put here on earth for a purpose, part of God's plan, and therefore part of the divine will that an ultimate realm of peace and harmony prevail in what is still a world all too sated with woe.

All of this takes us to the last blessing, on the theme of redemption, which we can now rename "hope." Because there is pattern, we have the right to plan with purpose, and because we have purpose, we dare to have hope. Again, however, projective thinking has attributed the hope of things to come to God's action in the universe, not to our own. But we can equally say that the final benediction around the *Sh'ma* is about hope in general: hope in the human condition, hope in world events, hope in

the presence of an unseen power that we call God—all working harmoniously through human purpose to perfect the world. The Epicureans
of antiquity denied God's beneficent concern for creation. There was no
personal afterlife to which they might aspire and no communal better
time to come toward which to contribute in an individual lifetime. Moderns worry about the future also. Only, the old-time word *redemption*
fails us; it does not convey the sense we have that hope for better times
is not misguided.

Creation, revelation, and redemption remain three basic Jewish
values, the essence of what we have been claiming about the universe
since the Rabbis first assembled the Jewish prayer service some two
thousand years ago. Leave them in their literal translated shape, and you
get an interesting précis of Jewish theology. Translate them into their
contextual backdrop, and you get some fascinating lessons in Jewish
history. Translate them into modern-day concepts, and you get a spiritual affirmation of pattern, purpose, and hope.

Spiritual thinking is the attempt to say more about the universe
than science can, without saying anything that science cannot at least
grant as possible and maybe even probable. It is consistent with ancient
thought, but couched in the language of today. It connects us with our
past, but speaks to our present. It is intellectually sophisticated, but not
academically distant from what matters to us most.

Chapter Seven

When It Is Night: Spirituality for the Suffering

> *Illness is the night-side of life, a more onerous citizenship.*
> *Everyone who is born holds dual citizenship, in the kingdom of the well*
> *and the kingdom of the sick. Although we all prefer to use only the good*
> *passport, sooner or later each of us is obliged, at least for a spell,*
> *to identify ourselves as citizens of that other place.*
> SUSAN SONTAG

Not long ago, I heard a preacher expound on the value of Psalm 23, with its well-known promise, "Yea though I walk through the valley of the shadow of death, I will fear no evil, for Thou art with me." Why does the psalm emphasize the valley of the "shadow" of death? the preacher wanted to know; why not just "the valley of death"? The answer, he contended, is that shadows are often more frightening than the real thing; and because where there is a shadow, there is also a light. Turn toward the light and the shadow vanishes. Our greatest fears dissipate with the coming of the day.

Light and Darkness; Up and Down

Would that all the darkness in our lives could vanish so easily! As a Christian, the preacher urged believers to remember that "Jesus Christ is the light of the world." Jews might equally have recollected promises of light, some of them precisely parallel to the Christian claim. As we have seen, Jesus of Nazareth plays the same role in Christianity that Torah does in Judaism. An old Hebrew expression therefore announces, *Torah orah,* "Torah is light." But light as a symbol of redemption ante-

dates both Christianity and rabbinic Judaism. We see it in biblical poetry composed after the Israelites returned from Babylonian exile in the
sixth century B.C.E.: Psalm 97:11, for instance, "Light is sown for the
righteous," or Psalm 36:10, "In your light, O God, do we see light." But
already two hundred years before that, the prophet Isaiah had looked to
the end of days by announcing, "O House of Jacob, come let us walk in
the light of the Lord," a phrase that was not lost even twenty-eight hundred years later on secular Zionist settlers, who called their immigration
movement BILU, an acronym formed by the first four Hebrew initials of
Isaiah's invitation.

If the postexilic psalms are especially saturated with light imagery,
that is because the light/dark dichotomy became ever more prominent
as time went on. We have seen already how the light/darkness opposition characterized Gnostic thinking in late antiquity. In Greece, it had
already dominated the fifth-century thought of Socrates; Plato, like his
teacher, no devotee of the cruder aspects of ancient Greek religion, reports Socrates' use of the metaphor of a dark cave for the abode of people
who fail to see the eternal truths toward which the mind naturally as-
pires, and a realm of light that attracts the soul as it seeks to apprehend
reality. In the first few centuries of the common era, the light/darkness
motif is everywhere: a synagogue in Israel's northern Galilee displays a
Jewish version of Helios the sun god as its promise that God brings light
into the universe; catacomb art under the ancient city of Rome gives us
sun–God imagery as the Church's way of imagining the risen Christ; the
Dead Sea Scroll community in Qumran pictured the coming Armaged-
don as a war between "the sons of light and the sons of darkness."

Whether he knew it or not, therefore, the preacher was playing on
imagery that everyone in his audience, not just Christians, must have
encountered, and not only in study of ancient history or even of Scripture. Cultural symbolism enters common consciousness in subtle ways:
Christmas lights, for instance, that light up the winter solstice season,
or Hanukkah candles shining into the darkness from Jewish homes. In

our time, we get the continuing appeal of the double movie trilogy *Star Wars.* Its hero is Luke Skywalker (*Luke* is from *lux,* Latin for "light"); he is locked in mortal combat with Darth Vader (Dark Father), a modern version of the Prince of Darkness, Satan himself. The depth of American racism owes its existence, in part, to the negative imagery associated with darkness and the positive value Western men and women have attached to light. Light is safety, goodness, a path to certainty; darkness is shadow land, where bugs and vermin lurk, the crawly spaces that we avoid when we can.

It may be that the cultural imagery of light and darkness is arbitrary. We might just as easily have emphasized the dichotomy of up/down, another set of opposites that we use to symbolize good and bad, the beneficial and the dangerous. Up, after all, is heaven, where our souls go after we die; we "elevate" people we admire to positions of power; ideas we esteem are called "lofty." Down is where we go if we "sink" in people's estimation because we have not been true to our "higher" selves. It is where even Hell is supposed to be. It is also where we say people are when they are "downcast" or just plain feeling "low."

Alternatively, both light/dark and up/down may be programmed into human nature to some extent by our evolutionary spiral "up" from animal life, away from the dark crevices where we used to be; they may be remnants of age-old fears of what lurked for us in the dark and on the ground when we managed, somewhere in Africa about 1.5 million years ago, to become *homo erectus,* the species most at home standing erect on our two hind legs. Part of that odyssey entailed the loss of a snout to burrow in the earth and of night vision for seeing in the dark. We became instead dependent on light and masters of the bodily stance that provides us a view downward on animals that still crawl on all fours. If you close your eyes and try to imagine an experience in which you recently found yourself—even sitting and reading this book now—the odds are that you will "see" yourself from the perspective of surveying the scene from above. People who report near-death experiences combine up/

down with light/darkness, saying that their souls were suddenly seized by a great light as they left the bodies that had hitherto been their earthly homes. They then had a panoramic view of their inert remains lying on the operating table and surrounded by doctors or emergency caregivers trying vainly to resuscitate them.

Either way, whether purely arbitrary or rooted in human evolution, human experience at its most promising presupposes standing tall, enjoying the clarity that comes from being bathed in light and surveying the pattern all around us. On a clear day, we say, you can see forever, and when we do, we feel "up" or "on a high." By contrast, when we are depressed, we feel "low," unable to "rise" to the occasion and see beyond the present moment. Robert Frost writes chillingly, "I have been one acquainted with the night." *Night* is also Elie Wiesel's haunting title for his chronicle of Auschwitz. In ancient mythology, day is what happens when the sun god pulls the chariot of cosmic light up from below the earth; night is the name we give to the awful hours when the light dips down below the horizon. Night, then is both darkness and down. It is what we all fear most.

I have been saying here that spirituality is the recognition of our perceived connectedness to all that is. We have seen how the meaning we seek depends on the success with which we establish patterns that deny universal entropy and cosmic chaos. But that view of things assumes we see a pattern. What happens when we do not? When we cannot see at all, because night has become our normal condition?

I refer to those unfortunate souls with incurable disease, chronic illness, mourners for innocent sons and daughters who have died before their time—not to mention the victims of incessant persecution: the *Night* inhabitants Wiesel describes. Can there be spirituality for them as well? Or is spirituality a luxury of the fortunate, the lucky folk whose momentary, not momentous, problems vanish with the light of a new day?

The Standard Answers

A starting point is a consideration of the age-old question of why we suffer. Western religion has emphasized a certain type of answer to that question. It still gets preached even though it is not the only answer possible and despite the fact that it is bad for people in the first place and not at all believable in the second. For some reason, normally competent adults who run families and businesses and who are at home in the many complex features of modern life, tend toward infantilization in the presence of religion, to the point where they accept this answer even though every fiber of their reason argues otherwise. I mention it here, therefore, not because I believe it, but because other people, knowing I am a rabbi, think I do and because, before we reconstruct a spiritual perspective on Night, we first must deconstruct what passes falsely for the proper religious way to view it. This common view is religion at its worst.

It comes in various guises, but it boils down to a particular theology (doctrine of God) and anthropology (doctrine of human nature) that conspire to blame people for their own suffering or to create the illusion that suffering is justified, usually as punishment for human sin or as appropriate divine chastisement. In either case, people deserve what they get. God, meanwhile, is held to be all powerful, all knowing, and all good; if we only pray hard enough and rectify our evil ways, we will be rewarded for our virtue by a God who cannot fail to make Night vanish. Even elementary experience ought to be enough to show us that God does not work this way. Let us look in greater detail at this claim and where it came from before we dismiss it.

This Western doctrine goes back to the Bible, particularly Deuteronomy, usually described as a book that was composed over a lengthy period of time during the seventh and sixth centuries B.C.E. Near the end of Deuteronomy, a section known in Jewish tradition as "the blessings and the curses" establishes the book's essential message:

> Now if you obey the Lord your God to observe faithfully all of his
> commandments which I enjoin upon you this day . . . all these
> blessings shall come upon you and take effect. . . . But if you do
> not obey the Lord your God to observe faithfully all of his com-
> mandments and laws which I enjoin upon you this day, all these
> curses shall come upon you and take effect.

In Deuteronomic theology, then, we always get what we deserve.

That is not the Hebrew Bible's final statement on the subject, however. Two late compositions cast suspicion on Deuteronomy's simpleminded calculus of blessing and curse. Ecclesiastes, for example, recognizes the futility of imagining that if we are only good, we will prosper.
In truth, we all die eventually, so "the same fate is in store for all, for the
righteous and for the wicked . . . that is the sad thing about all that goes
on under the sun: that the same fate is in store for all" (9:2–3). Even in
this life, "The race is not won by the swift, nor the battle by the valiant,
nor is bread won by the wise, nor wealth by the intelligent, nor favor by
the learned, for a time of mischance comes to all, and a man cannot even
know his time" (9:11–12). In the end, no matter what merit we may pos-
sess, "A man cannot know what will happen; who can tell him what the
future holds?" (10:12). By the end of the book, however, either a second
author appended a pious corrective, or the original author "lost the
courage of his lack of convictions." The great skepticism of Ecclesiastes
is denied in a simple one-line conclusion that reasserts Deuteronomy's
promise of justice: "The sum of the matter, when all is said and done:
revere God and observe his commandments, for this applies to all man-
kind, that God will call every creature to account for everything unknown be it good or bad" (12:12–13).

The Bible's classic challenge to Deuteronomy comes with the Book
of Job, whose author did not lose his courage, but instead steadfastly
denied the simple belief that we get what we deserve. Job is introduced
to us at the very outset as "blameless and upright; he feared God and

shunned evil" (1:1). Nonetheless, in almost whimsical fashion, God permits Satan, portrayed here as one of God's heavenly hosts, to try Job's faith. Here is a God who plays games with people's lives. In short order, Job loses his possessions; his children die in a freak windstorm; and he himself is plagued with painful boils all over his body. In utter despair, Job voices the theme of Night: "Perish the day on which I was born. . . . May that day be darkness. . . . May light not shine upon it. May darkness and deep gloom reclaim it" (3:3, 4, 5). He had "hoped for light, but darkness came" (30:26).

The ostensible point of the book is Job's unswerving faith in God despite his sufferings. But though he refuses throughout to curse God, he refuses equally to blame himself for his afflictions. Most of the book is given over to visits by would-be comforters, who plead with Job to understand that we get what we deserve: Job must have sinned somehow. "What innocent man ever perished?" the first visitor asks (4:7–8). "Where have the upright been destroyed? As I have seen, those who plow evil and sow mischief reap them." Job must be suffering "the discipline of the Almighty" (5:17). He should "accept instruction from God's mouth" (22:22). Job's own claim to righteousness is used against him: "Your sinfulness dictates your speech," says one of his visitors (15:5–6). "Your own mouth condemns you, not I." Only the truly evil "are thrust," as Job is, "from light to darkness" (18:18).

Throughout the book, different permutations of the same basic theme occur. Simply put, if we suffer, it is on account of our sins. But one need not be outright perverse to merit God's corrective measures. We all sin a little, even though we may not know it. If we accept God's discipline, we will eventually emerge all the happier for it.

But Job admits to nothing. In the end, he insists on confronting God, who appears in a whirlwind to question what Job knows about the laws of the universe (38:4, 12, 16). "Where were you when I laid the earth's foundations?" God demands. "Have you ever commanded the day to break, assigned the dawn its place? Have you penetrated to the sources of the sea or walked in the recesses of the deep?" What, really, does a mere mortal know about the ways of the universe?

This is hardly a fair contest, and the author of Job knows it. Elsewhere in the Bible, God appears in a "still small voice" to converse with Elijah (1 Kings 19:12). God initiates conversations with the patriarchs in simple visions (Gen. 15:1). Not here. Here, God chooses to confront poor Job, sitting half dead on a dunghill, from the middle of a raging storm. Predictably, Job quickly concludes, "I am of small worth. What can I answer You? . . . I spoke without understanding of things beyond me, which I did not know" (40:4; 42:3). It is perfectly apparent that this mighty God "can do everything. Nothing You propose is impossible for You. . . . Therefore I recant and relent, being but dust and ashes" (42: 1, 6).

But this is no solution. It is just a restatement of the problem, still unsolved. God's might was never in question. Indeed, God's omnipotence is precisely what raised the ethical issue to start with: why a good God uses such might to bring suffering on the Jobs of the world who are, remember, by definition, "blameless and upright; fearing God and shunning evil" (1:1). Nowhere does Job admit to evildoing. Nowhere does he grant one iota of his comforters' charges. He contends in the end only that he does not understand God's ways. More to the point, even God ends up condemning the comforters. "I am incensed," God says to the first of them, "at you and your friends, for you have not spoken the truth about Me as did my servant Job" (42:7). God admits, then, how *wrong* it is to hold that only the guilty experience tragedy and how equally mistaken to argue that God offers suffering as a loving corrective to human beings. That was not "the truth about me." God, who "laid the earth's foundations," may understand the rationale behind pain and suffering (if there even is one). But the simple Deuteronomic calculus of reaping our just rewards is simply untenable.

As the inheritors of both Deuteronomy and Job, the Rabbis display ambivalence on the question of suffering. They echo Deuteronomy by speaking of "measure for measure," the doctrine that we reap what we sow in carefully calibrated measurements. Sufferings can be *yisurin shel ahavah*, divine chastisements administered out of love. We are said to be punished in this life so that we may enjoy the rapture of the afterlife. All humans sin, and our fate is determined on Yom Kippur, the day set aside for repentance. On that day, "penitence prayer and charity cancel a decree of punishment."

On the other hand, they tell stories suggesting they are not altogether happy with this simplistic scheme. On one occasion, a Rabbi loses a son, and, like Job's visitors, his friends come to comfort him. When one of them says that somehow the mourning father must deserve what he is getting, the Talmud objects, "He came to comfort him but he only troubled him all the more." As we saw previously in our discussion of Gnosticism, the Rabbis' thoroughgoing monotheism made them concede that somehow, even the evil in the universe must come ultimately from God. But their balanced estimate of human character prevented their painting everyone as a complete sinner, and they seem to have recognized that suffering cannot be explained solely as punishment that is never undeserved or even that it is a blessing in disguise, a mild rebuke that is ultimately for our own benefit.

Is There Meaning behind Pain?

The beauty of the interpretations offered by Deuteronomy or by Job's comforters is that suffering is given meaning. It has been said that if religion cannot cure suffering, it should at least make suffering sufferable, and the way to do that is to put it in some context where it at least has meaning. The problem is that pain, real pain, is so insufferable that no attempt to give it meaning appears credible. The fact is, pain is everywhere, in various forms. In 1988, for instance, "one-quarter of the American population experienced moderate to excruciating pain requiring major therapy such as opioid narcotics. Nineteen percent of Americans were partially disabled by pain for periods of weeks or months, while another 2 percent were permanently disabled. . . . In 1989, Americans spent $1 billion for prescription analgesics and another $2.2 billion for over-the-counter painkillers. Meanwhile, the annual world output of aspirin stands at a staggering thirty thousand tons." And this is just the tip of the iceberg. What about parents mourning children who were gunned down in a school? Or people born with terrible disorders that are not painful, perhaps, but are lifelong and debilitating? The list goes on and on. How do we find meaning in all of that?

Make no mistake about it: The human spirit is driven by the search to find meaning in everything. The history of meaning-making methods knows no bounds. Biblical priests consulted an oracle called *Urim v'tumim.* The Greeks examined the entrails of birds. Master psychologist C. J. Jung adopted *I Ching,* an Eastern device by which sticks of various lengths are thrown randomly to the ground and their pattern interpreted. Even today, otherwise rational human beings consult the position of the stars to get their horoscopes or steal off to learn their fate from tarot cards, palm lines, and tea leaves. Just what method should we use to find meaning in pain? Is there meaning, for instance, in sickness? Is it possible, moreover, that all methods are doomed to failure because sickness has no meaning to start with?

Master essayist Annie Dillard asks, "What things have meaning?" and supplies a memorable illustration of the problem in finding meaning in everything:

Hans Prinzhorn is a psychotherapist [who] asserted, "Even the
smallest loop . . . can be understood . . . and interpreted." Happy
Hans Prinzhorn! For he has found a method (presumably Freudian) for the finding of meaning in "even the smallest loop." He
will never run out of objects for which meaning can be derived, so
long as schizophrenics keep doodling. In the happiness of his situ-

ation . . . he is matched only by the schizophrenics on the other side of the desk, who were presumably hospitalized in the first place for, among other things, the creepy habit of finding meaning in even the smallest loop of everything. . . .

Schematically, we could see an asylum as a meaning factory. The schizophrenics understand and interpret the world's smallest loops. The only question is, why is Prinzhorn on one side of the desk and the schizophrenics on the other? How do we decide who belongs on which side of the desk? . . . Why is it sane to find meaning in a doodle and insane to find meaning in a puddle of rain?

We should ask if pain, illness, and suffering are more like doodles or puddles of rain. For Dillard, only human phenomena have meaning, not the natural world, which is just what it is: functioning according to natural law, perhaps, but not on that account meaningful. That is to say, illness teaches us nothing about the makeup of reality, the grand plans of the universe, the relationship between morality and punishment, or the nature of God. Deuteronomy is wrong; Job is right.

Given the human penchant for finding meaning, we should wonder for a moment why the schizophrenics get institutionalized but people who attend séances or visit fortunetellers do not. Schizophrenics find meaning in globs of water; readers of tea leaves find it in globs of used tea. Clearly, from a scientific perspective, there is no difference. So, in practice, we adopt a simple criterion: As long as seekers of meaning do not hurt anyone, we allow them to function within the law. We close them down only when we judge their pursuits to be dangerous to their own health or the health of others. Schizophrenics get institutionalized when we judge their solitary view of life's meanings as preventing them from getting on in life, or if we suspect that the messages they intuit in puddles are likely to cause them to inflict actual damage on themselves or others. Presumably, then, whether illness has meaning or not, we have at least the right to see some meaning in it, as long as our efforts cause no harm.

That is what is ultimately wrong with the traditional approach one finds in Deuteronomy: It harms people. And Deuteronomy is only one version of it. The Greeks, as well, believed illness was sent by the gods, though not always because people deserved it; and Christianity joined the Greek view to Deuteronomy, overlaying the resulting scheme with the moral claim that sickness is always deserved because it fits the patient's character: We are all sinners after all. If, then, sickness is meaningful because we bring it on ourselves with our moral failures, illness is not just God-sent but self-sent. Susan Sontag argues convincingly against this method of assigning meaning to pain. It "assigns to the luckless ill the ultimate responsibility both for falling ill and for getting well." That is to say: It causes damage.

This religious scheme, however, is not the only perpetrator of secondary damage to these "luckless ill." Secular society has been no less at fault. Sontag cites psychologist Karl Menninger as saying, "Illness is in part what the world has done to a victim, but in a larger part it is what the victim has done with his world and with himself." That was Freud's position as well. He famously treated a woman named Dora, whose father, Phillip, was having an affair with a certain Mrs. K.; Phillip thereupon tacitly encouraged Mr. K., his mistress's husband, to attempt to seduce his daughter Dora! Freud knew all this, but badgered Dora repeatedly into seeing her hysterical symptoms as her own doing, a manifestation of her own libidinous fantasies.

And psychoanalysis was actually an improvement on nineteenth-century meaning-making on the subject of sickness. No longer willing to blame illness on the gods who recompense sin, society pinned the blame directly on the victim. Sickness was said to express the character or makeup of the sufferer. Victorian economics emphasized investment as the only "healthy" thing to do with your money, and Victorian society called tuberculosis "consumption," with which the victim just "wastes away." Tuberculosis attacks women like La Bohème's Mimi as well as poets and artists, Bohemian sorts who are not perceived as productive economic agents. That century's romantic turn refused to see the true pathos in this disease, which could in fact kill all kinds of people just as surely as cancer or heart attacks do today. It was rampant: For the first time, "the sick" as a social entity was imprinted onto people's minds. Before, people "got sick" but they remained who they had always been. With the epidemic of tuberculosis, "the figure of the sick person crystallized . . . into a social phenomenon. Henceforth, the sick person was to be defined by his or her place in society." These unfortunates were romantically named "melancholics"—which is really depression (depression being "melancholy minus its charms").

Women, in particular, were charged with manufacturing their own illnesses, just by virtue of their anatomy. They suffered naturally from hysteria, it was said, a disease named after the Greek word for "uterus." Male doctors imagined a free-floating female organ and blamed its evil results on women who, among other things, lazily avoided proper women's work raising children and keeping a house; excess energies then moved the uterus unduly, causing bizarre symptoms. They treated it by outright punishment, more akin to torture than to medicine, shocking the women with actual electric current or with hydrotherapy, bursts of freezing water on the patient's skin to bring about severe shuddering from the cold.

Our attitude toward sickness is tied to the larger issue of how we deal with unwanted suffering in general. Sometimes, relatively minor pain is necessary (a vaccination, say) or even desirable (as when we exercise to stretch our muscles and welcome a bit of pain as a sign that we are succeeding). But the meaning our society imbues pain with— "no pain, no gain"—can imply that even the pain of illness is ultimately worthwhile. Our society virtually trades in pain. Young women training for Olympic gymnastics mistreat their bodies terribly, often with long-term consequences. Less emphatically, we have come to valorize eighty-hour workweeks for lawyers and other professionals. Samuel Wilson Fussell, a successful bodybuilder in the 1980s, wrote a memoir of how he managed to go from a "ninety-pound weakling" to a veritable

"Charles Atlas man of muscle." It was, he said, "because no one else was willing to suffer this kind of pain." A less extreme, but nonetheless parallel, case of opting for pain are the myriads of Americans who exercise obsessively: not to enhance their health, but to improve their appearance beyond what is good for them and despite the cost of whatever suffering it causes. Fussell had begun his training in order to overcome fears that he might be mugged; but his trainer had it figured out right when he commented, "Big man, this is about looking good, not feeling good." "No pain, no gain" even forms the rationale for punishing children with beatings and ignoring their tears because, after all, suffering builds character. From there, it is only a small step to believe that sickness builds character, too, as when we fail to empathize with pain and, instead, emphasize admiration for how well a sick person bears up under trial.

In sum, suffering may have meaning. People want to believe that it does. But the dominant meaning-making schemes that surround it are morally unsavory. Sickness is not sent by God; it is not God's way of punishing us; we are not responsible for it ourselves; it does not express our inner character; and pain is not good for anyone. "Theories that diseases are caused by mental states and can be cured by will power are always an index of how much is not understood about the physical terrain of the disease," concludes Susan Sontag. When one of Job's comforters tells Job he must be guilty of something, if not in deed, then in his psyche—his will, at least, to sin—Archibald MacLeish has his modern Job, J. B., retort, "Yours is the cruelest comfort of them all." He recalls, by contrast, some halcyon era of "finding each other in the night." The spirituality of night begins by denying all of these (and similar) further victimizations of the victims. It requires a system of making sense of suffering that helps us find each other in the night, that our comfort be not cruel.

Dots Again; and Metaphors, Too

We have now come full circle. In chapter 2, we saw that life is made of dots that we connect into meaningful patterns; that meaning may not inhere objectively in the world we inhabit; but that we ourselves, as partners with God in creation, provide the connective tissue that makes one thing cohere with another. Spiritual thinking, we said, posits meaningful patterns in the face of randomness or blind fate. Meaning itself is the way one dot fits neatly with another. It is worth recollecting the lesson that the word *seven* can mean winning or losing at dice, the number of days in a week, or any number of other things with the meaning provided by context, without which the lone word *seven* means nothing at all.

Connecting diverse experiences is the way we manufacture a meaningful story of who we are. Also, it is the only way to make sense of suffering. The experience of night cannot be isolated from the rest of our biographies in the making. Meaning here is neither moral nor metaphysical. That was the problem with the negative systems we looked at. In framing a successful philosophical case for illness, they ignored the lives of the real people who are ill, thereby solving a hypothetical dilemma but only at the cost of adding to the pain of those already pained. Our question should be, From the personal perspective of the sufferers, what is the meaning of suffering? How, for instance, can people fit illness into their lives so that they have biographies like everyone else? They are not freaks: "the sick among us." They are people who happen to have pain, which overwhelms them. Meaning is what they make of it in the context of their lives as a whole.

And what they make of it depends on which metaphor they use. When the Rabbis try to solve the problem of illness metaphysically, they fail, just as other religions, the psychoanalysts, and secular society do. When, however, they enter the "world of the sick" and empathize with the people in hospitals, the dying, and those mourning for loved ones—

then they give us spiritual insight. The Jewish spirituality of night is like the spirituality of everything else. It is the Jew's way of being in the world, in this case, being in the world where pain and trauma are dots looming large in life's landscape.

Again, we appreciate how genuine spirituality differs from the popularized versions served up by the majority of self-help books and the media. Spirituality is widely perceived as a feel-good, euphoric, and even ecstatic experience. Our era has been aptly dubbed "a great awakening of experiential spirituality" and even "a self-satisfying rush of soul adrenaline." It is this yearning for experiential highs that makes the ritual of "mainline" Jewish and Christian denominations seem rather tame relative to Pentecostal churches, which grew from 75.4 million adherents in 1970 to 446.5 million in 1994. Pentecostal services are described as featuring ecstatic music born of a "mix of jazz and rock 'n' roll animated enough to make the rafters shake and worshipers dance." A *Newsweek* poll in 1994 turned up the news that 26 percent of Americans find "a sense of the sacred during sex."

It is of the utmost importance that we recognize just how recent and how secular that definition of *spirituality* is. The term comes from the Latin noun *spiritus* and its cognate *spiritualis,* meaning "spiritual." It is a translation from the Greek *pneuma* or *pneumatikos*—terms used by the apostle Paul to describe people who were led or influenced by the spirit of God as opposed to people merely of the flesh (*carnalis*). He had in mind a life devoted to the highest moral principles. The abstract noun *spirituality* (*spiritualitas*) was first coined by a fifth-century Latin translation of Gregory of Nyssa, a Greek-speaking bishop from Constantinople (c. 331–395), and is used commonly in the writings of the church from the ninth to the thirteenth century. By the twelfth century, however, it had lost its moral implications and meant the shunning of material well-being, that is, a life devoted to asceticism. Simultaneously, the term was politicized to stand for the ecclesiastical realm as opposed to the lords and kings of the feudal age who were not bishops—that is, it denoted "the lords spiritual" as opposed to "the lords temporal." Seventeenth-century France used *spiritual* generally to mean "devout," while social critics like Voltaire spoke pejoratively of people who wore their "new spirituality" on their sleeve. By the late nineteenth and early twentieth century, Western observers were discovering Eastern religions and began reserving the term for the true experience of religion that they thought Buddhism, especially, offered, and that is the source of our own popular view that spirituality is experiential, the kind of thing one feels rather than knows.

With all these competing meanings, we can define spirituality any way we like, of course, but the popularized view, so influenced by Madison Avenue marketing of experience, does not permit any kind of spirituality for people who are not seeking or not psychologically desirous of ecstasy. This popular view sees spirituality in Native American vision quests, community retreats, communing with nature, having a baby, and (as mentioned previously) even having sex—all experiences of transcendence or at least a psychological "high." With this definition, the best advice we could give people experiencing Night is to get over it, after which they might move on to the eclectic psychedelic circus of potential highs all around them.

Seeing spirituality as our way of being in the world avoids the troubling notion that soul-moving experience is everything. It allows us to reach out to the inhabitants of Night and say something other than it is high time they felt better. There is indeed a Jewish spirituality of Night, and it comes from taking Jewish metaphors seriously.

We have already looked at metaphors and seen their impact on the world we experience. For instance, we saw a foundational metaphor of "landedness/exile." Originally, landedness and its opposite defined where one lived—though even then, such designations were metaphoric since *exile* is not necessarily the opposite of "being at home." One could equally imagine the opposite as "visiting," say, or "touring," or "observing the strangers." But Judaism chose *exile*. Now, the beautiful thing about metaphors is that they stretch. They spawn secondary metaphoric colonies beyond the home territory that they occupied originally. *Well-being* and its opposite, *illness*, are just such an outpost, a derivative of landedness and exile. Susan Sontag intuits this relationship without, perhaps, realizing its harmony with Jewish tradition. She begins her classic study of illness and its metaphors by describing precisely what the chronically or seriously ill know to be the case: Health is our home country; illness is another place far away; it is exile from the place we want to be. "Illness . . . the night side of life," she says, is "a more oner-ous citizenship. Everyone who is born holds dual citizenship, in the kingdom of the well and the kingdom of the sick. Although we all prefer to use only the good passport, sooner or later each of us is obliged, at least for a spell, to identify ourselves as citizens of that other place."

This is not a phenomenon that is confined to illness alone. It goes also for mourners of tragic losses, say, or people rejected by would-be lovers. They, too, are temporarily (and sometimes permanently) exiled from a feeling of being at home. Those at home, meanwhile, the people who continue seeing movies, going out for dinner, and enjoying ordi-nary laughter, friendship, and fun resist hearing news from that "other country." The natural human tendency is to deny such evidence of night, so as to protect ourselves from the certain knowledge that we too own secret passports there.

The most tragic example of this may have been the inability of some Jews to hear reports of Hitler's systematic genocide. Elie Wiesel de-scribes the torment of Moshe the Beadle, who returns to his hometown, Sighet, with nightmarish news. Trucks of deportees had been driven to a forest in Poland. Then:

The Jews were made to get out. They were made to dig huge graves.
And when they were finished with their work the Gestapo began
theirs. Without passion, without haste, they slaughtered their pris-
oners. Each one had to go up to the hole and present his neck. Ba-

bies were thrown into the air and the machine gunners used them as targets. This was in the forest of Galicia, near Kolomaye. How had Moshe the Beadle escaped? Miraculously. He was wounded in the leg and taken for dead. . . .

Through long days and nights, he went from one Jewish house to another, telling the story of Malka, the young girl who had taken three days to die, and of Tobias, the tailor, who had begged to be killed before his sons. . . .

People refused not only to believe his stories, but even to listen to them.

Judaism insists that we listen—and not just to news of horrendous proportions like the tale told by Moshe the Beadle. We must listen to everyday news bulletins from that exilic kingdom called Night, and we must not offer the so-called comfort of Job's visitors who talked but did not listen, but just be present. In Jewish tradition, God's presence, the *Sh'khinah*, accompanies Israel into exile. Another Talmudic passage, as we saw, locates the messiah bandaging wounds of the lepers at the city's gates—again, an idiom for "outside the city," which is to say, the land of the sick that is "not at home." We bring spirituality to that land by emulating God and the messiah—by being there.

Visiting the Kingdom of Night

In the year I spent working with the United States Navy, I was enormously impressed with the time and commitment that chaplains of all faiths showed the young men and women aboard ship. For a period of months, even years, these recruits live in crowded conditions, working long hours not only in regular readiness for battle, but also miles away from spouses, parents, and friends—the normal support network that most people take for granted. On an aircraft carrier, a team of three chaplains may have to offer solace to six thousand sailors. Mostly, what they do is just "be there." They think of it as a "ministry of presence."

Long ago, Judaism demanded just that: a ministry of presence, not only for professionally trained chaplains, but for everyone. Sociologist Robert Putnam cites Woody Allen as saying, "80 percent of life is simply showing up." Putnam gives us a portrait of an America that no longer shows up very much. By contrast, Jewish spirituality arises from showing up, from making it a point of being there. Particularly, this is true for the Kingdom of Night, which residents of the Kingdom of Day are not just encouraged but actively commanded to visit.

Judaism is passionate about the need personally to visit the sick. The Talmud rules, for instance, "There is no measure for visiting the sick. What does 'no measure' mean? . . . Rava said: A person must visit the sick even a hundred times a day." The sick, moreover, are broadly defined to include more than just those with physical ailments. A Talmudic tale describes a Rabbi chancing upon Elijah the prophet, who is revisiting one of the market places on earth. Anxious to take advantage of the holy man's presence, the Rabbi inquires, "Does anybody in this market have a share in the world to come?" Pointing out two ordinary-looking passersby, Elijah responds, "Those two have a share in the world to come." The Rabbi approaches them and asks, "What do you do?" They respond, "We are jesters. When we see people depressed, we try to cheer them up. And when we see two people quarreling, we work hard to make peace between them."

Visiting is commanded also in the case of mourners. Recognizing the toll that the death of a loved one has on an entire family, Jewish law advises, "When a family member dies, the entire family has cause for concern. To what can this be compared? To an arch made of stone; when one stone shakes, all of them are insecure." The result is that, "It is a great commandment to console mourners. We find that the Holy Blessed One consoled mourners." Visiting a house of mourning is part of *imitatio dei*, the commandment to imitate the ways of God.

Unsurprisingly, Jewish law multiplies the rules of proper visiting. Job's would-be comforters are ubiquitous to every age, as we see from a story taken from modern Jewish folklore: A visitor came to see a patient and asked what was wrong. After the patient told him, the visitor said, "Oh my father died of the same disease." When the patient reacted with distress, the visitor said, "Don't worry, I'll pray to God to heal you." To which the patient answered, "And when you pray, add that I may be spared visits from other fools like you."

Our tale says much about the Jewish ideal of visiting. Clearly, the visitor's main error was the appalling suggestion that the disease might prove fatal. A second mistake, however, was the attempt to cover up the first one with the assurance, "Don't worry. I will pray for you." Judaism does offer the comfort of prayer, but on no account imagines that God necessarily or even usually grants petitions for health. First, the empirical evidence does not support such a claim. Recent investigation does demonstrate some benefit if the sick pray on their own behalf, pray with someone else, or even just know that others are praying for them. But successful explanations for these phenomena need not invoke God. Healing, here, could equally well be a result of mind–body interaction. So, researchers set on proving prayer's efficacy turn to cases in which that explanation is impossible: healing at a distance, that is, having worshipers pray randomly for patients they do not know, and not informing those patients that they are being prayed over. Preliminary results suggest that prayer may be helpful here, too, but the experiments are questionable methodologically and are being repeated to see if they are replicable. In any event, even if it turns out that prayer at a distance is helpful, it is not clear that this would be altogether good news. Suppose the normal rate of recovery from a given illness is 50 percent; suppose further that when people are prayed over, it rises to 60 percent. What shall we tell the other 40 percent, who received the same prayers but did not get better? Either God is surprisingly whimsical or we are back where we started: suggesting that God must have had good reason for passing over the people whose conditions did not improve—that is, blaming the victims.

Many Jews are surprised to hear that by and large Judaism does not emphasize prayer as the sole, or even the primary, purpose of the visit. That is because Jewish opinion has evolved over time, giving us more than a single unanimous view. Maimonides, for instance, was not just a legal scholar and philosopher but also a physician; he knew firsthand the tragedy of illness, especially in an age when doctors knew so little about what caused disease. In his summary of Jewish law on the subject of healing, he mentions prayer only once and actually paraphrases his Talmudic sources on occasion so as to leave prayer out. Maimonides represents an early Spanish tradition influenced by Islamic rationalism. Northern European rabbis saw things somewhat differently. They were influenced by a strain of Christian piety rooted in monastic reform and the papal dispatch of new religious orders to minister to the cities. Like the Christian monks, urban rabbis in France and Germany mentioned prayer more favorably. By the sixteenth century, the mystical doctrine of cabala had swept down from France to what was then Christian Spain and was carried throughout the Mediterranean by Jews expelled from the Iberian peninsula. Cabalistic cosmology saw the universe as a vast machine in which prayer outfitted with the proper mystical intentions worked to turn the cogs in the direction of making the universe work better. Cabalists therefore gave us the familiar modern image of continual prayer as the quintessential religious contribution to healing.

But even these pietists admitted that prayer had its limits. Their writings never speak of miraculous healing, but only of seeking God's mercy, perhaps successfully, perhaps not—who knows? A contemporary Hasidic teaching advises the sick to consult a physician first; then, if that fails, to depend on prayer; and if that fails, to hope for a miracle. Apparently the science of medicine is the preferable path. And God may answer prayer, so try that as well. But that also regularly fails; in which case, miracles still can happen—in the form of what doctors call a spontaneous (and inexplicable) recovery. And remaining alive is not the be-all and end-all in any case. Sometimes, we pray for death to come. "It seems to me," says Spanish pietist Nissim Gerondi (1310–c. 1375), "that at times, we ought to pray that the sick may die; for instance, if they are terribly pained by a disease, and they will not possibly recuperate." His point is twofold: not only that we sometimes pray for death, but that we have the right to deduce the probability that prayers for life will fail as other forms of medicine have. Deciding that the patient will die anyway, we pray to hasten the end. So, even though prayer *became* critical with the triumph of the cabala, classical Talmudic sources include prayer only alongside other more subtle components of the fine art of "being there."

Most important, "being there" means physically being present. One of the most outstanding rabbis of the twentieth century, Moshe Feinstein, was asked if a telephone call suffices as a visit, especially if the call includes a prayer. His answer is instructive: It is better than nothing, and if you really cannot visit, by all means do call. But a call can at best achieve some of the ends of visiting. Only a personal visit can do it all.

The first and foremost purpose of visiting is not to offer prayer but to ease the discomfort of the patient by cleaning the room or straightening the bedcovers. If conversation is impossible, you may say nothing; but conversation is desirable, especially on ordinary business affairs, so as to assure the patient that the illness is no punishment for a business practice that may have involved hurting another party. If death is near, you should help the patient face the end with the prior warning that merely discussing death does not bring it about; patients should get their moral affairs in order, confess any sins they do not wish to die with, and have hope in God and the promise of a life beyond the grave. If even just being in the room is hard for the patient, you should leave, but remain in the anteroom, so that the patient knows you are in attendance. If you pray for the patient, Hebrew, the normal language of Jewish prayer, should be used; but only if you are outside the sick room. If you are with the patient, you may use the vernacular, so that the patient understands what you are saying. You are to visit non-Jews also, not just Jews.

And we are not to expect too much. Just being there is said to remove a sixtieth of a patient's infirmity. (One-sixtieth, however, is the fraction that the Rabbis used to suggest the bare minimum of anything. For instance, Jewish law prohibits eating milk with meat. This is a very strong taboo, the breaking of which virtually horrifies those Jews who keep it. Yet it may happen that the tiniest amount of milk contaminates a soup made with meat, in which case, the Talmud does allow the soup to be eaten. That infinitesimally small drop is called one-sixtieth of the total liquid.) Visiting the sick, then, is not likely to make a patient better. But we do it anyway, over and over again, even to ease just one-sixtieth of the pain. The reason is striking. Once again, it is a metaphor.

Sharing the Pathway of Life: The Spirituality of Meeting

One of the reasons cited by Jewish tradition for visiting the sick is the practical advice from Exodus 18:20, "Teach them the way on which they should walk." The Hebrew for "should walk" can also mean "will walk," however, so the Talmud interprets the verse not only as what we should do but what we will do, just because we are human. Our moral obligations remind us of our own inevitable life cycle.

Rav Joseph interprets the passage in the following manner: "Teach them" is the home of their life. "The way" means the practice of deeds of loving kindness. "They will walk" implies visiting the sick. "On which" refers to the grave. Here is, first, the Jewish metaphor of home that we observed in our discussion of landedness. And we shall return to it again shortly.

But life is also "a way . . . that we will walk." It is a journey. And our walking on our way is linked to our obligation to visit the sick. If we do not visit the sick, we will fail ultimately to walk on our own path of life. Fail to visit the sick, and you fail to apprehend your own journey from birth to death. (The beginning of Jewish wisdom is the simple truth that life is a path that we all walk, a path with death at its end.) Thus, when Rav Hiyya lost his son, a rabbinic visitor advised, "It has always been thus, a *pathway* from the time of creation. Many have drunk this cup, many will drink it; the drinking of those who came before is the same as the drinking of those who come after."

Visiting the sick is an affirmation of a common human destiny, a path shared by those who find it difficult and those who do not—not yet anyway, but who will. Rabbi Meir cited Ecclesiastes 7:1, "It is better to go to the house of mourning than the house of feasting, for this is the way of all humanity." It means, he said, "Do for others, and they will do for you; accompany others to the grave, and they will accompany you; eulogize others, they will eulogize you; bury others, they will bury you."

So, life is a shared journey. Visits to the sick entail catching up with those ahead of us who have been slowed by illness. We pause to share the moment. It follows that visitors must be physically present for the visit to count, and that is why actually being there is required. Visiting is, literally, sharing the physical space of a common road.

The journey metaphor transcends the Jewish tradition. It is pervasive in Jewish, Christian, and even the Pagan traditions in the Greco-Roman world. Elsewhere in rabbinic literature, Rabbi Akaviah ben Mehalalel says, "Know whence you came, whither you are going and before whom you will have to render account." Abraham the nomad is Paul's ideal precisely because he is on a journey from his native Ur to "the land that God will show him," but until such time, he is the quintessential pilgrim here on earth. The journey was frequently fixed by stages, "a time to be born and a time to die," as Ecclesiastes 3:2 puts it. The second-century astronomer, Ptolemy codified seven such stages, which, as we saw, Shakespeare later popularized in *As You Like It*. John Bunyan's *Pilgrim's Progress* catapulted the metaphor of life's journey into American folklore in 1684. So, Judaism is not alone in emphasizing journeying. It does, however, apply the journey metaphor in its own unique way.

Four such applications mark the Jewish use of the journey metaphor. We have so far looked at the pathway of life from the perspective of the visitor. But what about those being visited? Visitors may, at best, be able to take away one-sixtieth of the pain—not much hope there. But people who are sick in body, mind, heart, or soul know that already. What they want is to avoid isolation, on one hand, and Job's comforters, on the other: people who add to their pain with metaphors that hurt, or who try to make sense out of their agony philosophically. That is why visitors are not to preach theology to those in anguish. They ask how patients feel, talk of ordinary affairs, and if talk is difficult, they shrink into the background to let their presence speak for itself as they fluff pillows, sweep the floor, do what they can. They position themselves, in other words, not as someone who is well and therefore above the patient in some regard, but as someone who is on the same level as the patient, knowing nothing more than the patient knows about this traumatic illness, but at least sharing the ultimately unfathomable road of life and refusing to let the patient stumble and be left behind all alone. A person on whom Night inexplicably descends has a right to an unfailing series of visits from those in the Kingdom of Day, who arrive not to explain anything, but to be there.

Crucial to this "being there" is what human beings share above all other animals: communication through speech. Speech is commonly associated with prayer, but we saw that prayer is underrepresented in the classical Jewish account of visiting. So, the point of visiting is not just to pray, but to engage the patient, when possible, with the magic quality of words. Hence my second point: Jewish sources assume not only a common path, but a path that is marked by the sharing of words. It is precisely when words become difficult for the patient that we are instructed to leave the room. As long as that is not the case, we share the path as only humans can: trying to find words that bind fellow travelers on a common road.

Of late, American culture has increasingly appreciated the motif of a journey and the value of shared speech. Approximately 40 percent of all Americans report belonging to "a small group that meets regularly and provides caring and support for those who participate in it." Sociologist Robert Wuthnow explains, "Advocates of small groups have drawn heavily on the language of journeys." Indeed, 50 percent of those involved in small groups say they are on such a journey. Ninety percent say they have grown spiritually in their group, and 92 percent say they have received support, mostly the feeling that they are not alone and encouragement when they were feeling down. Those concerned with spiritual growth and with their own healing are especially apt to cite the positive value of a confidant, a member of the group who is understood to be on the journey with them. And what makes groups work is the common sharing that is established by words, most notably, the sharing of stories and prayers. The Jewish metaphorical tradition may now have important points of contact with a thoroughly American world of discourse.

Philosophers have long wondered whether humans have minds distinct from the network of neurons and synapses called the brain. Either way, it appears that humans alone have self-conscious awareness of existing through a life and being linked thereby to other lives, past, present, and future. This sense of connecting the dots within our many selves as we grow through life becomes the meaning we attribute to our days. The meaning of life is thus the shape of the path; and the shape of the path is given to us in conversation, stories, words, and metaphors. Aristotle thought that to be human is to be rational; more likely, it is to be self-conscious, interpretive, in search of life's meaning. Medieval Jewish philosophers called that the gift of being *m'daber*—blessed with the gift of speech. The plant kingdom is *tsame'ach*—"that which grows." Higher species, sentient animals are *chayah*—"that which lives" more or less as we do. Only human beings are *m'daber*—"the species that speaks."

Modern critics agree. Nobel Prize winner Francis Crick, for example, doubted that human beings had such a thing as mind or soul, but he assures us that we and we alone have consciousness and the ability to handle complex linguistic problems. Consciousness is the path; language is the way we live it. Telling stories, sharing thoughts, provoking laughter, evoking memories, and even praying—these are among our ways with words. Seeing sickness metaphorically as a meeting place on life's path at which point the patients and visitors exchange words on the nature of the journey and both visitor and patient leave the meeting with a deeper sense of the journey's meaning is, I think, a model of Jewish spirituality for when Night strikes.

The Jewish sense of journey is saturated with yet another Jewish metaphor, "home," a construct we discussed with regard to the woman who inquired about the meaning of the final Yom Kippur service (chapter 2). We saw also that Rav Joseph taught "Teach them"—this is the *home* of their life. How can a journey, a way, be a home? And even more puzzling, if Night is exile, and exile is the opposite of home, then how can the Night moments of life be integrated into the master metaphor of "being at home"? We should say then that visiting is intended to convert Night into at least a temporary Day. We remove what we can of the patient's pain. Using words, we construct a relationship at this temporary stopping-off place along the road. Our visit can help those who suffer know that they are not entirely outside the realm of home. Remember the messiah who bandages up the wounds at the city gate. We said at first that the meaning here may be right outside the entrance gate to the home city. But it could as easily be that liminal boundary of the gateway itself—not inside, but not altogether outside either. It may be too much to expect that the sick can feel wholly inside the comforts of home, where altogether different rules of well-being reign supreme. But they need not feel like pariahs, utterly beyond the conventional normalcy they once experienced when they were well.

Then, too, death, for a Jew, leads to almost instant burial. In antiquity, bodies were interred right away, the whole community joining in the passing cortege to see the deceased to a final resting place. Why the rush? Other cultures have a wake; they delay the time of burial as much as possible. Jews, however, see burial as a final blessing: It is the return of the body to the *bet olamim,* the cemetery, which is called "an eternal home." Is it possible for us to welcome death when it comes? We all know it is. Judaism encourages it, since it will happen to us all when the journey of this life ends.

We need a name for this ministry of being there, the means by which the healthy and the ill share a common Jewish journey through the gift of language and the yearning for home. Martin Buber, the great theologian of the twentieth century, gave us one. He differentiated ways of knowing. We know most of the world scientifically. It is a thing we measure, weigh, experiment with, or use for our own ends. Another way of knowing, however, assumes we meet and treat each other not as things to know objectively, but as primary consciousnesses that exist for no other purpose than to be there for each other, if only for a brief moment. Buber acknowledges that sometimes we interact with each other for mutual advantage, and properly so, as when I buy something from you—you, the seller, and I, the buyer, together benefit. But Buber calls on us to be distinctively human in a sacred vein as well: to live the life of meeting.

Especially in the ordeal of Night, we should remember the potential for the spirituality of meeting. Unable to cure disease, remove people's pain, explain away great suffering, or bring back the dead, we can at least deliver that shared moment of "being there," which is the way to transform the exile of illness into at least the gateway to home; the way also to identify with the suffering of others because we know we will be where they are soon enough; and, in due course, the way we help them (as we hope others will one day help us) make their way in peace to a final home beyond the lifetime that we know.

The spirituality of meeting cannot deny the Kingdom of Night. But it can soften its inevitable arrival. By filling in for God, we can show those with pain (and by suggestion, ourselves as well) that even at night, "God does not leave us comfortless."

Chapter Eight

A Fourth Generation: Spirituality of Community

Such is the generation that seek out God.
PSALMS 24:6

Authentic Jewish spirituality does exist. It is real, not just rhetoric, and it is not anti-intellectual. It is a genuine part of life, akin to art, reflected in ritual, celebrated in moments of personal transcendence, and implicit in the recognition that life has direction, purpose, and hope. It is particularly the concern of our generation, the generation of men and women who inhabit the beginning of the twenty-first century. We should pause in awe of the magnitude of the spiritual project that our generation has initiated.

Generations and Their Projects

A generation is more than a random group of people who happen to be born at the same time. That is just a statistical category called a cohort. We are all, by chance, a particular cohort, like the millennial cohort born between 1975 and 1980, and, by chance reaching adulthood as the year 2000 dawned. *Cohort* attribution is arbitrary and potentially insignificant. By contrast, the *generation* to which we belong is a matter of choice, and it matters supremely. A generation is a group of people who may never have met, but who know they share a patch of history that directs their lives. They may be of different cohorts—born, that is, at different times, related as parents and children (or even as grandchildren) to each other. But they are one generation nonetheless, if they witness together the unfolding of their own unique chapter in time. They may be "local generations," such as the generation of the great San Francisco fire or the generation of one of the great Midwest floods. But generations may be broader in scope as well, as when we say that most of us were once the Cold War generation; or now, that we are the generation that saw the Iron Curtain fall. We may also be the Vietnam generation, as our parents and grandparents, perhaps, were the generation of the Great Depression, or, now, the generation that knows terrorism.

Our generation leaves its mark on us. Depression generations do not throw things out; they save them in dusty attics or moldy basements in case they are ever needed. Soldiers of the Cold War never quite fade away—they forever keep guard over American democracy, suspecting always that the sleeping Russian Bear will bestir itself again. The Vietnam generation will never trust its government with the same naive passion that the Roosevelt generation invested in their great FDR.

Attribution of generation is a subtle thing, however, because a generation's mark need not last forever. Healthy people who move on to experience more than one historic moment need not be fixated at reliving old ones. They carry their old experience with them, but apply what they have learned to the new task of a new generation that they join as passionately as they did the old one. Identity is constructed out of several generational pivot points.

As an American and a Jew, for instance, I have known the Holocaust, the revolutionary sixties, Kennedy's Camelot, Israel's many wars, and, most recently, its hope for peace. I chart my life as the coordinates of all these generational events. I am autonomous; I decide my own destiny— as much as possible—but I react necessarily to the cataclysmic affairs into which I am born and which swirl around me so long as I live.

What we are is more than what we individually plan on being. Life is what happens while we are busy doing something else, as the saying goes. We are regularly buffeted by waves of history that we neither plan nor anticipate. They mold the generations and define their projects.

A *project* is the way we determine our place in history. By *project*, we mean something greater in scope and in design than just work. We do not all have the luxury of conceptualizing a project. Slave laborers in Auschwitz made do from moment to moment, lucky just to stay alive. The poor who huddle beneath New York's Brooklyn Bridge have no project; they struggle to make it through each night. Children have no project; they move as directed by parental whim. But adults who manage to surpass the most elemental stage of animal needs do make up projects; that is our glory. God had projects; so do we: We were created in the image of God. A project is the connective tissue that gives enduring worth to the individual acts of labor that fill our days. When we despair of what we are about, it is because we have lost sight of our project. When we know somehow we matter, it is because we glimpse a larger pattern to our work. We "project" ourselves on the screen of human history, or at least on some temporal expanse beyond the moment.

Human conduct is absolutely filled with the divining of a project. We join causes that stand for something larger than ourselves. We build homes and decorate them with mementos of a life: family photos on the wall, and scrapbook pictures of happy times—the sacred relics of times and spaces we touched and that touched us in return. These remind us of the links that make us who we are.

When people die, we feel obliged to take stock of who they were, what they did, what they amounted to, and what others say of them. "He loved his family more than anything else on earth," the rabbi says in a eulogy that captures someone's project; or, "What a mother, daughter, sister, our beloved was." Our eulogies would no doubt surprise us, could we hear them. "Your father was a builder, patriarch, and hero," says the rabbi to the grieving daughter. "Was he?" she wonders briefly? "Is that what made him do whatever it was he did when he left home each morning?" Her father has been granted a posthumous project; his life makes sense now; the children put closure on who he was, maybe identify his project with their own, or move on to consider what they shall become.

Without a project, we are barely human: servants of time and circumstance. We seek something more of life, the momentous, not the momentary.

People of a single generation share a project. That is what unites them. Their lives take shape along a single vector. Take the Vietnam generation: They were for the war or against it, but they cannot thereafter live without considering what war is. Just so, the Roosevelt generation never quite gives up on the promise of the New Deal; just as people of the Kennedy generation ask over and over again what they can do for their country, not what their country can do for them. Projects differ within generational representatives, naturally. It is not the same for men as for women; for whites and for blacks; for old-timers and for newcomers; for the young and the old—that is because we occupy our own point in time and space where several generational currents intersect. But despite our differences, if we share a generation, we share also the everlasting impact of the historical waves that comprise it, and we cannot avoid sharing, too, the projects that those waves of time have dumped on the shores of our lives.

Jews today share a new project because they are a new generation: the fourth generation in North American Jewish history. Before describing the fourth-generation project, we should glance back at the generations that came before us to see how much our project is a continuation of theirs and how much it differs.

Generation One: The Founders

It helps to have some dates in mind, even if they are arbitrary. Dating by decades is convenient, starting with our own and looking backward. Also helpful is the Bible's generational calculus. There we find "generations": the generation of the flood, as the Rabbis put it, or the generation of the dispersion, meaning those who lived at history's putative beginning, touched forever after by their failure to erect a Tower of

Babel. Assume that both are myths; there never was a Noah (though there may have been a flood), and there was no Tower of Babel. But there must have been generations whose projects were the kind of thing that floods and towers can explain. Live through a flood and you never again take life's steady course for granted. Your project is to build a stable settlement on the shores of an eroded past. Babel is the Bible's "just so" explanation of human particularity. Why should we all be different? Why are we not all one people, with one language and one scrapbook of the things that made us who we are? The generation of the dispersion formulated the human project that anthropologists call "culture."

By biblical count, generations come and go every forty years. After leaving Egypt, for instance, the first generation of Israelites wandered in the desert for forty years. So, let us count back forty years from where we are today, then forty years more, and forty years more to get back to the first generation of the four that concern us here. If the high-water mark of our generation is roughly the first decade of the new millennium, then generation three (to which we are heir) reached maturity in the 1960s, and its parental generation left its mark from about 1920 to 1930, while the generation of the founders notched its project in the stones of time somewhere in the 1880s.

To be sure, Jews had been coming to America for a long time prior. Sefardi immigrants (those of Spanish-Portuguese heritage) arrived from the Brazilian port city of Recife as early as 1654. They had moved there from Holland when the Dutch controlled the area (1630–1654), but had to leave when Catholic Portugal took it from the Dutch and imported the hated Inquisition. Threatened now with criminal investigation leading to the *auto da fé* (burning at the stake), Jewish refugees made their way by ship to what lay still in Dutch control, the city of New Amsterdam (later New York), which was under the governorship of Peter Stuyvesant. Against his will, Stuyvesant was forced to admit these first Jewish settlers, and with that act, North American Jewish history began.

But the Recife Jews were few in number and America was just being born, so outside their own circle, the Sefardi founders left relatively little lasting impact on the ultimate shape of North American Jewish life. They were overrun by German immigrants, who began arriving shortly after 1815 when the Congress of Vienna ended the Napoleonic Wars. Napoleon had led Jews to believe that all things were possible. He had convened a council of Jewish elders to hail the new era in which Jews as French citizens of the Jewish faith had a place. With Napoleon's demise, Jewish hopes collapsed. The following era of reactionary politics and nascent racism relegated Jews again to the margins of European life. No wonder so many of them immigrated to the New World. Napoleonic enlightenment still ruled for Thomas Jefferson and James Madison. While German statesmen went about the business of returning Germany to the Germans, Jefferson outfitted Washington with neoclassical architecture reflecting universal reason. The first German Jews to arrive were enraptured by America's promise. Their project, simply put, was to make it here.

European liberals tried one more time to wrest Europe from the hands of the reactionaries. When their attempted revolution of 1848 died, a second stream of German Jews admitted defeat and headed to America to join the German émigrés already here. The latter had followed the course of the revolution in the press, which reported the battles fought by democratic partisans on the ramparts of the very cities where America's Jewish readers had once lived and whose curves and alleyways they knew by heart. Some even went back to Europe to usher in the messianic era that they hoped was on its way. When no messiah came, they washed their hands of Europe once and for all and returned home to New York, Boston, or Baltimore. This time, they were joined by the second wave of Germans migrating westward. If they met on the boat crossing the Atlantic, these two groups of Germans would have discovered much in common, but something subtle divided them as well. Unlike the Jews who had left immediately after Napoleon's defeat, the second wave arrived proudly imbued with the experience of nineteenth-century German art and literature. They, too, adopted the project of making it here, but for them, making it meant doing so as Germans in America. Thus was born the ambivalent project of German Jewry: to succeed in the New World without actually giving up the Old; to be a Jew by religion, but of German culture and American loyalty.

What it meant to be American was clear enough. It was to be a citizen of a modern state, just as Napoleon had foreseen in his abortive fling with modernity. But what did it mean to be Jewish? In Europe, it had many meanings: religion, certainly, but also peoplehood, ethnicity, separatist community, way of life. America in the 1800s, however, was especially enamored of religion. Founded by religious people from the very beginning, America insisted on religious identity for its citizens. As the nineteenth century dawned, the largest religious gathering ever massed in Cane Ridge, Kentucky, where Evangelical Protestantism made its greatest one-time stand. By 1830, America was in the throes of a Great Awakening that Cane Ridge had begun: Revivalist preachers were steadily migrating westward, gathering enormous crowds wherever they went. That same year, Joseph Smith announced that he had been visited by an angel with the good news that the United States was actually the land of promise, the new Israel, and the people he would lead were the ten lost tribes.

Thanks to President Madison, who had rejected a state religion, Catholics, Protestants, and Jews all found a welcome foothold here, even though Protestantism vastly outnumbered, outranked, and outdid the others in shaping the American experience. But Protestants were anything but united. American religion was becoming a family of independent churches, such as the Baptists and Methodists who stormed the south and midwest frontiers making souls. Jews of the time took it as part of their project, too, that they should become a "church," American style.

Epitomizing generation one was the founder of founders, Isaac Mayer Wise. As early as 1855, just one year after he had left Albany for

Cincinnati, and only eight years after arriving from his native Bohemia, he had called a conference in Cleveland for the purpose of forging America's disparate Jews into a union. He failed at first, but in the 1870s, he tried again, and by 1875, he was the president not only of the Union of American Hebrew Congregations (a national alliance for synagogues) but also of the Hebrew Union College, whose mission it was to educate and create Jewish clergy—just as Princeton did for Presbyterians or Harvard, Unitarians. By the 1880s, the project of the founders had reached fruition. With its institutional bastions firmly set in place, it issued an official doctrinal statement in 1885 called the Pittsburgh Platform. Roughly one hundred years after America was born, its Jewish founders served institutional notice that they too had arrived. Their project was successful; they had indeed made it here.

Generation Two: Preserving Peoplehood

What the German founders never did appreciate was the positive pull of peoplehood on the Jewish psyche. How could they? When they arrived here, their claim to belonging was precisely the fact that they were not a people at all; they were a religion. That claim had been implicit in the Enlightenment all along. Even Moses Mendelssohn had known that. Back in the early 1700s, this exceptional Jew had been singled out for permission to dwell in Berlin, a city that was still officially off limits to Jews. A philosopher and scholar, Mendelssohn typified the Enlightenment ideal. He would meet on a Shabbat afternoon for a friendly game of chess with his friend, a Catholic priest, Johann Caspar Lavater, rejoicing in his newfound Prussian residency, which he could and did justify on the grounds that he was a man of reason. As to nationality, however, he was a German. He spoke German and even translated the Bible into German so that his fellow German Jews could learn to speak it also. When Lavater tried nonetheless to convert him to Christianity, Mendelssohn responded that he preferred to remain a Jew, not because the Jewish *People* had any claim on him, but because Judaism as a *religion* was so perfectly rational that he could think of no reason why any rational soul would want to leave it.

The French Revolution furthered this Enlightenment goal with shouts of "Liberty! Equality! Fraternity!"—all true if (and only if) all human beings really are free, equal, and fraternally related, which is to say, members of the same human family and divided into national enclaves called states purely for purposes of administration. Napoleon redrew the European map, dividing Europe into geographical entities called consistories, which corresponded to nothing deeper than lines of arbitrary latitude and longitude. The age-old nationalist claims of Europe's several peoples were being overturned even as the group of learned Jews assembled in Paris on February 4, 1807. They told Napoleon exactly what he wanted to hear: Jews are a religion, not a nation.

To some extent the second migration of Germans had watered down these radical claims of the Enlightenment. Having lived through the reactionary era that denied Napoleonic geography, they had experienced the reassertion of the German *Volk*. Only in the 1880s would that nationalism flare up into full-fledged anti-Semitism, so the Jews who arrived earlier than that were free to celebrate their identity as Americans (by citizenship), Jews (by religion), and Germans (by national culture) all at the same time. Until the First World War, German Americans (Jews included) saw no conflict between their European culture and their American home. As late as 1900, 90 percent of Lutherans in the Midwest still worshiped in their European language, not in English. In 1816, the philosopher Hegel was appointed to the coveted chair of philosophy at the University of Heidelberg, where he taught that history reached its zenith in the German state. By 1870, Hegel had been dead for thirty-nine years, but he was alive and well among German Jews who agreed with him, to the point of doubting whether anything worthwhile could be expected from a cultural backwater such as the United States, without Germanic culture to help it along.

As much as German Jews celebrated their German heritage, they were ambivalent about their Jewish tradition, which looked far too medieval to be proudly displayed as the equal of what Germanic culture offered. Modern Jewish scholars therefore spent the century redeploying the literary output of the Rabbis, featuring the things they liked and ignoring what they didn't. They called medieval Spanish Jewry a "golden age" because it had produced philosophy and poetry, the highest cultural carriers from the perspective of German aesthetics. Rabbi David Einhorn of Baltimore composed the liturgical forerunner for the *Union Prayer Book* (the first official prayer book for America's liberal German Jews) almost solely in German, and he epitomized his generation of rabbis by delivering flowery (and long!) German sermons to German worshipers. He was by no means ashamed of his Jewish heritage, especially since the heritage he championed was a selective perception of what Judaism really had been. He preached a kind of Judaism that resembled Germanism, which he regarded as the standard toward which Jewish creativity should aspire.

By the end of our high-water decade of the 1880s, that purely religious view of Judaism was being challenged by the largest wave of Jewish immigrants ever to move to one place at one time. They would stand the entire German scheme of things on its head. Whereas the German project entailed building Judaism as a religion, the new immigrants, from eastern Europe, arrived with almost no regard for religion at all. We distort reality if we picture only pious Hasidic synagogues on New York's Lower East Side. It takes a mere instant to discover that the old tenement district is dominated by the building that once housed *The Daily Forward*, the Jewish Socialist press of the time, so, hardly a bastion of religion. Its stone facade now carries Korean characters affixed by new owners, who bought it from the Chinese, who bought it from the Jews. But scrape away the Korean and you find the carved-out images of the people who really mattered to the eastern Europeans: not Moses and Miriam, but the American socialist leader who ran for president five times, Eugene V. Debs (1855–1926), and his German equivalent Rosa Luxemburg (1871–1990). Like their eastern European cousins who moved to Israel rather than America and who observed May Day rather than Yom Kippur, some of these Russian Jews trashed the whole Jewish project, so enamored were they of the rival Marxist promise of a classless society. But most remained true to Jewish identity, being careful only to differentiate *Jewish* from *religious.* It was religion that they despised. They were Jewish as a matter of peoplehood.

They arrived at that conclusion because Napoleon did not triumph in eastern Europe. The transformation of Judaism into a matter of modern Western faith occurred only in the Western orbit of the Parisian Assembly, never in the traditional Talmudic academies of Vilna and Volhynia, and certainly not among the rank-and-file socialists, the intellectual Yiddishists, the land-intoxicated Zionists, or any of the other ideological *luftmenschen* (a Yiddish term for perpetually unemployed intellectuals who lived off the air itself, apparently), who debated their way through every passing day. Certainly, the idea that Jews are just a religion never dawned on the masses, whether or not they attended the storefront and threadbare synagogues of the time. Neither classical Hebrew nor Yiddish even has a native "Jewish" word for "religion" as Western thought understands it. Religion is a Western concept through and through, a generalization offered up by eighteenth- and nineteenth-century academe in its admiration of European Protestantism. It is what Western Jews decided they must be, if Napoleon was not to kick them out; what German Jews had to aspire to, if they were to deserve citizenship in the Prussian state.

Eastern European Jews knew instead they were a people, a nationality like the other groups constituting czarist Russia and, after that, the Union of Soviet Socialist Republics. "Republics," note! Like Latvians, Lithuanians, Ukrainians, and Bessarabians—national groupings all, peoples, with their own distinctive customs, languages, and land. Debate among the Jews who filled the eastern European coffeehouses focused not on religion but on the Zionist question of land, the missing ingredient in the Jewish equation if Jews, like the others, were to be a licit people.

Both in the west and in the east, therefore, modern Jewish strategy revolved around the question of how to justify inclusion in the body politic. In the west, inclusion meant being a religion, so the west gave us religious reform, a means by which Jews could retool their inherited religious traditions and make them come out looking modern and Western. In the east, it was land, not religion, that was missing; so Jewish thinkers there divided into "territorialists," the group that wanted to carve out a Jewish state in eastern Europe (where Yiddish, the language of the masses, would be spoken), and Zionists, the opposing group, which insisted on returning to the Land of Israel and speaking Hebrew, the language of the Bible. In any case, *religious* reform did not capture the attention of those in generation two, who came to these shores not to seek religion but to celebrate peoplehood. Here they needed no separate land, but they did establish Yiddish theater, a Yiddish press, and a fully Yiddish ambience without much religion, for which most of them, as socialists, had little regard.

But they quickly found that Jews here were expected to have a religion. This was a Protestant country and Protestants knew a religion when they saw one. The Germans, who looked down on their Greenhorn eastern European cousins, were aghast at the prospect that these new immigrants would join them in their Reform temples, but eastern Europeans were equally offended by the purely religious Judaism that German Reform had become. So, a compromise was reached. Wealthy Reform bankers bailed out a bankrupt school called the Jewish Theological Seminary and made it the home for eastern European Jewish strivings. By 1920, the beginning of the decade that we chose as emblematic of generation two, Jews had settled into a happy divide: western European Jews in Reform temples that preached Judaism as a faith like Protestantism; and eastern European Jews in Conservative synagogues, where Judaism as an ethnic enterprise reigned supreme.

One outstanding teacher at the Jewish Theological Seminary was Mordecai Kaplan, the founder of a philosophy called Reconstructionism. If Judaism is essentially a people's ethnic folkways, he reasoned, it must be not just a religion but a civilization. In America, where people ought to have religions, it must be a religious civilization. Synagogues should be more than places to pray. They should be gathering places for the clan, houses of assembly, even community centers of a mildly religious sort. How ironic that Kaplan, the most American of all Jewish thinkers, influenced above all by Thomas Dewey and American pragmatism, should have missed the very essence of America: its insistence on religion as the dominating hallmark of what Jews must be. Much later, his Reconstructionist descendants would modify his radicalism, inviting Arthur Green, a religious seeker rooted in the very Hasidic mystical tradition that Kaplan's rationalism fought, to be its president. But in the heyday of generation two, the era when Conservative Judaism was just being born and Kaplan's ideas were only coming into being, no one would have predicted just how much American Jews would return to religion as a source of their identity. That return is the essence of the spiritual quest that dominates the fourth generation—our own. Before discussing that, however, we must analyze the third generation, which reached its pinnacle in the American suburbs of the 1950s.

Generation Three: Suburban Survival

By 1950, American Jews had settled down into two competing Jewish visions. Intermarriage between Germans and Russians veiled the divide to some extent, as did the very vastness of the eastern European numbers that overflowed into German temples despite their organ music, strict decorum, and other trappings of a liturgy redesigned to look Western. Jews had to join some synagogue after all, as Eisenhower himself made clear when he announced that all Americans should join the place of worship of their choice—and he didn't care which it was. The Eisenhower decade was to rival even the 1830s in its reclamation of religion as a grand American pastime.

This mid-century religious revival had many causes, not the least of which was the Red Scare, which promoted air-raid drills and a senator from Wisconsin shouting wild accusations from the House Un-American Activities Committee. Eisenhower shared Joseph McCarthy's fear of godless communism, as we can see from his refusal to grant clemency to Julius and Ethel Rosenberg. But Eisenhower was also religious in his own right. He was a personal friend of Billy Graham, whom he invited to the White House. He referred to himself as "the most religious man I have ever met." Religion was good; Communists were bad. Communists had no religion— so Americans must. End of matter.

Americans flocked in droves to church and synagogue, then, and they did so not just to the places their parents had built. They used postwar largesse to buy all the things they had done without for six years, not to mention all the things just invented and being newly peddled as part of a postwar economy retooled to serve a ravenous peacetime hunger: refrigerators, washing machines, television sets, new cars, and suburban homes. Most Americans who were alive back then remember to this day the commercials featuring Dinah Shore singing, "See the USA, in your Chevrolet." Most of us missed the point. She was actually selling us the interstate highway system, whose ribbons of roads brought Jews to the beltway and beyond, often into communities that hitherto had belonged to the American elite who could afford second homes and country club addresses for the weekend. Now the Jews were coming.

Philip Roth explores the phenomenon in his *Goodbye, Columbus*. The Potamkins live on Long Island, New York, where, once, only people like F. Scott Fitzgerald's Jay Gatsby could reside. Gatsby's neighbor is now Potamkin, the stereotypical nouveau-rich (or at least, "comfortable") Jewish junk dealer who has made good financially, but who lacks Gentile civility. Roth's characters are caricatures, of course, but they tell the tale of Jews who had to learn the ways of the country and did so, in part, by building synagogues across the street from wherever their Protestant neighbors built churches. Children of Russian immigrants who had little use for religion, they now rediscovered Judaism—but Conservative Judaism, mostly, with an accent on peoplehood and ethnicity above all.

The Jewish response to the suburbs was partly like that of everyone else at the time; but it was also uniquely Jewish. Both Jews and non-Jews had children in record numbers. Women who had postponed having children during the war years joined their younger sisters in together producing the largest cohort of children America had ever seen: the baby-boom generation. The boomers were raised by parents who had discovered Dr. Spock. Madison Avenue targeted them as likely consumer prospects for the rest of their lives. Synagogues responded by constructing spanking new school wings that dwarfed the tiny sanctuaries, which went largely unattended anyway.

The parents wanted religion for their children, not for themselves. They had joined the religious enterprise mostly because Eisenhower said they should; belonging was the American thing to do. Going, however, was another matter, especially since services were held on Friday night and Saturday morning when suburban life offered more appealing options in keeping with the children-first ethos: take the kids to little league, or shopping, or piano lessons. Everything for the children.

That much was shared with Christian suburbanites. Churches, too, catered to the not-yet-adult crowd. But Jews had their own take on the situation. Only Jews had to come to terms with the Holocaust. Jews had lost six million, a number higher than anyone had ever counted. Nowadays, we throw around meganumbers with abandon: billions of kilowatts, bytes, even dollars. But back then, six million was a huge number. It meant more than it does now. And it meant Jews, a lot of them, killed under our noses, while American warplanes didn't bomb the gas chambers.

So, American Jews had a special reason to want children, to educate them Jewishly, and to shower every benefit on them. Theologian Emil Fackenheim captured their poignant anguish when he charged his generation with a novel postwar commandment: not to give Hitler a posthumous victory. Consumed with responsibility for a next generation, Jews, especially, manufactured what can only be called "pediatric religion": Judaism for the children.

Simultaneously, Jews turned to saving Jews elsewhere. The war was over; the killing of Jews was not. There were "DPs," as they were called —displaced persons—in refugee camps in Cyprus and wandering throughout Poland, all of them looking for a home when there was none. If generation three had been raised on peoplehood, that emphasis seemed doubly or triply important now. The gathering Jewish project was unmistakable. It had to save the Jewish People. Having and educating Jewish children was the priority at home. Securing the State of Israel and marching for Soviet Jewry became our foreign policy. Synagogues were practically abandoned except as way stations for their children's Jewish education. And in their place, they invented what historians call Jewish Civil Religion, a religious complex that revolved around saving other Jews.

Central to this new civil religion were the United Jewish Appeal (UJA) and a social service network called Federation. The former raised money for Israel, and the latter supported a series of agencies to help needy people domestically in the United States. Especially after the Six Day War of 1968, UJA-Federation attracted enormous support. It represented the Jewish People as a corporate entity with its own corporate economy allocated with corporate efficiency. American Jews thus invented corporate Judaism, complete with new holidays such as Israel Independence Day, Holocaust Memorial Day, and something called Super Sunday—a day not for football, but for phone banks staffed by volunteers soliciting Jewish pledges for the work of saving Jews worldwide. For rituals, this civil religion invented "missions," guided tours where prospective donors could see the remnants of the death camps and then visit Israel to witness how the Jewish People, like the phoenix, rose from the ashes to be reborn. There were marches, too—my own children learned early to say "Let my people go," the annual chant of the New

York March to Save Soviet Jewry. Spirituality was unimportant, compared to the life-saving necessities of the time. The fourth generation's spiritual project is a luxury earned by the third generation's success at securing Israel's safety; airlifting whole Jewish populations out of Yemen, Ethiopia, Chechnya, and elsewhere; and keeping Soviet Jews alive until the Soviet Union collapsed.

But life moves on and so do generations. Generation four, raised on marches by their parents, has launched a Jewish project of its own.

The secret of that project comes from a tale told by Rabbi Sheldon Zimmerman, immediate past president of the Hebrew Union College, who remembers his mother feeding him castor oil regularly. One day, he says, he had an epiphany. It dawned on him that his mother gave *him* the castor oil; she never took it herself. So, too, through all those years of childhood education in the synagogue, despite the millions of dollars poured into classrooms, the kids of generation four got one overarching message: Judaism is like castor oil; parents do not take it.

Jews in generation four, therefore, have had to pioneer religion all over again. Their grandparents who came from Russia had no use for it; their parents never took it. Yet simultaneous with this insight has come an unprecedented American spirituality: As we saw in chapter 1, mature baby boomers particularly began searching for the spiritual.

Generation Four: Spirituality Seekers

The search for spirituality is inextricably linked to demographic changes that began to be felt in the 1960s when the first phalanx of baby boomers came of age. The boomers are just one of three cohorts that stand out as altogether novel in the annals of American history. They are distinguished most obviously because they outnumber everyone else, and they are entering the age range of 45 to 60, which is when people acquire power in our society. As they become successful executives, they set the agenda for the country as a whole. They learned early that the world was supposed to provide them with their needs, and their need now is spirituality: They want to know that their lives have meaning.

Then there are the other two cohorts, the men and women just older and just younger than the boomers. The former are the boomers' parents, blessed with old age beyond what anyone could have predicted prior to the invention of miracle drugs and computer medicine. We have never known as many old people, especially old people who have spent virtually their entire adult lives working for their children, giving little thought to themselves. They are not accustomed to building their own lives as if they themselves mattered. But aging is not for the faint-hearted. It is hard to watch the next generation take over and be yourself dismissed to play golf or otherwise putter around as if you have nothing productive to add to tomorrow. The death of friends, your own more frequent trips to the doctor, and the reality of your demise just around the corner are spiritual issues of the highest magnitude.

Then there are the twenty-somethings. Middle-class Americans used to know by age twenty-five what they probably would be doing for the rest of their lives. Not anymore. Very frequently people in their twenties are still going to school, trying out careers or even live-in mates, but are still uncertain of when and how they will settle into a stable life trajectory. This third cadre of society makes up our final challenge. Just the opposite of their aging grandparents, who look back on lives that ought to have meaning, our youngest adult cohort has the spiritual task of looking ahead to the certainty that life will matter.

Noteworthy in all three cases is the element of free choice, which simply did not exist in the first half of the twentieth century. Until the revolution that gave us rock 'n' roll, birth control pills, and the baby boomers who benefited from them both, middle-class roles were largely fixed according to stereotypes bequeathed us by our Victorian elders.

One element of that legacy was religious denominationalism. The "Church" had become a bastion of American life. It was something people were expected to belong to for life. When Eisenhower called on all

Americans to belong to "a church, any church," he was urging us to return to the mentality that had preceded World War II and that we all considered normal. You knew in those days that you were a Catholic, a Lutheran, a Methodist, or a Jew. You went to church or synagogue school, mixed with others like yourself, and later married one of them. Jews lived in Jewish areas, met other Jews at college, married in synagogues, and had Jewish children; Catholics did the same with Catholics; and Protestants, too, kept their distance not only from Jews and Catholics but even from each other. People settled down in the same churches that their parents had joined and their grandparents had built. Religious denominations were hermetic structures sealed off from strangers who frequented other religions and were held to be different not just in belief but in their very being. Religious conversion was rare; intermarriage was even more rare.

For a variety of reasons, the hermetic seals that surrounded religious identity began to crack during the 1960s and 1970s, mostly because of religious polarization into political right and left, conservative and liberal factions. In the 1950s and 1960s, the mainline churches had taken leading roles in furthering liberal social issues; in the 1970s, conservatives fought back. Within their once-stable religious denominations, conservatives and liberals looked out at each other across fault lines that began to seem unbridgeable. With the bifurcation of denominations, conservative Baptists and conservative Episcopalians, for instance, began to side with each other but against the liberals in their respective camps. The same was true of liberals, of course, so that instead of thinking first and foremost of themselves as Lutherans, Catholics, or even Jews, Americans began identifying as conservative or liberal, fighting a holy war for the good and the just in conjunction with like-minded citizens across religious lines.

Except in new immigrant communities, therefore, the social solidarity of religious ethnic life is now gone. Longstanding Reform Jews on Long Island's south shore, for instance, will tell you that they have little in common with the newly arrived Hasidim who regularly make them unsolicited offers to buy their homes and lock up the area as an Orthodox citadel. But these same Jewish liberals share a lot with the liberal Christians they meet at work or at parties and who are equally threatened by the right wing of their own religious denominations. What goes for liberals goes for conservatives as well. The *New York Times* in June 1993 reported that New York's late Cardinal O'Connor was using Pat Robertson's list of evangelical Protestants for his mailings against abortion—a moral position supported by Hasidic Jews as well. Once upon a time, Robertson had fulminated against papists, and the only thing right-wing Protestants and Catholics agreed on was the need to convert Jews. Now all three parties are in agreement on a host of political positions: the illegitimacy of abortion, prayer in public places, and school vouchers, to name a few. On the left and on the right, we have thus reached the point at which the ethnic or religious community that we have inherited is not the group with whom we count on sharing our deepest commitments.

But if ethnic Jewish solidarity is a thing of the past, so too is Catholic and Protestant solidarity. Religious identity is thus up for grabs. Instead of something into which we are born, religion is increasingly seen as something we choose; it becomes less something to which we feel an allegiance, and more something on which we feel we can make a claim. It owes us, and if it doesn't deliver, we abandon it.

Alongside the demise of certain and lifelong religious identity, we have seen the death of guaranteed family and gender roles. Women, therefore, constitute a special case in this new world where free choice and marketplace options have replaced traditional loyalties and inherited roles.

In the fifties, Jewish women had few choices in life. They were expected to attend college, meet husbands, get married, and have children—all within a few years' time. What happened after that, no one very much noticed. It was widely assumed that women's very nature outfitted them as nurturers of the family.

The notion that it is part of women's genetic makeup to stay home and care for the family does not go back as far as people imagine. It has its origins in the Victorian era. Since, however, the high-water mark of generation one was in the 1880s when Victorian values were rampant in urban centers, the Victorian view of women was inculcated in synagogue culture. Men did not attend synagogue very much in those days. They preferred their men's clubs: the B'nai B'rith, for instance, or lodges like the Freemasons or the Oddfellows. Women, however, were expected to take their children to the synagogue for moral training and also to serve as synagogue volunteers in various charitable projects. Until the turn of the twentieth century, these projects were often large civic endeavors— the equivalent of the Christian Temperance League among non-Jewish women, for instance—but as the migrations of the 1900s swelled the ranks of the urban poor, professional social workers displaced the volunteer women, moving them into subsidiary positions within the churches and synagogues. Our sisterhoods arose, therefore, as a consequence of women's charity role being deflected from the urban crises that professionals were handling into the local efforts of synagogue maintenance and programs.

By the 1920s (the high-water mark for generation two), women had been relegated to the role of Victorian or Edwardian mothers on one hand, and synagogue volunteers on the other. Take Boston's venerable Temple Israel, for instance. Already in 1898, Saturday attendance was noted as including one man, eight married women, six young women, five girls, and two boys. What was true of Boston was true elsewhere as well, to the point that one contemporary observer opined that without the women who attended, sanctuaries would be empty. Rabbis preached largely to women as mothers and wives.

The best metaphor I can use to explain what happened when traditional American society collapsed in the sixties is the revolution in clothing that accompanied it. I think particularly of the staple of Victorian wear: the corset, designed to hold you in, but to make your constriction look natural. In the 1920s, Americans flirted with freedom and demonstrated it by the freer styles of the flapper generation. The conservative fifties saw a return to suburban stolidity, but the corset effect was permanently withdrawn by the Vietnam years, when men and women began dressing the same way, making a sartorial point to their elders who clucked their tongues at the impertinence of unisex styles.

My father once warned me not to say *forever*. "Forever is a long time," he would remark. It may well be, however, that the corset effect is gone forever. At least it is gone for the foreseeable future. And with it, we have lost much of the certainty of life. Instead of inheriting our identities, we choose them. The world in which we live arrives un-pre-packaged now. Whereas once it came to us in the recognizable shapes of old familiar neighborhoods and predictable relationships that claimed you for life (whether you liked it or not), the only thing we can say for sure now is that nothing much is for sure. Instead of fitting into the cozy confines of the way things necessarily are, we are left to decide how we want to sort out the world and the way we want things to be. Even the Army advertises, "Be all that you can be." We civilians want at least that much.

At its core, spirituality is the sense that things all fit together despite momentary fears that they are falling apart. It posits connectedness where there seems to be none. The search for spirituality is the yearning for shape when old contours have eroded; for belonging when the old structures (such as family) to which we belonged have broken down all around us; for meaning in a world so fragmented that we ask again and again, with the hit song of the baby-boomer generation, "What's it all about, Alfie?"

Part of us wants to return to the old days when families could be counted on and the streets were safe for walking. Another part of us, however, knows that the new world of elective identity is not all bad. It does, however, require that we find something to hold us together and connect us beyond ourselves, as we go about choosing the paths that will take us through the labyrinth of life.

I return, then, to the notion of a migration. We have embarked on a spiritual journey no less real than the one taken by Sarah and Abraham at the beginning of the Jewish saga. Ours is internal, however: It is a journey to a new internal life of the soul. I address women especially, for whom choice has opened as never before, but men, too, who are no longer corseted in to the way things have to be and who therefore may as well welcome the new era in which choice is crucial to our destiny. I mean adult Jews, old and young, who have been indifferent to or even alienated by a religious tradition whose spirituality was never explained to them, through all those years of Mr. McChoakumchild's schooling. And I mean people raised outside of Judaism, who nonetheless are curious about the distinctiveness of the Jewish spiritual road map along the rocky terrain of modern life where the old signposts no longer can be counted on to point our way.

Oddly enough, it turns out we can go home again: to a home we never knew we had. Not the ethnic home of European nostalgia; and not at the expense of freedom of inquiry and freedom of choice. But home to the deep-down insights of Jewish tradition: its liturgy of blessings, its metaphors that connect life's dots; its thrill of textual discovery; its rootedness in a sacred land; its honest spiritual thinking; and, at Night (ours or others'), its insistence on the simple presence of human meeting. It requires more than individual effort. It requires community.

Spiritual Community

What, then, is a spiritual community, the community, that is, that comes after "ethnic"? Discussion of community is everywhere. We all know we want it, but what is it? The problem is that we have not specified what kind of community we are talking about. Educator Parker Palmer, for instance, distinguishes four communities: therapeutic, civic, marketing, and academic. Therapeutic communities, such as the many twelve-step or self-help groups, feature a shared intimacy in which love and support can blossom into healing. Civic community is the democratic model of small-town life, where too much intimacy is avoided, but citizens band together in mutual civility to build a better commonweal. A marketing community knows neither intimacy nor civic virtue, but is organized around economic principles of maximizing profit, effectiveness, and a "bottom line." In an academic community, the search for truth is supreme. Professors publish papers and are immediately challenged by the responses of other professors. No one cares much about how the first professor feels. This is a hunt for truth, not therapy. To which of these communities are we returning home?

The old adage "You can't go home again" turns out largely to be true. The home we rediscover the second time around is not the home we left, or even the one we dreamed of from the pictures and stories our grandparents left behind. The home for which our generation yearns is a community of the sacred, the spiritual community that transcends the four communities described by Parker.

We saw that the sacred in Judaism is necessarily nonutilitarian. Insofar as market communities exist only to maximize profit, it is clear that as much as we live our business lives in a market environment, we can never hope to find the sacred there. Civic virtue, however, engenders stewardship for what we all hold dear in common; healing love is precisely the virtue that upholds the spirituality of night; and truth is the passion behind the spirituality of discovery. So, therapeutic, civic, and academic communities are all consistent with the larger goal of spiritual community. But they require something more: the transcendent sense of the ultimate.

Drawing the dots of life, we said, connects us to the disparate moments in time that we weave into our biographical selves. Similarly, the concept of landedness gives shape to geographical chaos, constructing places on a map as either homes or points of exile. The common road we travel toward our final resting place assures us of our common human heritage. And at its core, the spirituality of discovery knows that logical inquiry links up every truth into an all-connected whole where nothing stands alone, for truth, by definition, is a linkage between one thing and another, and every truth leads on to others, until at last, the grand scheme known only to God comes into distant focus.

The kind of mystical spirituality that I described as likely to lead to "going native" is not on that account altogether wrong. It is just so deep that it is easily misrepresented by lesser minds who mistake metaphor for literalism or otherwise fail to point our way to what the mystical mind so surely intuits: the ultimate connectedness of all that is, and the reality of God, therefore, as the final point of absolute connection. Mystics strive for union with the divine—literal union, not just metaphoric, a sense of oceanic disappearance of the solitary self in the cosmic wholeness to which all logic, space, and time must lead. If I have emphasized what I call "reasonable" spirituality, I do not on that account think that mystical consciousness is unreasonable. I mean only to say that most people do not start there, and, indeed, they need not end up there. But then again, they may—for the various forms of Jewish spirituality reveal reality as a multiconnected whole. Absolute coherence joins with absolute comprehensiveness to stretch out a universe of infinite design and meaning far beyond the paltry limits of a single human life, or even of human life in the aggregate—a mere speck in the totality of time. It takes one's breath away.

Even mystics cannot live each moment in that staggering vision. But each and every one of us, mystic or not, should be equally boggled by the implications of a world where stewardship, discovery, and "being at home" are real. It occurs to us that the connectedness we see goes on forever. The Jewish way of being in the world is, finally, a way of connecting with the infinite and knowing it as home. Here, then, is where the spiritual community takes shape: at the point where humans meet to find the infinite, where our minds meet God's, where all the universe is our home, because we are part of all the universe.

I suppose some solitary geniuses arrive at this conclusion and live it hourly as minorities of one; but most of us need others on this human voyage that even Jewish mystics described as dangerous to the psyche. The Talmud tells of four who entered paradise, the rabbinic term for speculation such as we are now engaged in. Only one escaped unscathed. If ordinary mortals shun the lonely search for ultimates, who can blame them? So, Judaism invents community, not market community, mind you, and something more than communities of truth, care, and virtue. The Jewish ideal is a sacred community, a community where our daily regimen together suggests that there is more in heaven and on earth than is dreamt of in most philosophies; where, in short, there are rumors of angels and moments when, angels or not, we are willing to posit the reality of God.

This is the community that generation four is even now reinventing. It begins in the mundane realities of care, virtue, truth, and other signs of the spiritual, as described in previous chapters. A Talmudic adage urges, *tafasta m'rubah lo tafasta*, "If you reach too far, you capture nothing." The successful beginning, then, is hardly a mission statement announcing the need to find God in an instant, or even a day, or a month, or a year. Sacred community begins with a modest but firm commitment to the project of our generation: to transcend ethnicity and seek out the holy in such things as the ways we think, the blessings we say, the truths we discover, and the homes we have or seek to find. Jewish spirituality is not just real. It is reasonable and it is deep. And it beckons us now more than ever to return home to find it.

Notes

1. RETURNING HOME

1   *The search for spirituality is endemic to North American society:* The literature on these trends is too vast to cite in toto. Specially influential studies for me include many sources, of which I mention only a few: Peter L.
Berger (*A Rumor of Angels* [New York: Anchor Books, 1970]) heralded
the rediscovery of the supernatural and the properly insistent individual search for the transcendent. The spiritual ferment of the 1960s is
well chronicled in Robert S. Ellwood, *The Sixties' Spiritual Awakening*
(New Brunswick, N.J.: Rutgers University Press, 1994), but the consequences of that era came vividly to life for most Americans in Robert N.
Bellah et al., *Habits of the Heart* (New York: Harper and Row, 1985),
a popular book that charted end-of-century individualism and the
search for one's own personal spiritual amalgam. In it, see, for example, the most famous case of "Sheila," a respondent who was manufacturing her own religious mix and naming it after herself: "Sheilaism"
(220–221). Almost simultaneous to Ellwood, Wade Clark Roof (*A Generation of Seekers* [New York: HarperCollins, 1993]) traced the spirituality
phenomenon to the baby boomers; and, somewhat later, Donald E.
Miller (*Reinventing American Protestantism* [Berkeley: University of California, 1997]) joined an epoch-making study by the Harvard Business
School in demonstrating the rise of new-paradigm churches in which
individualism, inner healing, and spirituality are paramount. The demise of the old Church structure has been amply demonstrated by Robert Wuthnow in *The Restructuring of American Religion* (Princeton, N.J.:
Princeton University Press, 1988). The individualistic loneliness and
failure of community had been predicted by the "grid/group theory"
of Mary Douglas (*Natural Symbols* [New York: Pantheon Books, 1970]);
and Robert D. Putnam (*Bowling Alone* [New York: Simon & Schuster,

2000]) amply demonstrates just how far individualism had pushed the religious quest in the direction of spirituality rather than the kind of formal religious affiliation that marked the 1950s. Richard Cimino and Don Lattin provide a good retrospective in their *Shopping for Faith: American Religion in the New Millennium* (San Francisco: Jossey-Bass, 1998). Probably more than anyone else, however, Thomas Moore captured the spiritual search for everyday seekers in his *Care of the Soul* (New York: HarperCollins, 1996).

2   *Spirituality was mainstreamed in the 1990s: Newsweek,* November 28, 1994; July 8, 1996; *Wall Street Journal,* July 20, 1998; *Fortune,* July 9, 2001.

4   *The 1990s spiritual revival is epitomized in Mollie:* Roof, *Generation of Seekers,* 63–88.

16 *All of that began to change in the 1960s for a variety of reasons:* Following Wuthnow, *Restructuring of American Religion.*

3. LIVING WITH BLESSINGS

55 *The most obvious examples are those occasions when language creates what are called "social facts":* John R. Searle, *The Construction of Social Reality* (New York: Free Press, 1995).

60 *Paul recognizes standard mealtime customs when he writes to the Corinthians:* 1 Corinthians 11:20–22.

61 *One-third of the entire tractate on blessings deals with food regulations:* M. Ber. 6:1. See standard translation, Jacob Neusner, *The Mishnah: A New Translation* (New Haven, Conn.: Yale University Press, 1988).

63 *It is written, "The earth is the Lord's and the fullness thereof":* Ber. 35a.

63 *A variant version of the same teaching instructs us, "One should eat nothing before saying a blessing":* T. Ber. 4:1. For full discussion of this and parallel texts, see Baruch M. Bokser, *"Ma'al* and Blessings over Food: Rabbinic Transformation of Cultic Terminology and Alternative Modes of Piety," *JBL* 100 (1981): 558–570.

66 *The classic Jewish prayer that acknowledges God speaks of "daily miracles, morning, noon and night"*: Philip Birnbaum, *Daily Prayer Book* (1942; reprint, New York: Hebrew Publishing Company, 1995), 91–92.

4. LIVING BY TORAH

83 *Know that Adam was already filled with wisdom*: Ibn Ezra, commentary to Genesis 2:17.

84 *The human thirst for knowledge is a constant theme in the history of science as well*: Bertold Brecht, *Galileo*, scene 8, end; Werner Heisenberg, *Tradition in Science* (New York: Seabury Press, 1983), 9.

85 *Regarding the oven*: B.M. 55b.

86 *One can imagine the same argument advanced by physicists against medieval authorities who feared where unfettered curiosity would lead*: Brecht, *Galileo*, scene 4, end.

89 *The Mishnah is explicit, even hyperbolic, on this point*: M. Avot 4:7.

90 *'The main categories of labor [that are prohibited on Shabbat] are forty less one"*: M. Shab. 7:2.

5. HAVING A HOME

98 *"My heart is in the east, and I am in the utmost west"*: Heinrich Brody, ed., Nina Salaman, trans., *Selected Poems of Jehudah Halevi* (Philadelphia: Jewish Publication Society, 1928), 2.

99 *Adam and Eve foreshadowed the Babylonian expulsion of 587 B.C.E.*: For this reading of the Bible, see Joseph Blenkinsopp, *The Pentateuch* (New York: Doubleday, 1992).

100 *"Comfort, oh comfort my People"*: Biblical poetry generally follows the translation of the Jewish Publication Society (JPS), 1999.

104 *In theory, Jewish law actually permitted a man who wanted to move to the Land but whose wife refused to go with him to sue for divorce*: See Marc Saperstein, "The Land of Israel in Pre-Modern Jewish Thought: A History

of Two Rabbinic Statements," in Lawrence A. Hoffman, *Land of Israel*, (Notre Dame, Ind.: University of Notre Dame Press, 1986), 191.

105 *In what can only be considered a form of mystical geography:* See Shalom Rosenberg, "The Link to the Land of Israel in Jewish Thought," in Hoffman, *Land of Israel*, 150–153.

107 *Massive government-sponsored pogroms in Russia in 1881 moved one Jewish observer, Leo Pinsker, to describe his people as "a nation long since dead":* Arthur Hertzberg, *The Zionist Idea* (Garden City, N.Y.: Doubleday and Company, 1959) 184.

117 *Psychologist C. G. Jung (1875–1961) got it right when he described "belief and disbelief in God" as "mere surrogates" of the real thing:* Gerhard Adler, ed., *Selected Letters of C. G. Jung, 1909–1961*, Bolingen Series (Princeton, N.J.: Princeton University Press, 1984), 101.

121 *Landed people are those who pray and study with full intentions of carrying out their consequences:* See Saperstein, in Hoffman, *Land of Israel*, 201–202.

121 *Polls reveal that one-third of Americans identify as spiritual a whole host of things:* George Gallup Jr. and Timothy Jones, *The Next American Spirituality: Finding God in the Twenty-First Century* (Colorado Springs: Victor Cook Communications, 2000), 49.

122 *Sociologist Robert Wuthnow sees this privatization of spirituality as the domestication of God:* Robert Wuthnow, *Sharing the Journey* (Princeton, N.J.: Princeton University Press, 1994), 239.

6. SPIRITUAL THINKING

123 *In 1989, the Gallup Poll constructed an index of religious belief:* George Gallup Jr. and Jim Castelli, *The People's Religion: American Faith in the 90s* (New York: Macmillan, 1989), 47; George Gallup Jr. and Sarah Jones, *100 Questions and Answers: Religion in America* (Princeton, N.J.: Princeton Religious Research Center, 1989), 44; Gallup and Jones, *Next American Spirituality*, 177–178.

124 *Polls tell us that from 1944 to 1999, the percentage of people who affirmed a*

belief in "God or a universal spirit" vacillated: Gallup and Jones,
100 Questions, 207; Gallup and Jones, *Next American Spirituality*, 177.

124 *In 1986, 93 percent of all Americans said that they were either "very
satisfied" or "mostly satisfied" with their family life:* Gallup and Jones,
100 Questions, 150.

125 *In 1960, John F. Kennedy, the first Catholic president, had to guarantee
American voters that his personal religious views would not influence public
policy:* Barry Kosmin and Seymour P. Lachman, *One Nation under God:
Religion in Contemporary American Society* (New York: Harmony Books,
1993), 179.

125 *And yet, through all of this, the Gallup poll finds that American churchgoing
patterns have remained the same:* Gallup and Jones, *100 Questions*, 204.

125 *It turns out that 42 percent of all Americans say they go to pray every week,
but only 21 percent really do:* See latest discussion in Robert D. Putnam,
Bowling Alone, 65–79.

128 *"This is what the whole course of history teaches us":* From *The Moral and
Intellectual Diversity of Races* (1853), cited in Marvin Harris, *The Rise of
Anthropological Theory* (New York: Harper and Row, 1968), 103–104.

132 *For example, 83 percent of Protestants and 81 percent of Catholics say they
are "sometimes very conscious of God's presence":* Gallup and Castelli,
People's Religion, 58–59.

149 *Leucippus of Elea or Miletus (450–370? b.c.e.) . . . posited innumerable elements in perpetual motion:* Simplicius, *Physics*; Aristotle, *On Democritus*;
cited in Walter Kaufman, *Philosophic Classics: Thales to St. Thomas* (En-
glewood Cliffs, N.J.: Prentice Hall, 1961), 59, 61.

150 *Epicurus thus held that "the whole of being consists of bodies and space . . .":*
T. V. Smith, *From Aristotle to Plotinus* (Chicago: University of Chicago
Press, 1934), 118, 119.

150 *"Death is nothing to us, for the body, when it is resolved into its elements,
has no feeling":* Smith, *From Aristotle to Plotinus*, 148, 149.

154 *How would we best translate into French (for instance) the book title* All the
President's Men: Douglas R. Hofstadter, *Metamagical Themas: Questing
for the Essence of Mind or Pattern* (New York: Basic Books, 1985), 24–25.

7. WHEN IT IS NIGHT

165 *"Now if you obey the Lord your God to observe faithfully all of his commandments which I enjoin upon you this day"*: Deut. 28:1, 2, 15.

165 *By the end of the book, however, either a second author appended a pious corrective, or the original author "lost the courage of his lack of convictions"*: A
phrase borrowed from Samuel Sandmel, *The Hebrew Scriptures: An Introduction to Their Literature and Religious Ideas* (New York: Alfred A.
Knopf, 1963), 270.

168 *On that day, "penitence prayer and charity cancel a decree of punishment"*:
From *Un'taneh Tokef*, a High Holy Day prayer from the Middle Ages.

168 *When one of them says that somehow the mourning father must deserve what
he is getting*: Ket. 8b.

168 *In 1988, for instance, "one-quarter of the American population experienced
moderate to excruciating pain requiring major therapy such as opioid narcotics"*: David B. Morris, *Illness and Culture in the Postmodern Age* (Berkeley:
University of California, 1998), 110.

169 *Master essayist Annie Dillard asks, "What things have meaning?"*: Annie
Dillard, *Living by Fiction* (New York: Harper and Row, 1982), 137–138.

171 *It "assigns to the luckless ill the ultimate responsibility both for falling ill and
for getting well"*: Susan Sontag, *Illness as Metaphor* (New York: Anchor
Doubleday, 1988), 46.

171 *Sontag cites psychologist Karl Menninger as saying, "Illness is in part what
the world has done to a victim"*: Sontag, *Illness as Metaphor*, 46–47.

171 *He famously treated a woman named Dora, whose father, Phillip, was having an affair with a certain Mrs. K.*: Hannah S. Decker, *Freud, Dora and
Vienna, 1900* (New York: Free Press, 1991), 79; Frederick Crews et al.,
The Memory Wars: Freud's Legacy in Dispute (New York: New York Times,
1995), 50–53.

172 *With the epidemic of tuberculosis, "the figure of the sick person crystallized
. . . into a social phenomenon"*: C. Herzlich and J. Pierret, *Illness and Self
in Society* (Baltimore: Johns Hopkins University Press, 1987), cited by

❧ Notes to Pages 155–172 ❧

220

Horatio Fabrega Jr., *Evolution of Sickness and Healing* (Berkeley: University of California, 1997), 16.

172 *These unfortunates were romantically named "melancholics"*: Sontag, *Illness as Metaphor*, 50.

172 *Women, in particular, were charged with manufacturing their own illnesses, just by virtue of their anatomy*: Decker, *Freud, Dora and Vienna*, 8–11.

172 *Samuel Wilson Fussell, a successful bodybuilder in the 1980s, wrote a memoir of how he managed to go from a "ninety-pound weakling" to a veritable "Charles Atlas man of muscle"*: Samuel Wilson Fussell, *Muscle: Confessions of an Unlikely Bodybuilder* (1991), cited by David B. Morris, *Illness and Culture in the Postmodern Age* (Berkeley: University of California Press, 1998), 143; Fussell, *Muscle*, 193.

173 *"Theories that diseases are caused by mental states"*: Sontag, *Illness as Metaphor*, 55.

173 *When one of Job's comforters tells Job he must be guilty of something, if not in deed, then in his psyche*: Scene 9.

175 *Spirituality is widely perceived as a feel-good, euphoric, and even ecstatic experience*: Richard Cimino and Don Lattin, *Shopping for Faith*, 17; Gallup and Jones, *Next American Spirituality*, 52.

175 *It is this yearning for experiential highs*: Larry Tye, "New Vigor for That Old-Time Religion," *San Francisco Examiner*, Sunday, December 11, 1994, p. A-14; Kenneth L. Woodward, "On the Road Again," in "In the Search of the Sacred," *Newsweek*, November 28, 1994, 61.

175 *It is of the utmost importance that we recognize just how recent and how secular the definition of spirituality is*: For survey of meanings, see Walter Principe, "Toward Defining Spirituality," *Sciences Religieuses/Studies in Religion* 12, no. 2 (1983): 127–141.

177 *"Illness . . . the night side of life"*: Sontag, *Illness as Metaphor*, 3.

177 *Elie Wiesel describes the torment of Moshe the Beadle*: Elie Wiesel, *Night* (New York: Bantam, 1982), 4.

179 *Sociologist Robert Putnam cites Woody Allen as saying, "80 percent of life is simply showing up"*: Robert D. Putnam, *Bowling Alone*, 60.

179 *The Talmud rules, for instance, "There is no measure for visiting the sick":* Ned. 39b.

179 *A Talmudic tale describes a Rabbi chancing upon Elijah the prophet:* Taan. 22a.

179 *Visiting is commanded also in the case of mourners:* Tur 215:2, 207:1, 2, 4.

180 *Recent investigation does demonstrate some benefit if the sick pray on their own behalf, pray with someone else, or even just know that others are praying for them:* Larry Dossey, *Healing Words: The Power of Prayer and the Practice of Medicine* (New York: HarperSanFrancisco, 1973).

181 *In his summary of Jewish law on the subject of healing, he mentions prayer only once:* Maimonides 14:6.

181 *"It seems to me," says Spanish pietist Nissim Gerondi:* RaN to Ned. 40a, d.h. *ein mevakesh alav rachamim.*

182 *Most important, "being there" means physically being present:* Igrot Moshe, Y.D. 223.

182 *The first and foremost purpose of visiting is not to offer prayer but to ease the discomfort of the patient by cleaning the room or straightening the bed covers:* Taken largely from *The Tur*, Y.D. 335, "Laws of Visiting the Sick."

183 *Rav Joseph interprets the passage in the following manner:* B.M. 30b.

183 *"It has always been thus, a* pathway *from the time of creation":* Ket. 8b.

184 *Visiting the sick is an affirmation of a common human destiny, a path shared by those who find it difficult and those who do not:* T. Ket. 7:6. Cf. Maimonides 14:1, which provides a similar lesson, concluding that all such meetings on the path of life fall into the category of "Love your neighbor as yourself."

184 *The journey metaphor transcends the Jewish tradition:* M. Avot, 3:1; Hebrews 11:8–10; William Shakespeare, *As You Like It*, act II, scene 7. See also Thomas R. Cole, *The Journey of Life: A Cultural History of Aging in America* (Cambridge, England: Cambridge University Press, 1992), 6, 14, 20–21, 40–47.

185 *It is precisely when words become difficult for the patient that we are instructed to leave the room:* Tur 338, middle.

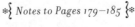

185 *Of late, American culture has increasingly appreciated the motif of a journey and the value of shared speech:* Robert Wuthnow, *Sharing the Journey*, 45, 170, 192, 223, 224, 273, 289–324.

186 *Nobel Prize winner Francis Crick, for example, doubted that human beings had such a thing as mind or soul:* Francis Crick, *The Astonishing Hypothesis: The Scientific Search for the Soul* (New York: Simon & Schuster, 1994).

8. A FOURTH GENERATION

193 *By biblical count, generations come and go every forty years:* Num. 14:33; 32:13; Deut. 2:7, 8:2, 4; Deut. 29:4; Josh. 5:6.

207 *For a variety of reasons, the hermetic seals that surrounded religious identity began to crack during the 1960s and 1970s:* Robert D. Wuthnow, *Restructuring of American Religion*, 71–99.

211 *Educator Parker Palmer, for instance, distinguishes four communities: therapeutic, civic, marketing, and academic:* Parker J. Palmer, *The Courage to Teach* (San Francisco: Jossey-Bass, 1998), 89–106.